FW
10/11

DATE DUE FOR RETURN

TRUE CRIME

2 6 AUG 2014

2 6 AUG 2015

Renewals
www.liverpool.gov.uk/libraries
0151 233 3000

THREAT

Palestinian Political Prisoners in Israel

Edited by Abeer Baker and Anat Matar

PlutoPress
www.plutobooks.com

First published 2011 by Pluto Press
345 Archway Road, London N6 5AA

www.plutobooks.com

Distributed in the United States of America exclusively by
Palgrave Macmillan, a division of St. Martin's Press LLC,
175 Fifth Avenue, New York, NY 10010

British Library Cataloguing in Publication Data
A catalogue record for this book is available from the British Library

ISBN   978 0 7453 3021 1   Hardback
ISBN   978 0 7453 3020 4   Paperback

Library of Congress Cataloging in Publication Data applied for

This book is printed on paper suitable for recycling and made from fully managed
and sustained forest sources. Logging, pulping and manufacturing processes are
expected to conform to the environmental standards of the country of origin.

10   9   8   7   6   5   4   3   2   1

Designed and produced for Pluto Press by Chase Publishing Services Ltd
Typeset from disk by Stanford DTP Services, Northampton, England
Simultaneously printed digitally by CPI Antony Rowe, Chippenham, UK and
Edwards Bros in the United States of America

Contents

Preface
The Palestinian Prisoners:
Politicization and Depoliticization

Abeer Baker and Anat Matar

A context is needed. A political context. That is a cliché, of course, but when it comes to the blind spots of Western mutual consciousness—to what is never challenged, being too obvious—it is doubly true. Think of the term "threat": an image is somehow implicitly already taken for granted when we use it; a picture of innocence in danger, of justified means of defense, and so on. But the contents of "innocence," "justified" and "defense" are far from being neutral. Questions should be posed, then: who threatens whom, and why? What is conceived and classified as a threat, and by whom? What is the reality behind images of threat? How is a threat to be eliminated, if at all? These questions and similar ones have many aspects: psychological, historical, criminological, legal, and others. But above all, they should be posed as political questions, deserving a political answer.

The present volume deals with a particular "threat": the Palestinians who are incarcerated in Israeli jails and are conceived as security threats. In general, prisoners in Israel are classified into two categories: "criminal" and "security" prisoners. The commands and directives of the Israel Prison Service (IPS) do not define a "criminal" prisoner, but they do define a "security" one. A "security" prisoner is defined as "a prisoner who was convicted and sentenced for committing a crime, or who is imprisoned on suspicion of committing a crime, which due to its nature or circumstances was defined as a security offense or whose motive was nationalistic." Already here, in this succinct albeit vague definition, the political is both explicit and implicit, both asserted and denied. For what is to be counted as a "security offense"? And are all offenses whose motive is "nationalistic" to be treated equally? First of all, it would be an understatement to note that most of the prisoners who fall under this category are Palestinians;

but moreover, a closer look discloses that the undertone of this term "security prisoner" stretches far beyond the IPS's administrative needs and ranges over the whole Israeli discourse relating to Palestinians: they are all "security threats," to one degree or another, and they should all be tucked away behind fences, bars, walls; they should all be disciplined and controlled.

The "security prisoner" rubric has become a code of identification for Palestinian prisoners in general and not only *vis-à-vis* the IPS or the law enforcement authorities. Applied in a blind, categorical manner, without distinction, it transforms thousands of Palestinians as they are seized, interrogated, detained and imprisoned in Israel into a single group that poses, as such, an identical level of danger which justifies special treatment: brutal arrest, prohibition from meeting a lawyer, torture and illegal interrogation methods, arrest without trial, lack of due process, disproportional sentencing, stricter living conditions, isolation, and also poor prospects of early release and parole. In contrast to the general approach towards prisoners, which is based on an individual assessment of a person and the extent of the danger he or she presents, the attitude of the State of Israel toward these "security prisoners" is based on their group identification as "threats." This is true of Palestinians—of all ages, including children—arrested and incarcerated in Israeli jails, independently of their alleged offense or their sentence. Administrative detainees and prisoners serving life sentences, prisoners sentenced for organizing or participating in demonstrations, for being active in political movements declared "illegal" by the occupying forces, for possessing ammunition, and for planning suicide bombing: all are categorized, *en bloc*, as "security prisoners," as threats.

What is resounding in its absence from this "security" discourse is its background: the long years of occupation of the Palestinian Territories, the prevention of livelihood, of freedom of movement, of personal and community development, of education, of autonomous economy; in short, of self-determination and national independence. It is inconceivable to examine the issue of Palestinian prisoners without keeping this background constantly in mind.

The blurring of prisoners' personal characteristics by attaching to them the "security" label hence not only violates their rights as individuals, but also denies them their political definition and motivation. An Israeli minister once said in relation to these "security threats": "Semantics do not interest me. Terror must be denounced even if one calls it resistance." It takes no more than a second to realize how politically biased and contextualized is this statement.

Think of the reverse wording: "Resistance must be denounced even if one calls it terror." It sounds, of course, completely absurd. But when does "resistance" end and "terror" begin? Who is the terrorized? The presumption to know the answers to these questions in an aloof, "neutral" manner is nothing but a gross distortion.

The term "security threat" combines two benefits for the Israeli authorities and public opinion: it enables Palestinian political prisoners to be stripped of their basic rights as diverse individuals, as they all belong to this large collective of "threats," and simultaneously it enables the depoliticization of their acts and the blurring of their political aims. What is common to both of these benefits is the rejection of the prisoners' subjectivity, both as individuals who deserve personal treatment, and as rational and essentially free beings who aspire to realize their freedom. In other words, regarding them all as "threats" erases the fact that they are *subjects* and turns them into *objects*: an object—like a collapsing wall, a roof on fire, a stone hurled from a slingshot, a knife, or even fingernails—can pose a threat, a security risk, a source of fear, from which we must protect our lives. A *subject*, on the other hand, deserves to be treated as a singular human being—as having aspirations, talents, emotions, and as forming an integral part of one's society; granting subjectivity—acknowledging one's aspirations, talents, emotions, the social texture into which one is woven—is political, always political. The depoliticization, therefore, is not only of the prisoners themselves: the IPS "administrative" classification reflects the fact that the entire Palestinian struggle is denied. All of Palestinian political existence is fossilized by means of the "security threat" label, turned into a type of dangerous *object* for the only subjects around, Israeli citizens.

* * *

The following essays have been written specifically for this volume, by prisoners, ex-prisoners, human rights defenders, political activists and academics, Palestinians from the Occupied Territories (1967), Palestinian and Jewish citizens of Israel, and others. Every major Palestinian political faction has a voice here. Yet although the writers brought under the present umbrella vary in their political visions, all are united in believing that any discussion of the Palestinian prisoners incarcerated in Israeli jails should not ignore its political nature. This is what the present volume aims at installing into the various discussions, in different discourses.

We have tried to encompass most of the crucial questions relevant to the topic of this volume. Unfortunately, this was revealed as an impossible task. Most painful for us is the omission of a separate chapter dedicated to the political incarceration of Palestinian children. At any given moment, hundreds of children are held in Israeli jails, interrogated with harsh methods, including humiliation and torture, and some declared as administrative detainees for long periods. All the hardships depicted in this book are doubly painful when it comes to detained children.

Restoring the political context means also positioning the problem which is the focus of this volume alongside others. Thus it is important for us to mention that Palestinian political prisoners are currently held also in Palestinian jails. They too deserve to be treated as subjects, with a full acknowledgment of their political motivation. The Israeli soldier Gilad Shalit has been held for years now in the Gaza Strip, his most basic rights denied. It would be a gross distortion to ignore all this; however, a thorough treatment of these additional topics goes much beyond the scope of this book and should hence remain as a necessary background.

* * *

The editors are grateful to the many people who helped on the way to materializing this volume. In January 2007, the Faculty of Law at Tel Aviv University hosted a conference on the question of classification of Palestinian prisoners. We wish to thank Guy Mundlak who chaired the Minerva Center for Human Rights at the time and Shai Lavi from the Cegla Center for Interdisciplinary Research of the Law for sponsoring and supporting that event in the face of attempts to curb it. For their endless cooperation and sense of solidarity, we wish to thank all our friends and colleagues from Adalah: The Legal Centre for Arab Minority Rights in Israel, Addameer Prisoners' Support and Human Rights Organization, B'Tselem—the Israeli Information Centre for Human Rights in the Occupied Territories, the Association for Civil Rights in Israel, Defense for Children International—Palestine Section (DCI), Al-Hak, Al Mezan Center for Human Rights, HaMoked—Center for the Defense of the Individual, the Israeli Association of Physicians for Human Rights (PHR), the Palestinian Center for Human Rights, the Public Committee against Torture in Israel (PCATI), Women's Organization for Political Prisoners, MachsomWatch team of observers in military courts, Yousef al-Sadeeq Association, and every individual and organization devoted to the issue of Palestinian prisoners. For their support of the Israeli Committee for the Palestinian Prisoners, we are indebted to Mr. and Mrs. Kroymann from the Palastina-Frieden Stiftung Rachel Corrie.

Some of the essays in this volume were written in Hebrew or Arabic and needed translation. Our gratitude goes to the following individuals who answered our call and volunteered to help with this difficult task: Thomas Aplin, Chaya Amir, Valentina Azarov, Uri Bitan, Katie Hesketh, Ali Issa, Matan Kaminer, Reuven Kaminer, Carmi Lecker, Ran Makleff, Inas Margieh, Rela Mazali, Michal Sapir, Nadav Sigal and Oded Wolkstein.

A continuous source of inspiration throughout many years has been the work of the late Riad Anis and of Hassan Jabarin, Amira Hass, Hussein abu Hussein, Felicia Langer, Gaby Lasky, Lea Tsemel, Saleem Wakeem, Iris Bar and Tirtza Tauber, to whom we wish to extend our gratitude. On a more personal level we wish to thank our friends Tamar Berger, Orna Kohn, Yael Lerer and Sanaa Salame; and most of all, our infinitely patient and supportive partners, Ala Hlehel and Doron Matar.

Notes on Contributors

Nahla Abdo is a Palestinian feminist activist, and professor of sociology at Carleton University, Ottawa, Canada. She has published extensively on women, racism, nationalism and the state in the Middle East, with special focus on Palestinian women. Among her recent publications: *Gender, Citizenship and the State: The Israeli Case* (2010, in Arabic); *Women and Poverty in the OPT: Some Conceptual and Methodological Notes*, 2007.

Sheikh Muhammad Abu Tir is a Member of the Palestinian Legislative Council, who was abducted by the Israeli Army in 2006, shortly after being elected. He was sentenced to four years' imprisonment for affiliation with the Hamas movement, and his residency in East Jerusalem was revoked. Sheikh Abu-Tir has spent a total of 30 years in Israeli prisons, in six different periods, for various activities, first with Fatah and then Hamas.

Itaf Aliyan (Hodaly) is a former political prisoner, currently living in Ramallah and studying for her Master's degree in psychology and administration. In 1987, she was arrested and accused of planning a suicide bombing and of affiliation with the Islamic Jihad Movement. She was sentenced to 15 years in prison, of which she served ten. In 1997, she was rearrested and declared an administrative detainee; she was released after a hunger strike of 40 days. In 2003, she was arrested again, but three years later she was acquitted and released.

Abeer Baker is a senior lawyer with Adalah: The Legal Centre for Arab Minority Rights in Israel and Chair of the Legal Clinic for Prisoners' Rights in the Law Faculty of Haifa University. Baker works mainly in litigation of Palestinian human rights issues, concentrating on cases of group discrimination, political rights, prisoners' and detainees' rights and victims of security force brutality. She has recently received her LLM (with Honors) from Northwestern University in the US.

Osama Barham is a Palestinian from the village of Ramin, who spent a total of some 20 years in Israeli prisons, the first half of them having been charged with activities in the Fatah movement. He was rearrested in 1993 and declared an administrative detainee. His detention was renewed several times, and in total reached a record of six years. In 2003, Barham was rearrested, charged with affiliation with the Islamic Jihad and trading in explosives, and sentenced to five years. Currently, he is manager of the Mental Support Unit in the Palestinian Ministry of Detainees' Affairs.

Anat Barsella holds an MA in human rights and an MA in political economy from the University of Essex, England. Following her studies, she did an internship with the UN Office of the High Commissioner for Human Rights. From mid 2005 to mid 2008, she worked as a researcher at B'Tselem—the Israeli Information Centre for Human Rights in the Occupied Territories, where she focused on the issue of family visits of Palestinian prisoners held in Israel. Since then, she has been working for the UN High Commissioner for Refugees in Israel, as a refugee status determination and protection officer.

Sigi Ben-Ari is a human rights lawyer working for the Israeli NGO HaMoked—Center for the Defense of the Individual.

Smadar Ben-Natan is an Israeli lawyer practicing in human rights and criminal law and a graduate of the University of Oxford in International Human Rights Law. She represents Palestinian prisoners before both civil and military courts. In 2006, she represented Hezbollah fighters captured by Israel during the war in Lebanon, arguing for them to be granted prisoner-of-war status when they were charged in Israel with offenses connected to the conflict.

Yael Berda is a human rights lawyer and PhD candidate at the Department of Sociology at Princeton University. She represented Palestinians in hundreds of cases against the military civil administration and recently won the case against prison privatization in Israel. Her first book, *The Bureaucracy of the Occupation* (in Hebrew), is forthcoming in 2011.

Walid Daka is a Palestinian citizen of Israel, serving a life sentence for his alleged involvement in the kidnap and murder of an Israeli soldier, and for belonging to the Popular Front for the Liberation of Palestine. He holds an MA degree in social science from the

Open University in Israel and routinely publishes articles in the Palestinian press.

Avigdor Feldman, the son of Holocaust survivors, graduated from Tel Aviv University's Law School in 1973. Along with Raji Sourani, he was awarded the Robert Kennedy Peace Prize in 1991 for his work on the violation of Israeli and international law in Israel and the Occupied Palestinian Territories. He has litigated cases opposing Israel's use of torture, arbitrary detention and extrajudicial assassinations against suspected Palestinian terrorists and political leaders. Among others, he represented now-prominent Palestinian negotiator Saeb Erekat, who as a student was accused of incitement; Feldman also represented the 400 Hamas activists who were expelled from Israel in 1991.

Sahar Francis is general director of the Addameer Prisoner Support and Human Rights Association in Ramallah, a position she has held since 2005. Previously, between 1996 and 2005, she worked as a lawyer for Addameer. She holds a Masters degree in international relations from Birzeit University.

Kathleen Gibson, JD from Case Western Reserve University School of Law (2008), is the international advocacy officer for the Addameer Prisoner Support and Human Rights Association in Ramallah.

Alon Harel holds the Phillip P. Mizock & Estelle Mizock Chair in Administrative and Criminal Law at the Hebrew University Law Faculty and is a member of the Center for Rationality at the Hebrew University Law School. He has written extensively in the fields of political and legal philosophy.

Alina Korn is a lecturer in the Department of Criminology at Ashkelon Academic College in Israel. Her research interests include social control and the links between crime, politics and the media. She has published articles on incarceration rates in Israeli prisons in *Criminal Justice* (2003), and on the ghettoization of the Palestinians in *Thinking Palestine* (2008).

Mounir Mansour is a Palestinian citizen of Israel, a former political prisoner who spent some 18 years in Israeli prisons. In 1972, at the age of 16, he was arrested and accused of affiliation with the Fatah and involvement in a military confrontation with Israeli soldiers.

Mansour was sentenced to life imprisonment, but released 13 years later (1985) as part of the Nawras ("Jibril") prisoner exchange deal. In 1991, Mansour was sentenced for supporting terror and sent again to prison. In 2001, he was appointed Chair of the Prisoners' Friends Association, which in 2006 was declared illegal by Israel's Minister of Defense.

Ruchama Marton is a psychiatrist, peace activist and feminist, and the founder and president of the Israeli Association of Physicians for Human Rights. She has edited and written chapters for *Torture: Human Rights, Medical Ethics and the Case of Israel* (1995). Marton received several peace and human rights awards, including the Emil Grunzweig Award for Human Rights, presented by the Association for Civil Rights in Israel, and the Jonathan Mann Award for Global Health and Human Rights. She is among the women nominated for the 1000 Women Nobel Peace Prize 2005.

Anat Matar, a Jewish Israeli citizen, is a senior lecturer at the Department of Philosophy, Tel Aviv University. Her latest book is *Modernism and the Language of Philosophy* (2006). Matar has been an anti-Occupation activist for many years, in particular in the refusal movement. She was a member of Open Doors, an activist group against administrative detention, and is co-founder and chair of the Israeli Committee for the Palestinian Prisoners. Matar serves on the steering committee of Who Profits?—Exposing the Israeli Occupation Industry.

Esmail Nashif, a Palestinian citizen of Israel, is a lecturer at the Department of Sociology and Anthropology, Ben Gurion University. He is the author of *Gradus for Opening the Episteme* (2010), and *Palestinian Political Prisoners: Identity and Community* (2008).

Tamar Pelleg-Sryck received her MA degree in humanities from the Hebrew University in 1949 and graduated from the Law Faculty at Tel Aviv University in 1985. Since December 1987, in the ranks of different human rights organizations and since 1997 on behalf of HaMoked—Center for the Defense of the Individual, she has defended Palestinians against assaults on their bodies, freedom and property by the Israeli military occupation authorities, while gradually specializing in the defense of administrative detainees.

Maya Rosenfeld is a research fellow at the Harry S. Truman Research Institute at the Hebrew University and a lecturer in sociology and anthropology. Her main field of study is the social and political history of the Palestinians in Palestine and the Diaspora. Her book, *Confronting the Occupation: Work, Education and Political Activism of Palestinian Families in a Refugee Camp* (2004) is based on her PhD research. Rosenfeld's latest publication is *From Emergency Relief Assistance to Human Development and Back: UNRWA and the Palestinian Refugees, 1950–2009* (2009).

Leslie Sebba is Lawrence D. Biele Professor of Law (Emeritus) at the Institute of Criminology at the Law Faculty of the Hebrew University in Jerusalem. He holds an MA in Jurisprudence from Queen's College, Oxford, an LLM from the London School of Economics and a Dr. Juris from the Hebrew University. Professor Sebba has published seven books and more than 90 articles on criminal justice policy, victimology and punishment and human rights. He is a founding member of the Association for Civil Rights in Israel.

Michael Sfard is an Israeli lawyer specializing in international human rights and humanitarian law. Sfard had litigated central cases regarding the separation wall and represented dozens of Israeli conscientious objectors. He has acted on behalf of the Bil'in village council and has initiated its lawsuit in Canada against the Canadian construction corporations involved in building settlements on village land. Sfard represents Palestinian prisoners in parole board hearings and in cases brought by the Israeli Committee for the Palestinian Prisoners. He has litigated the Yesh Din case, challenging the practice of incarceration of Palestinian prisoners in Israel.

Bana Shoughry-Badarne, a Palestinian citizen of Israel, is the Legal Director for the Public Committee against Torture in Israel (PCATI). She holds an LLB degree from the Hebrew University in Jerusalem and LLM degree in international law from the American University in Washington, DC. Prior to joining PCATI, she spent seven years working as a human rights attorney at the Association for Civil Rights in Israel. She is a member of the Coalition for Equality in Personal Status Issues for Palestinian-Arab Women Citizens of Israel.

Sharon Weill is a PhD Candidate in international humanitarian law at the University of Geneva and a researcher at the Geneva Academy of International Humanitarian Law and Human Rights. Her Master's thesis dealt with the jurisdiction of the military courts in the Occupied Territories. She also lectures at Tel Aviv and Paris II Universities.

Part I
Analyses

1

The Centrality of the Prisoners' Movement to the Palestinian Struggle against the Israeli Occupation: A Historical Perspective

Maya Rosenfeld

INTRODUCTION: A PERSISTENT ISRAELI POLICY OF MASS IMPRISONMENT

By the latter months of 2009, approximately 7,000 Palestinian prisoners, residents of the Occupied Palestinian Territories (OPT), were being held in Israeli jails, detention compounds and interrogation facilities. Some 5,000 of them (approx. 70 percent) had been sentenced to various imprisonment terms, around 1,500 (approx. 20 percent) were detainees awaiting their sentence and slightly less than 300 were administrative detainees (held without trial).[1] Nearly 85 percent of the prisoners were residents of the West Bank; Gaza residents comprised some 10 percent of the total and East Jerusalemites the remaining 5 percent.[2]

In comparison with most recent years, 2009 saw a decline in the number of prisoners, which ranged between 7,952 and 8,595 during 2008, and between 8,441 and 9,344 during 2007, and which reached a peak of around 9,600 in October 2006.[3]

Nonetheless, as is clearly evident from the above and additional figures, the "post-Oslo" era, which started with the outbreak of the second Intifada in late September 2000, was and remains marked by an especially high incidence of detentions of Palestinians by the Israeli army, police, and GSS (General Security Service) on the grounds of what is referred to as "security offences."[4] Indeed, it was recently estimated by the former statistician of the Palestinian National Authority's (PNA) Ministry of Prisoners and former Prisoners' Affairs that approximately 69,000 Palestinians were detained between October 2000 and November 2009, among them 7,800 children (youths under the age of 18) and 850 women.[5]

Yet, when placed within the broader perspective—that of 43 years of Israeli military occupation over the Palestinian territories—the figures on prisoners and detentions in the post-Oslo era appear as part of a continuum, evidently a striking one: According to another estimate by the Ministry of Prisoners and former Prisoners' Affairs, approximately 650,000 Palestinians had been arrested in the course of four decades of Israeli military control (between June 1967 and April 2006),[6] this with respect to a population that numbered around 1 million in 1967 and around 3.8 million in 2006. While this approximation is most probably far from accurate due to inadequate counting methods and to the lack of distinction between hours-long arrests and long-term imprisonment, it is nevertheless very important. No matter what the number of incidents that would be subtracted following the necessary adjustments, the final figure will remain extremely high by all standards.

The statistics are indicative, therefore, of the persistence of an Israeli policy of mass imprisonment in reaction to the varying manifestations of Palestinian resistance to Israel's military occupation. One main exception to this generalization is traced to the Oslo period (1994–October 2000), which opened with a mass release of political prisoners and continued with a marked decline (albeit not a complete cessation) in the scope of detentions and imprisonment.[7] A second major exception pertains to Palestinian women, who despite the noticeable role they have played in the ranks of all the political organizations and their widespread participation in grassroots anti-occupation activism, did not become subjected to mass imprisonment at any stage.[8]

Taking the persistence of an Israeli policy of wide-scale imprisonment as an overriding structural factor, then, the current chapter seeks to examine the effect that this condition has exerted upon the Palestinian struggle against the Israeli occupation from the time of its inception in the aftermath of the 1967 War to the second Intifada.

THE PERVASIVENESS OF THE PRISON EXPERIENCE: SOME SOCIAL MANIFESTATIONS

That mass imprisonment has had a fundamental impact on Palestinian society in the OPT is amply manifest in a range of spheres and areas. To start with, it is rare to find a family in the West Bank or in the Gaza Strip that has not experienced the incarceration (even if short-term) of at least one of its male members and many a family has faced the imprisonment of two or more members. In a survey that I conducted in 1993 among hundreds of households in the Dheisheh refugee camp, I found that 47.8 percent of the men who then belonged to the generation aged 25–40 had experienced some form of imprisonment for periods ranging from several weeks to 15 years; nearly 85 percent of the families of origin of these young men experienced the imprisonment of at least one male member and 58 percent of the families faced the imprisonment of two or more of their male members.[9]

The pervasiveness of imprisonment, including that of administrative detention, was particularly high during the first Intifada (December 1987 through 1992), during which time it significantly surpassed the current (post-October 2000 through 2009) incidence of the phenomenon. Cases wherein three and even four brothers were held simultaneously in Israeli jails (at times in the same prison) were not uncommon; I recall the words of a Dheisheian father to four sons, then in their early, mid and late twenties, all of whom had spent time in jail when they were in high school or at university, and all of whom were detained again during the first Intifada and held under administrative detention: "Just as it was clear to me that every living creature eventually dies, it became evident that every Palestinian man would eventually be taken to prison."[10] The lengthy—at times decades-long—active participation of the prisoner's family members, especially that of female members, in caring for their prisoners and their needs and the fact that similar experiences, toils and hardship were shared by the majority of families were grounds for profound socialization and politicization processes; this gave rise to novel social formations on the community and regional levels, first and foremost of which was the solidarity networks of prisoners' families.[11]

For the tens of thousands of families whose male members spent years behind bars, the imprisonment experience also implied an economic setback as a result of the prolonged absence of the imprisoned husband/son/brother and the subsequent loss of the latter's contribution to the household income. Such disruption commonly gave rise to a new, alternative division of labor in the family, often based on female primary providers, that is, the prisoner's wife, mother and/or sister. To this one should add the detrimental impact of the interrupted high school or college education of many a prisoner, and the enormous difficulties of finding employment encountered by former prisoners. Indeed, up until the establishment of the PNA and the subsequent mass recruitment of former prisoners into its security forces and to various other branches of its public sector, the overwhelming majority of former prisoners faced lengthy unemployment that often rendered them economically dependent on their families of origin (in the case of the unmarried) and/or on their wives (in the case of married ex-prisoners).[12]

Turning to the public political sphere, the impact of mass imprisonment is most directly discernible in the biographies of entire strata of political officials, public figures and community leaders in the West Bank and Gaza. The centrality of the imprisonment experience to their ascent became exposed to the Israeli public, albeit on a rather superficial level, during the Oslo years, when the media zoomed in on a rank of prominent political figures, most of them members of the middle and younger generation of al-Fatah movement, who grew up and came of age in the West Bank and the Gaza Strip of the 1960s, 1970s and 1980s: Jibril Rajoub, Kedura Fares, Marwan Barghuthi, Sufian Abu Zaida, Hisham Abd al-Razeq and Hussein al-Sheikh are just a few examples of the more well-known names. The common denominator for all included seniority in Israeli prisons (some had served prison terms of over 15 years), a most impressive command of Hebrew, remarkable familiarity with the dynamics of Israeli politics, and an unequivocal support of Palestinian participation in what was then "the peace process," in line with the political program of the PLO. The conspicuousness of "the prison years" in the life stories of this generation of leaders ran parallel, more or less, with the salience of events and episodes such as "Black September" (*aylul al aswad*), "the Beirut years" (*ayyam Beirut*) and the Lebanon War (1982) in the biographies of their peers, members of the military, political and administrative apparatus of the PLO, who returned to the OPT in the wake of the Oslo Accords after decades of exile.

THE FORMATIVE NATURE OF "THE PRISON YEARS"

As emerged unambiguously from the many dozens of interviews that I conducted with former political prisoners in Dheisheh, the formative nature of "the prison years" in terms of the contribution to the political education and maturation of the individual was not merely a derivative of the long time periods that activists spent in Israeli jails, although the latter factor was undoubtedly a weighty one. Rather, it is traced back to the process by which Palestinian prisoners succeeded in organizing themselves inside

Israeli prisons and building what they referred to as an "internal order/organization/regime" (*nitham dakhili*), which countered the imposed prison order and challenged it. While the roots of organizing in prison go back to the early years of the Occupation (the late 1960s and early 1970s), the prisoners' organization, or as it is alternatively named, the prisoners' movement, gained ground in the second decade of the occupation and possibly reached its peak in the mid- and late 1980s and the very early (pre-Oslo) 1990s.[13] What made the "counter-order" especially powerful was its all-inclusive, indeed "total" nature, embodied in the attempt and more so in the ability to encompass and address all spheres of the prisoner's daily life, starting from the material conditions and basic facilities in the prison cell and from the fundamental necessities of those confined to it, continuing with education (formal, non-formal, political), and culminating in the prisoner's ongoing (daily) participation in political discussion and democratic decision making.[14]

Much evidence appears to support the generalization that none of the organizations and movements that gained ground in the OPT during the 1970s and 1980s, not even the most progressive, socialist-oriented factions of the Palestinian left, was able to implant and sustain equally comprehensive programs and institutions as those that were upheld by the prisoners' organization.[15] This unique nature of the prisoners' organization received ample manifestation in the accounts of former prisoners, which attributed clear trans- formative qualities to their participation in the "prisoners' order" and in the organized studies program in particular. Indeed, dozens of my interviewees underscored similar aspects of the change they underwent and often employed similar expressions and metaphors when they evaluated the differences between "before" and "after" (the prison experience). For example:

> Before being in prison, I was connected emotionally to the national struggle, but in jail I became connected to it intellectually and ideologically. It was in prison that I read the theory. Love of the homeland became more rooted, for two reasons: my discussions with other people and my reading pamphlets and books ... .[16]

Given the pervasiveness of the prison experience in the life histories of generations of Palestinian activists and given the seminal impact that it bore for individuals and families, the main part of this chapter attempts to draw an outline for the analysis of the interrelation- ship between the development of the organization/movement of

Palestinian political prisoners inside Israeli prisons and between the development of the national-political struggle against the Israeli occupation in the West Bank and Gaza.

THE INTERRELATIONSHIP BETWEEN THE PRISONERS' MOVEMENT AND THE PALESTINIAN NATIONAL MOVEMENT IN THE OPT UP TO OSLO

The first general observation that I elaborate on is that, when put in historical perspective, the growth and consolidation of the prisoners' movement in the OPT coincided with the gradual transformation of local resistance to the Israeli occupation into a full-blown, mass-based, decentralized movement; a distinct yet indivisible branch of the Palestinian national movement and, as such, affiliated with the PLO. One should bear in mind that when Israel took over the West Bank and the Gaza Strip in the 1967 War, the two territories were ruled and administered by different regimes: the West Bank had been officially annexed to the Hashemite Kingdom in 1950, and the Gaza Strip was under Egyptian military rule. By that time, various shades of Palestinian nationalism had struck root in both territories, mainly through the influence and under the banners of three movements, all of which had been outlawed by the two regimes: the Movement of Arab Nationalists, which promoted Arab nationalism and upheld the ideal of Arab unity; the Fatah movement, then still in its infancy, which espoused particular Palestinian nationalism and an independent Palestinian struggle, and the Communists (the Jordanian Communist Party in the West Bank and the Palestinian Communist Organization in Gaza; both originating from the Palestine Communist Party), which continued to endorse the partition plan (the "two-state solution") throughout. Activism in the two territories took place separately, however, and was largely shaped and determined by local circumstances; by no means was there, at the time, a unified, cross-country platform of Palestinian national action.

The immediate aftermath of the 1967 War saw a steep decline in the popularity of Arab nationalism among Palestinians in Palestine and the Diaspora and a corresponding upsurge among them in the appeal of distinct Palestinian nationalism. Influenced by the anti-colonial, revolutionary struggles in Vietnam, Cuba, Algeria, and elsewhere the emergent independent Palestinian organizations— including the by-then senior al-Fatah and the nascent PFLP and DFLP—adopted guerrilla warfare as a core element in their strategies of national liberation. Yet the attempt by al-Fatah and others to build and sustain an infrastructure of armed struggle in the West Bank and Gaza was aborted, before long, by the Israeli army and intelligence, and thousands of young men who took part in this endeavor were quick to find themselves in prison.[17]

Alongside the latter group of "aborted" fighters, the first generation of Palestinian prisoners in Israeli jails, those imprisoned between 1967 and 1975, also included thousands of youths who had been apprehended by the Israeli army on grounds of their association with locally based and often locally initiated clandestine formations that engaged in sporadic, most often uncoordinated acts of violence against the army, and yet others, much fewer in number, who were involved in terrorist action against Israeli civilians. The great majority of these prisoners were very young and inexperienced, lacked military and political training, and exhibited only a loose affiliation with the factions of the Palestinian resistance movement.[18] In prison, they met with a particularly harsh regime that denied them the most basic human needs and rights; extremely over-crowded, cramped rooms, lacking, or rather, absent facilities, unhygienic conditions, insufficient and bad-quality food, a prohibition on books and on writing utensils, the excessive use of violence and physical punishment on a regular basis, were among the most common features.[19] On top of this, they were denied official recognition as political prisoners and were dealt with instead by the Israel Prison Service (IPS) as "security" prisoners, more commonly referred to as terrorists. As emerged from the accounts of veteran former prisoners, the attempts to build a prisoners' organization/counter-order during these early years centered mainly on the struggle to improve prison conditions. The following excerpt from the panoramic testimony of Noah Salameh, a former prisoner who entered prison in 1970 at the age of 17 and was released in 1985, is revealing:

> One can say that our struggle was conducted hour by hour and day by day around every "right" and every subject. We paid a high price for the notebook, the book, the mattress, the blanket, the shower and for food and health care. It is important to remember that conditions differed from one prison to another, and this too was a deliberate policy adopted by the authorities. You found that something that you had fought for in one prison for months was a recognized "right" in another prison.[20]

Starting in the latter part of the 1970s and increasingly so in the 1980s, the population of Palestinian prisoners underwent some noticeable changes, reflecting the broader transformations and developments that affected the political arena in the OPT at the time. Most conspicuous among the latter were the rise of the PLO to prominence as the widely recognized, legitimate representative of the national aspirations of the Palestinians; the emergence in the West Bank and Gaza Strip of public political formations, specifically the Palestinian National Front (PNF) and the National Guidance Committee (NGC), which openly accepted the leadership of the PLO, rallied on a day-to-day basis against the military occupation and supported (in the 1970s) a platform for a political settlement along the lines of the two-state solution; and the subsequent demilitarization, decentralization and diversification of the resistance to the occupation, which was led by all factions of the Palestinian national movement from the early 1980s onwards, and which found expression in the proliferation of popular committees and unionist formations, among students, women, workers, local communities and so forth.[21]

In contrast with his predecessors from the late 1960s and early 1970s, then, the prisoner of the 1980s was most unlikely to have taken part in an attempt to launch a guerrilla attack (as such attempts had been all but liquidated by 1970) and neither was he likely to have been engaged in clandestine armed activity or terrorist action. Rather, he was prone to have been imprisoned on the grounds of affiliation with al-Fatah, the PFLP, DFLP, or the Communist Party (all of which had been banned), and of activism in the network of associations and institutions that were set up by each of the factions. Among the most dynamic and appealing of these were the committees of high school students and the unions of university students, which had taken root in the early 1980s and were behind much of the popular protest action at the time. The decentralization of the national movement and the diversification of its spheres of action implied, therefore, that the prisoners of the 1980s came from all sectors of society and from all geographic locations and boasted a high representation of secondary school students and a considerable representation of university students and graduates. These interrelated changes in the background of imprisonment and in the composition of the prisoners' population empowered the internal organization inside prison; the youngest, least experienced and least educated among the prisoners directly benefited from the presence of the more veteran activists and especially of those with higher levels of education. The latter now contributed significantly to the education programs that were developed and run in prison: they taught languages, history, economics, and even natural sciences and mathematics to their fellow cell and ward-mates and they usually played an instructive role in the political education programs of the organizations with which they were affiliated.

However, and this is the second observation I propose, while the prisoners' movement was certainly affected by the affairs and factors that shaped the national movement at large, its course of development was determined to a no lesser degree by internal affairs, namely, by the day-to-day struggle of the prisoners to maintain a united and effective organization and to pursue the fight for basic rights in the face of the prison order and the IPS. This struggle was in many respects autonomous of the movement outside, because it was conducted under the extreme conditions of the prison cell, the prison ward and the prison regime, because it centered around the material and intellectual survival of those who sustained it, and because it demanded and depended on an especially high level of discipline and commitment. As already mentioned above, perhaps the most unique achievement, the "flagship" of the prisoners' movement at the time, was in the sphere of education. Education programs, including general studies (history, languages, sciences) and studies of political theory and ideology, were introduced in prison through the fostering, and indeed through the enforcement, of daily schedules that allocated special time-slots for individual studies, instructed reading, group discussions of study materials, political meetings for the discussion of current (external and internal) affairs, and so forth. Political meetings, as well as studies of political ideology, were conducted separately on the basis of organizational (factional) affiliation, whereas participation in the study of general academic subjects was voluntary and open to all ("cross-factional") and organized on the level of the cell or section. The building and upholding of the education enterprise inside Israeli prisons rested, therefore, on three pillars. First, a very tight, union-like, cooperation between the political factions that comprised the prisoners' movement ran all the way through, from cell and ward level to that of cross-prison coordination. Secondly, within each faction, a highly animated, highly compelling group life centered around ongoing discussion, debate and democratic decision making. Third, foremost priority was accorded not merely to educational attainments but rather to the educational process itself (the enlightening impact of knowledge building) and to the resultant transformation of consciousness.[22] It was the sustenance of the education venture as part and parcel of the all-embracing "internal order" that enabled a powerful prisoners' collective to be forged and that continuously gave rise to highly esteemed leaders and leaderships from within its ranks.

Building on this premise, I maintain further, and this is a third observation, that during a critical time period in the history of the Palestinian struggle against the Occupation, starting in the mid 1980s and culminating with the first Intifada, the prisoners' movement enjoyed a prominent position within the OPT-based branch of the Palestinian national movement and in the public at large. In the backdrop of this ascent stood the relocation of the central arena of the Palestinian resistance movement in the aftermath of the 1982 Israeli invasion of Lebanon, from exile to the OPT. To recall, between the end of the 1960s and the invasion of 1982, the central leadership, the bureaucracy, the military apparatus and the intricate network of institutions of the PLO and of each of its constituting organizations were allowed to operate on Lebanese soil, in accordance with the Cairo Agreement.[23] This Palestinian enterprise was brought to an end in the wake of the mass destruction that was wrought by the Israeli aggression and the concomitant expulsion of the PLO, rank and file. Thereafter, Palestinian institution building and popular resistance became confined mainly to the occupied West Bank and the Gaza Strip. Here, the coupling of the omni-presence of the Israeli military throughout the territory with the weakened position of the exiled PLO leadership pushed the local leaderships away from armed struggle and in the direction of further reliance on mass-based structures, of setting up broad coalitions, and of articulating a joint political agenda that accorded major priority to ending the occupation and achieving independence.[24]

The culmination of this trend of development is epitomized by two of the formations that were most commonly identified with the first Intifada: the United National Leadership of the Uprising (UNLU, *al qiyada al wataniya al-muwahada*, known by the initials "QWM") and the popular committees. The UNLU, which comprised prominent representatives of all the OPT-based factions of the PLO, directed and "scheduled" the day-to-day program of the Intifada by means of bi-weekly communiqués and formulated the political message of the revolt. Locale, region and sector-based popular committees had already proliferated in the mid 1980s as the grassroots branches of the political organizations. Following the eruption of the Intifada, the number of locally based committees multiplied sevenfold and they assumed the major role in running the day-to-day affairs of communities in the face of Israeli military measures such as prolonged curfews, denial of utilities and services, army raids, mass arrests, school closures, and so forth, as well as in organizing community-based protest activities, such as demonstrations, processions, commemorations, etc; hence the committees constituted both the building-blocks and the backbone of the uprising.[25]

Returning to the prisoners' movement in light of all the above, it appears justified to review it as both a forerunner and an extension of the Intifada-related structures: a tight and effective cross-factional cooperation underscored the leadership and the rank and file of the prisoners' organization from its very early days, years before cross-factional coalitions materialized at large and decades before the emergence of the UNLU. Similarly, the operation of a network of committees that covered all affairs of the prisoners constituted the "nuts and bolts" of the prisoners' internal order more than a decade before popular committees appeared on the horizons of West Bank and Gaza Strip activism. In this respect, both the underlying features of the leadership and the organizational structure of the prisoners' movement served as a model for the development of the major formations that enabled the uprising and led it. At the same time, however, the prisoners' movement was constantly being fed by the growth and spread of the popular committees, especially after the latter were officially declared illegal in a decree that the Israeli military government issued in August 1988, eight months into the Intifada.[26] In the wake of this Israeli policy, thousands of activists, very young, young and older, who had joined the ranks of the committees ended up in prison, where they were soon absorbed in the existing prisoners' organization or in the establishment of similar structures in the newly erected detention compounds, such as the Ketziot prison that had been set up in the midst of the Negev Desert especially to accommodate the inflow of Intifada detainees. In this latter respect, then, the prisoner's movement constituted an extension of the struggle against the occupation in the West Bank and Gaza Strip. To conclude, then, there existed an empowering dialectical relationship, wherein the organization that Palestinian political prisoners set up inside Israeli prisons was pivotal to the formation of the key structures that led and sustained the popular struggle against the Israeli occupation, and where, at the same time, the mass imprisonment of grassroots activists eventually led to the reinforcement of the prisoners' organization.

A complementary factor that continuously enhanced the position of the prisoners' movement in the Palestinian public sphere was the ongoing interaction between prisoners and their families back home. Contact was facilitated mainly through the relatives' visiting days at the prison sites, which took place on a regular, bi-weekly basis, albeit under a host of restrictions.[27] Tens of thousands of visitors from all regions and locales of the West Bank and the Gaza Strip, consisting mainly of female family members of the prisoners, took part in these bi-weekly journeys to the prison and detention compounds on a continuous, durable basis. In the great majority of cases, family visits developed over the course of time into junctures of transmission, wherein a measure of the prisoners' culture and ethos was passed on to the regular visitors, in particular their mothers, sisters and wives. Whatever had been captured by visitors in the moments of union and exchange with their loved ones, be it a description of the deteriorating imprisonment conditions, a hint about a possible hunger strike, the story of an ill mate that had been denied proper medical treatment, or the title of a recommended book, was eventually rendered subject for further discussion or action either in the circle of the family and kin group or in the wider support networks that were set up in solidarity with the prisoners and in concern over their needs.[28] Consequently, the prisoners' issues and cause were being relentlessly addressed, constantly acted upon, so to say, by a significant and, at the time, an ever growing portion of Palestinian society.

A good indication of just how elevated was the status of the prisoner's movement in the years under review can be obtained from the scope of the public reaction to prisoners' related affairs and events. To take the most salient case, prisoners' strikes, especially hunger strikes—the ultimate manifestation of the organized struggle of political prisoners—seldom remained an internal matter confined within the prison's boundaries. Rather, no sooner did a strike successfully cross the initial days of trial and gain some momentum then the public began to mobilize in solidarity with the striking prisoners and their demands: the political factions would call out for protest action; committees in each and every town, village and refugee camp would organize daily rallies, demonstrations and processions in support of the strikers, events which were regularly met with violent reaction on the part of the Israeli military, including the use of live ammunition, and which ended, at times, with fatalities. An illuminating example of the stimulating, indeed galvanizing, impact of the prisoners' movement is that of the hunger strike initiated by the central leadership of the prisoners' organization in September 1992, which lasted for 15 days (September 27 through October 12). It was estimated that more than 12,000 prisoners were held in Israeli prisons at that time, but the Intifada was long past its peak and popular action of the form that characterized the first two years of the uprising had almost died out. Yet news of the hunger strike and the fact that it was observed simultaneously in all the prisons and detention centers sufficed to bring back to life the by-then dormant popular structures. Most spectacular, perhaps, in the chain of the prisoner-centered activities were the sit-in solidarity hunger strikes of prisoners' mothers, which took place in front of the International Red Cross offices in Jerusalem, Bethlehem, Nablus and Gaza City. The cross-country solidarity campaign accompanied the hunger strike for more than two weeks until its successful conclusion with the acceptance of a majority of the prisoners' demands by the Israeli authorities.[29]

IN THE WAKE OF THE OSLO ACCORDS: MASS RELEASE OF PRISONERS, INCORPORATION INTO THE PNA APPARATUS, AND DISINTEGRATION OF THE MASS-BASED POPULAR STRUCTURES

If the mass mobilization that followed the prisoners' strike of October 1992 signaled a revitalization of the empowering interaction between the prisoners' movement and the OPT-based branch of the Palestinian national movement, then this revival did not last for long, as both constituent components of the interrelationship were soon to undergo far-reaching changes. In September 1993, the until then secret channel of Israeli-Palestinian negotiation that took place in Oslo culminated in the signing of the Declaration of Principals (DoP) between the government of Israel and the PLO, which was subsequently followed by a series of interim agreements between the parties. And while the Oslo Accords did not bring about an end to Israel's military control over the West Bank and Gaza, the Accords nevertheless gave rise to two major developments that critically affected both the national movement at large and the prisoners' movement, namely, the establishment of the PNA and the mass release of political prisoners. This, then, is my fourth observation, on which I elaborate below.

The founding of the PNA in 1994 set in motion three contradictory processes that directly bore on the national movement, and which can only be addressed very briefly here. First, nation-building, partial and restricted as it was, entailed a vast incorporation of tens of thousands of political activists, among them thousands of the then "just-released" political prisoners, into the nascent state apparatus, first and foremost the branches of the security forces and the administration of the government ministries. Among the latter was the Ministry for Prisoners' and former Prisoners' Affairs, which was set up especially to take care of the welfare needs of prisoners' families and for the socioeconomic rehabilitation of former prisoners, and which was headed and staffed by former prisoners. While the majority of the new recruits were affiliated with the Fatah organization, which subsequently became the ruling party, members of other factions of the national movement were by no means excluded.[30]

Secondly, at the same time, Palestinian state building, coupled with the weakening of PLO institutions and with the decline of the Palestinian left (PFLP, PDFLP and Communists), contributed to the dissolution of the popular, mass-based structures that formed the backbone of the national movement during the latter part of the 1980s and the first Intifada. While this process had already been set in motion in the later years of the uprising, disintegration and the concomitant demobilization of large segments of society became much more rapid and visible in the mid-1990s, by which time membership in formations such as the women's organizations, workers' federations, and voluntary committees had significantly diminished if not evaporated altogether. Together with demobilization came "NGO-ization" and depoliticization, that is, the substitution of the former politically affiliated and politically motivated formations with a myriad of supposedly politically neutral services and community-centered organizations that depended entirely on the support of external donors and subsequently also—at least to some extent—on donors' agendas. Interestingly enough, many of the proliferating NGOs of the 1990s were headed by former leaders of the mass-based political structures of the 1980s and the first Intifada, in particular leaders that had been affiliated with the left-wing factions so that, in a way, NGO-ization signified a competing channel to participation in PNA-led state building.[31]

Thirdly, and concurrently, state building also stimulated the emergence and rooting of a powerful and violent Islamist opposition, under the leadership of the Hamas and Jihad movements. These organizations, which developed outside the unifying umbrella of the PLO and which played a relatively marginal role in the resistance to the Israeli occupation up until the late 1980s, now waged an open war against the PNA, the Palestinian Israeli negotiations and the further implementation of the Oslo Accords.

As for the mass release of prisoners in the wake of the Oslo Accords and its impact: it is estimated that at the time of the signing of the Declaration of Principles in September 1993, more than 10,000 prisoners were being held in Israeli jails.[32] In the wake of each of the interim agreements that were signed between the Government of Israel and the PLO between 1994 and 1999—the "Agreement on the Gaza Strip and Jericho Area" ("Cairo Agreement"), in May 1994; the "Interim Agreement on the West Bank and Gaza Strip" (Oslo II) in September 1995, and then the "Wye River Memorandum", in October 1998 and "Sharm el-Sheikh Memorandum", in September 1999—thousands of prisoners were released. By September 2000, at the eve of the second Intifada, the number of the most veteran prisoners, that is, those who were detained and sentenced prior to the establishment of the PNA, which were still being held in Israeli prisons, was approximately 400.[33]

Critics of the Oslo Accords have repeatedly blamed the PLO negotiator for two major flaws in the agreements that pertained to prisoners' release. First, it was claimed that the absence of monitoring mechanisms allowed for large discrepancies between the terms of prisoners' release that were specified in each of the agreements and the actual implementation on the part of the Israeli side. This implied lengthy delays, particularly in the release of the more vulnerable among the prisoners, the elderly and ill, the veteran, the very young, women, and so forth. Secondly, it was claimed that the PLO negotiator surrendered to the dictates of the Israeli party by accepting the exclusion of several categories of prisoners from the release agreements, among them Jerusalemites, Palestinian citizens of Israel, and hundreds of individual cases that were denied pardon. By willing to forgo the principal of an all-inclusive prisoners' release, critics maintained, the Palestinian negotiator stirred a division among the until then united body of political prisoners and induced deep mistrust among those who remained behind bars.[34] Without downplaying these contentions altogether, the attempt to attribute the demise of the prisoners' movement in the post-Oslo era to deficiencies on the part of the Palestinian negotiator appears unsubstantiated, at the very least. Moreover, the case under review appears to be one of the relatively rare examples in which numbers do speak for themselves; it is an indisputable fact that the Oslo Accords gave rise to the release of the greater majority of the prisoners that had been imprisoned prior to the establishment of the PNA.

At the same time as the mass release of "pre-Oslo" prisoners was taking place, however, fresh arrests were being carried out and detainees were sent to prison on a daily basis. However, this time very few of the new inmates came from the ranks of the national movement. Rather, the majority was affiliated with the Islamic opposition forces and with the terror waged by the latter in attempt to sabotage the implementation of the Oslo Accords. Still, the scope of imprisonment during the Oslo era was far from comparable with the Intifada and pre-Intifada years; according to the IPS, in 2000, prior to the outbreak of the second Intifada, the total number of Palestinian "security" prisoners that were being held in Israeli jails (not including detainees held in IDF facilities) stood at approximately 800.[35]

To conclude then, the establishment of the PNA and the mass release of Palestinian prisoners yielded complementary repercussions for the Palestinian national movement and for the prisoners' movement. By 1996, following the Oslo II agreement, only a small fraction of the prisoners that were detained in the pre-Oslo years remained behind bars. This inevitably implied that the prisoners' movement ceased to exist, if not altogether, then in the vital, comprehensive and authoritative format and role that it assumed in the pre-Oslo era. Many of the released, former members of the prisoners' movement were incorporated thereafter into the apparatus of the PNA and thus into the state-building process, which at one and the same time absorbed or "consumed" the rank and file of the national movement, and induced the disintegration and demobilization of the popular structures that had sustained this movement for decades. Finally, and this is the fifth observation, in light of the concomitant dissolution of the two movements, the interrelationship that empowered them both in the 1980s and early 1990s no longer existed. It is this decline of the movements and the severance of the connection between them that would face the incoming generation of prisoners of the post-Oslo era.

THE SECOND INTIFADA: THE RETURN OF MASS IMPRISONMENT AND THE PREDICAMENT OF THE PRISONERS' MOVEMENT

The second Intifada, which broke out in late September 2000, was met with a fierce Israeli military reaction of a then unprecedented level. Yet, mass detentions and imprisonment of the scope that characterized the first Intifada were not employed in the early stage of the confrontation, that is, precisely at the phase that was marked by popular Palestinian participation in sizeable demonstrations. In fact, according to data provided by the IDF and the IPS, the number of Palestinian detainees and prisoners that were held in their custody during 2001 ranged between 1500 and 2000.[36] It was the reoccupation of "Zone A" by the IDF in March–April 2002 (Operation Defensive Shield) and the subsequent resumption of full Israeli military control over the West Bank that prepared the ground for the return of the Israeli policy of wide-scale imprisonment, which persists in the West Bank until this very day. The situation in the Gaza Strip differed in this respect (as in many others) from the outset: Israel refrained from a full reoccupation of this territory and opted for a policy of recurring massive incursions accompanied by airstrikes and the enforcement of an ongoing siege. And while the military operations often resulted in an extremely high number of Palestinian casualties, very few arrests were regularly made. The persistence of this policy up until the "Disengagement" of August 2005 and the adherence to similar practices in the years that followed since resulted in the low rate of Gaza Strip residents among the total population of prisoners, which remained around 10 percent throughout most of the past decade.[37]

Unlike my analysis of the interrelationship between the prisoners' movement and the national movement in the pre-Oslo and Oslo years, which is grounded in a thorough socio-anthropological study, my observations with respect to the developments that took place in the post-Oslo era are not supported with a similar body of research; rather they represent an attempt to contemplate the present situation in light of the conclusions that were drawn from the review of the past.[38] I will therefore confine myself to very general remarks. My main contention is that notwithstanding the re-employment by the Israeli occupation forces of wide-scale imprisonment in the West Bank, the prisoners' movement that developed inside Israeli prisons in the post-Oslo era failed to gain a position of comparable impact, magnitude and authority to that of its pre-Oslo predecessor. This failure should be attributed to two major factors: the fact that the majority of the new prisoners of the second Intifada lacked or nearly lacked a background of political activism, and the fact that this uprising lacked a unified leadership and a political program.

Broadly speaking, the majority of the people who were imprisoned since October 2000 were born in the 1980s and grew up in the 1990s; that is, they belonged to a generation that matured during the Oslo years and had barely experienced, if at all, active participation in the political movements and popular structures that shaped the youth of their elders. The want of such experience necessarily entailed lack or near lack of political education and training. An exception to this generalization applies to the youth that came under the influence of the Hamas and Jihad movements, in light of the semi-clandestine existence that characterized these organizations under the PNA rule and the corresponding "organizational discipline" that they instilled in their members. A much smaller group, indeed a small minority among the post-Oslo prisoners, consisted of senior activists and leaders whose histories in the ranks of a political organization dated back to the 1970s, 1980s, and early 1990s. This "older guard", which included members of both the factions of the national movement and of the Islamic opposition, together with the nucleus of the pre-Oslo prisoners who had remained in prison throughout, now formed the core of a new leadership, which was subsequently faced with the daunting task of rebuilding the prisoners' movement.

If the dearth of political education and the paucity of organizational experience that characterized most of the post-Oslo prisoners were detrimental for the rebuilding of the prisoners' movement, then the absence of a unified leadership and of a guiding political agenda to the uprising constituted an obstacle that proved to be insurmountable. This predicament received evident manifestation in the failure of the "National Conciliation Document," a prisoners' initiative to mark a way out of the divide that haunts the Palestinian political system. The "Document" was drafted in May 2006 at Hadarim Prison by senior prisoners' leaders of five political factions/parties: Fatah, Hamas, Islamic Jihad, PFLP and DFLP.[39] At the background of the venture was the escalating conflict between Hamas, which won the parliamentary elections of January 2006 and had subsequently formed a government under the premiership of Isma'il Haniyeh, and between the until then ruling party, Fatah, which retained the presidency of the PNA (Mahmoud Abbas) as well as its hegemonic position in the PLO. Key provisions of the document included a declaration of the right of the Palestinian people to establish their independent state on all territories occupied in the 1967 War (an implicit recognition of the Israeli state); support for popular resistance to the occupation alongside with political action and negotiations and an explicit opting for the focusing of resistance in the OPT (that is, outside Israel proper); a call for the incorporation of Hamas and the Islamic Jihad into the ranks of the PLO and for the subsequent reactivation of the PLO. While the Document did stir a strong reaction at the time, and while it won the considerable support of the Palestinian public, it failed to gather sufficient leverage to effect political change. However, a full evaluation of the current downturn of the prisoners' movement and of the successive developments that brought it about awaits and deserves separate research.

NOTES

1. See B'Tselem, "Prisoners and Detainees," statistics on Palestinians in the custody of the Israeli security forces for the last months of 2009 (the data is provided to B'Tselem by the IPS and the IDF).
2. See <www.Palestinebehindbars.org>, a release dated November 24, 2009: A comprehensive statistical report presented by Abdel Nasser Ferwana.
3. See B'Tselem's data for 2006 through 2008. Note however that major data for the months of February through June 2006 is lacking. See also a comprehensive report prepared by Nadi al-Aseer, on the occasion of Palestinian Prisoner's Day (report number 059-2006).
4. All Palestinian prisoners charged by the Israeli military law of having committed a security offence against the State are hereby referred to as *political* prisoners. This definition is not based on the intention, aim or justification that detainees attribute to their deeds or their consequences, but rather on the means and procedures—military and legal—employed and enforced by the occupation authorities against the detainees.
5. See Ferwana report, November 24, 2009.
6. This estimate appeared in a special publication by the Palestinian Prisoner's Society on the occasion of Palestinian Prisoner's Day (059-2006). It is based on a report published by the statistical department of the Ministry of Prisoners and former Prisoners' Affairs, in March 2006.
7. It is estimated that at the time of the signing of the Declaration of Principles in September 1993, more than 10,000 prisoners were being held in Israeli jails. In the wake of each of the interim agreements that were signed between the Government of Israel and the Palestine Liberation Organization (PLO) over the years 1994–99, thousands of prisoners were released. Much fewer arrests were carried out by the IDF and other Israeli security forces during that time period, and they were targeted mainly against Hamas and Jihad militants.
8. For more on Palestinian women prisoners, see Nahla Abdo's chapter in this volume and the website of Women's Organization for Political Prisoners <www.wofpp.org>.
9. M. Rosenfeld, *Confronting the Occupation: Work, Education and Political Activism of Palestinian Families in a Refugee Camp*, Stanford, CA: Stanford University Press, 2004, p. 232.
10. Ibid.
11. Ibid., Chapter 11.
12. For an analysis of the development of the PNA's government sector and data on the scope of recruitment into the PNA security services during the years 1994–98, see J. Hilal, *Palestinian Society and the Problems of Democracy*, Nablus: Center for Palestine Research and Studies (CPRS), 1999 (in Arabic),

pp. 54–6. For elaboration on the situation of former prisoners in the wake of their release from jail, see Rosenfeld, *Confronting the Occupation*, Chapter 12.

13. See K. al-Hindi, *The Democratic Practice of the Palestinian Prisoners Movement*, Ramallah: Muwatin—The Palestinian Institute for the Study of Democracy, 2000 (in Arabic).

14. The prisoners' "counter-order" and its impact on the process of politicization are discussed in Rosenfeld, *Confronting the Occupation*, Chapter 10.

15. This generalization is not based on comparative research but emerged from recollections of political prisoners that pertained to their activism prior to their imprisonment. Ongoing persecution and harassment were among the prime factors that hampered the experience of activism and rendered it lacking in many respects; the development of group life, group solidarity, democratic decision making, the acquisition of political education and political consciousness, and so on, all suffered as a result.

16. Rosenfeld, *Confronting the Occupation*, p. 252.

17. On the Palestinian guerilla organizations in the wake of the 1967 war and into the early 1970s, see G. Chaliand, *The Palestinian Resistance*, Middlesex: Penguin Books, 1972. See also Abu-Iyad (Salah Khalaf), *Palestinian without a Homeland Conversations with Eric Rolo*, Tel Aviv: Mifras, 1979, pp. 92–4 (Hebrew translation); H. Cobban, *The PLO: People, Power and Politics*, London: Cambridge University Press, 1984, pp. 37–9. On armed and civilian resistance in the Gaza Strip from 1967 through 1971, see A.M. Lesch, "Gaza: History and Politics," in *Israel, Egypt and the Palestinians: From Camp David to Intifada*, A.M. Lesch and M. Tessler (eds), Bloomington: Indiana University Press, pp. 229–30.

18. On the background and "profiles" of the first generation of prisoners, see Rosenfeld, *Confronting the Occupation*, pp. 218–24.

19. See al-Hindi, *The Democratic Practice of the Palestinian Prisoners Movement*, Chapter 1.

20. Rosenfeld, *Confronting the Occupation*, pp. 244–5.

21. On the development of the Palestinian National Movement in the OPT during the late 1970s and the 1980s, see, for example, E. Sahliyeh, *In Search of Leadership: West Bank Politics since 1967*, Washington, DC: Brookings Institution, 1988; L. Taraki, "The Development of Political Consciousness Among Palestinians in the West Bank and Gaza Strip, 1967–1987," in *Intifada: Palestine at the Crossroads*, J. Nassar and R. Heacock (eds), New York: Birzeit University and Praeger Publishers, 1991, pp. 53–72.

22. For elaboration on the education enterprise, see Rosenfeld, *Confronting the Occupation*, pp. 252–63. On the upholding of democratic practices by the political factions and by the (joint) cross-factional prisoners' structures, see al-Hindi, *The Democratic Practice of the Palestinian Prisoners Movement*, Chapters 2 and 3.

23. The Cairo Agreement, brokered by Egyptian President Gamal Abdel Nasser, was signed by Yasser Arafat, head of the PLO, and Emil Bustani, Lebanese chief of staff, on November 2, 1969. It guaranteed the Palestinian resistance movement autonomy to organize and operate within specified zones in Lebanon, especially in refugee camps. In return, the PLO was obligated to refrain from intervention in internal Lebanese affairs. The Agreement was violated during the peak of the Lebanese Civil War (1975–76) but was nevertheless restored thereafter. The

Israeli invasion of 1982 nullified the Cairo Agreement. See R. Brynen, *Sanctuary and Survival: The PLO in Lebanon*, Boulder, CO: Westview Press, 1990.

24. For a critical analysis of this transition, see S. Tamari, "The Palestinian Movement in Transition: Historical Reversals and the Uprising," *Journal of Palestine Studies* 20(2), 1991: 57–70.

25. On the role of the UNLU and the popular committees, see. F. Hunter, *The Palestinian Uprising: A War by Other Means*, Berkeley: University of California Press, 1991. See also, J. Nassar and R. Heacock, "The Revolutionary Transformation of the Palestinians under Occupation," in Nassar and Heacock (eds), *Intifada*, pp. 191–206. See also S. Mishal and R. Aharoni, *Speaking Stones: Communiqués from the Intifada Underground*, Syracuse, NY: Syracuse University Press, 1994.

26. Nassar and Heacock, "The Revolutionary Transformation of the Palestinians," p. 202.

27. On these and other difficulties regarding family visits, see Anat Barsella and Sigi Ben-Ari's chapter in this volume.

28. Rosenfeld, *Confronting the Occupation*, Chapter 11.

29. For more on the October 1992 strike and its impact, see, for example, Washington Report on Middle East Affairs, Special Report, "All-prison Hunger Strike by Palestinian Political Prisoners Ignites Widespread Demonstrations," November 1992, pp. 50–51.

30. It should be noted that absorption into the PNA apparatus, which was very rapid in the first five years (1994–98), was later significantly attenuated under a host of external pressures that were exerted on the PNA, first and foremost by the World Bank.

31. See R. Hammami, "NGOs: the Professionalization of Politics," *Race and Class*, Vol. 37, No. 2, 1995, pp. 51–63; M. Abdul Hadi, "NGO Action and the Question of Palestine: Sharing Experiences, Developing New Strategies," in M. Abdul Hadi (ed.), *Dialogue on Palestinian State-Building and Identity, PASSIA Meetings and Lectures 1995-8*, Jerusalem: Passia, 1999.

32. According to the figures provided by the IPS and the IDF, the number of Palestinian prisoners that were held in Israeli prisons in May 1993 was 10,045. See N. Carmi, *Oslo: Before and After, the Status of Human Rights in the Occupied Territories*, Jerusalem: B'Tselem, 1999, pp. 12–13. According to the PNA Ministry of Prisoners and former Prisoners' Affairs, the number of prisoners in September 1993 was approximately 12,500. See Abdel Nasser Ferwana, *A Comprehensive Study: the Peace Process and the Prisoners*, December 2007 (in Arabic) (republished May 2009).

33. According to Ferwana's calculations, more than 11,000 were released in the wake of the agreements that were signed in the context of the Oslo Accords, that is, between the DoP and the Sharm el-Sheikh Memorandum. A detailed review of the prisoners' release that followed each of the agreements is found in Ferwana, *A Comprehensive Study*.

34. See, for example, Rasem 'Abeidat, *Oslo and its Impact on the Palestinian Prisoners' Movement* (in Arabic), July 12, 2009 <http://www.alasra.ps/news.php?maa=PrintMe&id=8179>.

35. See IPS, *Palestinian Security Prisoners at the Custody of the Prison Authorities*, July 2005 published on the IPS website <http://www.ips.gov.il/shabas> (in Hebrew).

36. See B'Tselem's statistics. The relatively low scale of imprisonment through 2001 can be traced to the "redeployment" of the IDF from "Zone A" (namely, withdrawal from all major Palestinian population centers, except from Hebron) back in the mid-1990s, in the framework of the Oslo Accords. The absence of Israeli Army troops from Palestinian towns rendered arrest raids a less frequent occurrence.

37. Israel conducted a different type of "warfare" in Gaza than in the West Bank, one based on a much more intensive use of heavy ammunition: missile strikes from the air, tanks, cannons, and so forth. It would not be far-fetched to suggest that, at the time, especially in 2003–04, the annihilation of militants was more commonplace than their arrest and imprisonment. Consequently, not only is the relative share of Gaza Strip residents among the overall population of prisoners small, but also, a large proportion of the Gaza prisoners are veterans, who were sentenced during the pre-Oslo and Oslo periods. Among other things, the "under-representation" of Gazans in prison implied that the strength that Hamas accumulated in Gaza over these years was not correlated with an equivalent increase in the strength of Hamas inside prison.

38. For a different analysis of the causes that affected the current demise of the prisoners' movement, see Walid Daka's chapter in this volume.

39. A revised version was ratified by the Fatah and Hamas leaderships in June 28, 2006.

2
Towards a Materialist Reading of Political Imprisonment in Palestine

Esmail Nashif

One of the major arenas of the political imprisonment processes in Palestine is the material conditions in and through which these processes occur. These material conditions are what make it possible for the colonial prison to exist as such. All of the three major categories of actors, namely, Palestinians, Israelis and foreigners (politicians and professionals), experience and simultaneously shape these material conditions differently, yet they agree that these conditions are the foundation upon which political imprisonment is constructed and conditioned.[1] Moreover, most of the crucial formative moments of the complexity of real life in prison are resolved, negotiated, contended over and determined in material terms and conditions.[2]

In contrast to these realities of political imprisonment in Palestine, the different literatures on them appear to displace, and at times conceal, their material constitutive logic. The socio-historical and politico-legal knowledge and their discursive apparatuses regarding the colonial prison in Palestine stand on different grounds. These are, mostly, abstract categories of who is the individual human, and what are his or her basic rights in different contexts of crises. In this regard, for example, the right to eat differs from, or may even contradict in its inner organizing principle, the material condition of eating. Hence, the hypostatization of rights could result in negating the practice of the right in certain concrete processes of social realities, of which the colonial prison is the exemplar. In this short chapter, I do not intend to deconstruct these bodies of knowledge; rather I will try to illuminate the primacy of the material conditions and the materiality of the colonial prison in approaching the realities of the colonial prison in Palestine. In this way I will attempt to broaden our understanding of its complexities.

The journey of this chapter takes us to two major sites. The first is the main characteristics of the material conditions of the colonial prison in Palestine. In this site, we will critically demarcate the main dynamics that characterize the histories of political imprisonment in Palestine since the early Mandate period until now. The second site will be the conceptualization of materiality as an analytical tool, and the possibilities of its application to the realities of the colonial prison in Palestine. The insights from these two sites will lead us to explore particularity as the major formative agent of materiality, and the ways it is suspended in the colonial prison by the different agents who occupy it. In the final section, we will come back to revisit our understanding regarding the specific dynamic interrelations, materialities and systematization(s) in and around the Israeli colonial prison.

1.

The main characteristic of the material conditions of the colonial prison in Palestine is its totality. This is a totality of the quantitative and qualitative aspects of political imprisonment, a totality that powerfully engulfs the whole bodies of Palestine and Palestinians, and hence their Israeli counterparts. Through various accumulative and formative processes, totality came to reign as an organizing principle. In order to explicate the basic features and workings of this principle, I will attempt to delineate the totality, first, on the seemingly empirical level.

The totality seems to start with the material nexus of the prisons as sites and buildings spread all over the territory of Palestine. In many respects, this nexus creates a geography of imprisonment that parallels the body sovereign of the colonial state. In the relevant literature, it is customary to chart the material and spatial layers of the colonial prison system starting from the late Ottoman period. The beginning is conceived as a threshold point in time that divides the pre-modern from the modern era.[3] Hence, the material conditions of the prison system in the late Ottoman period are described in terms of a pre-modern materiality. It is argued that the difference lies in that the Ottoman period was bounded to localities; prison was a local matter in its materiality as well as in its manners of functioning. In contrast, the British colonial administration systematized the prison, and hence material conditions were standardized in such a way that matter became irrelevant. It took the British Mandate authorities a decade or so to initiate and accomplish their master plan for the prison system in Palestine. Once built, though, all Tegart forts—the network of buildings erected by the Mandate authorities in the 1930s as part of their attempt to control Palestine—looked almost exactly the same regardless of the locality in which they were erected.[4] But despite these de/recoding processes, the Ottoman material and symbolic regimes did not disappear; rather, one could sense them visually and hear their stories in the narrative related by the different occupants of these buildings. The ostensible systematization and the hybrid, and at times conflictive, realities of the material conditions of imprisonment were processes that could be discerned at other tense colonial sites of that period, such as the landscape, the sanitation system and the hospitals.[5]

Although this is one of the unspoken areas in the Zionist discourse, the Israeli regime inherited the British one at many levels and in different ways, and the prison system is no exception in this regard. To this day, most of the prison system is based on the British one. It is beyond the scope of this essay to depict the different stages through which this part of the inheritance—that is, the prison system—has evolved and taken shape since the establishment of Israel. However, one cannot fail to notice that the logic of the systematization of material conditions, and by extension its bureaucratic sibling, are the main dynamics of forming and instituting the Israeli prison system.[6] The most relevant current example, on this level of systematization, is the transfer of most of the prisons that were under the military (IDF) authority to the Israel Prison Service. After this reorganization of the IPS, there is one authority in charge of imprisonment in Israel. However, this systematization did not negate the hybrid realities of the material conditions in the Israeli prison system. For, in addition to the particular realities of each prison and its unique historical layers, these realities seem to interact differently with the processes of systematization initiated on the higher level of the system as a whole. The actual material conditions of Ofer Prison interact with the general systematization processes differently, than, say, the Gilboa Prison, although both of them are subordinated to the same process simultaneously.[7]

The duality of systematization and hybridity in the Israeli prison system is reminiscent of the British colonial era. It seems, though, that the Israeli prison system is more intensive and vigorous in attempting to resolve the tensions that result from this duality. The systematization for the purpose of total recoding of the material conditions is apparently conditioned by different political events. Examples of this are the closing and reopening of different prisons

during the two Intifadas and the differential attitudes and (de)
privileging of different Palestinian factions by the prison authorities
according to the faction's position towards the Oslo Accords. This
impression may be misleading if one looks at longer stretches of
time sequences. Seen from this perspective, the systematization has
been and still is the main organizing behavior pattern of the Israeli
authorities in charge of the prison system. Contrarily, though, this
indicates the dominance of the material conditions and materiality
as the major force in shaping the opposite pole of systematization.

On their side, the collectivity of Palestinian political prisoners
has repeatedly tried to dismantle the systematizing processes by
constantly returning to the material conditions and materiality. The
question that concerns us here is the manner of this return. The
basic perception among the prisoners is that only at the level of
collective return, that is, systematized return, can they renegotiate
and redirect the systematization processes imposed on them by the
prison authorities. From this understanding, they have invested
most of their resources in forming a certain community based on
a dual process of systematization, consisting of (a) organizing the
community systematically,[8] and (b) developing systematic modes of
returning to the material conditions in order to divert the imposed
systematization processes of the prison authorities. As I have shown
in detail elsewhere, the history of systematization of the community
has been told and written by the prisoners' collectivity via different
stations of return to the material conditions. For example:

> The history of the political captive's community is narrated in
> verbal and written accounts by the captives themselves, a time/
> space continuum punctuated by the landmarks of its materiality.
> The hunger strike after which the captives received beds, the
> date when the Red Cross stopped bringing fruit, the opening
> of grilles in the cell doors, are examples of history narrated
> as a changing materiality. Thus the community's struggle and
> resistance are constructed in a historical narrative around the
> material conditions and the demands to change them.[9]

However, this pattern of return has not succeeded in negating
the prison authorities' systematization. Rather, by struggling for
control over the power structure of the systematization of the
imprisonment spatio-temporal matrices—as is evident from the
organizational charts and documents from different organizations
and periods[10]—the collectivity of prisoners has largely negated the

material conditions through which it struggles to liberate itself. Despite these processes, as is the case with the prison authorities but probably more intensely so, several moments/sites of the material conditions seem to slip away from, or even resist such attempts of the community to systematize them. Notable among these are the interrogation, the hunger strike and the body.[11]

To conclude this section, we could argue that the material conditions are the main arena of the conflictive/merging interrelations between the prison authorities and the collectivity of the political prisoners. Yet, both sides negate the material conditions while systematizing them in their struggle over control of the prison's power structure. For the colonial prison authorities, this mode of government, namely the constant expansion of systematization, is a necessary condition for its survival. For the political prisoners' community, it is a socio-historical choice that has so far failed to put an end to its conditions of incarceration. The stubborn return of the negated material conditions as a moment/site of fracture for the parallel processes of systematization obliges us to rethink these material conditions in terms of a formative third pole in this specific colonial condition. For that, we will now turn to materiality.

2.

At the planning and designing stages of each prison, the Prisons Authority creates and defines the material conditions. Moreover, it formalizes the rules as to who can use it, when, and in what manner. Although it aims at total control of the prisons through such planning and design, it fails time and time again to achieve such a total systematization. The systematized struggle of the collectivity of political prisoners starts at those moments of fracture when the colonial prison fails to systematize. But the prisoners' systematic return to the material conditions fails for the very same reasons that obstructed the attempts of the prison authorities. As for the human rights organizations, they accept a priori the principle of systematization and deal only with what could be termed "improving systematization," that is, systematization that actually improves prisoners' lives. The failure to totally systematize the prison complex, then, is not due to the struggle of the collectivity of political prisoners and/or the human rights organizations' watchdog roles. Rather, it seems that the material conditions themselves have resistive aspects that elude planning, design and formalizations by both the prison authorities and the collectivity of political prisoners. Now, let's look more closely at the deeper dynamics that cause these failures of systematization.

Seen from a certain rational perspective, materiality is a vague concept.[12] One way to overcome its vagueness is to reconceptualize it as the different possible modes through which the material conditions (re)present themselves as a formative agent in sociohistorical processes.[13] In the context of political imprisonment, the formative charge of materiality is its particularity, in contrast to the universality of systematization characteristic of modern rational modes of agency. In a sense, this particularity pierces the body universal, thus forming an approximation towards a colonial difference. It is an approximation because it cannot be articulated and elaborated on; the structural conditions of systematization are aimed precisely at eliminating such a return of the particular of materiality. Hence, it is formative by recurrently opening the heavy screenings of systematization without itself being subjugated either to the apparatuses of the colonial prison system or to the ones developed by the collectivity of the Palestinian political prisoners.

By this reframing of our understanding of materiality, the concept of particularity turns out to be a core concept which requires further elaboration. One could start by relying on the Gramscian insight that no system of domination can contain all of that which it is aimed to dominate. In our case of the colonial prison, indomitability stems from the nature of the system of domination itself, that is, the incessant systematization to eliminate the material conditions of possibility of Palestinian-ness. For that particularity is initially perceived as the domain of accumulative socio-material activities that could negate systematization. The problematic of such an understanding is that it frames particularity as a dependent, interrelated construct of the systematization processes. In other words, it systematizes particularity, and in such a move it empties it of its critical charge. And, I argue, the collectivity of the Palestinian political prisoners could not fail to fall into this trap due to the nature of the national ideological infrastructure upon which it was built.

It is no coincidence that the literature on colonial difference usually starts by deconstructing the intellectual inheritance of Enlightenment regarding the interrelation of the abstract human, his or her rights and freedom(s).[14] The interesting twist in this junction, though, is the critique raised by many scholars who reposition these humanistic themes back in the social history of capital. What is relevant to us here, from this corpus of critique, is the argument that there are at least two histories that cannot be reduced to the single formal history of capital.[15] While the humanistic themes, including their later offshoots of rationalization and systematization, are inherent parts of the formal history of capital, the other histories have different organizing principles. Termed differently by different readers of these histories, the different socio-historical processes that occur parallel to the history of capital resonate with what is described here as particularity. These frames of analysis may help us in peeling the different dynamic layers that are at work in the Israeli colonial prison context.

Of these different readings, the most relevant to our context is Dipesh Chakrabarty's *Provincializing Europe* (2000), especially Chapter 2. Chakrabarty directly addresses the issues of systematization and materiality/particularity as the basis for colonial difference. Moreover, he links the disciplinary nature of the factory and the prison as two sites of regeneration of the capitalist relations of domination.[16] Chakrabarty builds his argument about the history that is not subsumed by the formal history of capital by re-reading Marx's analytical apparatus that is based on the main concept of the Enlightenment, the abstract human. He argues that the Marxian concept of abstract labor is a derivative from the abstract human. Moreover, Chakrabarty argues that abstract labor *à la* Marx does not negate concrete labor but suspends it continuously and infinitely. In his attempt to explicate from Marx the dynamic process of transforming all concrete particular labor and the use-value of the particularities into abstract labor, which is built at least partly on systematization, Chakrabarty quotes the following paragraph from *Capital*:

If ... we disregard the use-value of the commodities, the only one property remains, that of products of labour ... If we make abstraction from its use value, we also abstract from the material constituents and forms which make it a use-value. It is no longer a table, a house, a piece of yarn or any other useful thing. All its sensuous characteristics are extinguished ... With the disappearance of the useful character of the products of labour, the useful character of the kinds of labour embodied in them also disappears; this in turn entails the disappearance of the different concrete forms of labour. They can no longer be distinguished, but are all reduced to the same kind of labour, human labour in the abstract.[17]

Particularity, as the main characteristic of materiality, is the concrete labor that accumulates or is objectified as a use-value. The bed, the house, or the yarn of the socio-material production in general are not the particularities of the colonial prison. Rather, the individual and the collective concrete bodies of the political prisoners are both the producers/performers of the concrete labor and the objectified use-value that the systematization (namely, the apparatus upon which stands the abstract human labor) aims at. But these concrete material socio-historical formations—the bodies—cannot be totally abstracted. What is abstracted is the "political prisoner." Therefore, the processes of systematization are accomplished through two simultaneous restructuring mechanisms. We can locate the dual movement first in suspending the concrete bodies/particularities, and second in systematizing an abstract political prisoner. It is this abstract entity that is signified, invoked, imprisoned and fought for by the different discourses of the colonial authority, the collectivity of political prisoners, and the human rights organizations. The question then arises as to the nature of the interrelations between the suspended particularity and the abstract systemized entity.

After establishing these two domains of different histories, Chakrabarty moves on to generalize regarding the interrelations between them. Mainly, he argues that there is no single discernible manner of interrelations. Rather, he names them H1 and H2, the formal history of capital and the one not subsumed by it, respectively, and claims that:

> History 2 does not spell out a program of writing histories that are alternative to the narratives of capital. That is, History 2s do not constitute a dialectical Other of the necessary logic of History 1. To think thus would be to subsume History 2 to History 1. History 2 is better thought of as a category charged with the function of constantly interrupting the totalizing thrusts of History 1.[18]

Chakrabarty is right in differentiating H2 from the inner logic of H1, which dictates the dialectical Other. But the problematic of thinking of H2 as a "category" that has a "function" seems to bring us back to H1. The return of H2, or particularity, can be seen as a category with function only if it is looked at through the lenses of H1. Put differently, particularity is not constituted by suspension, and with this Chakrabarty agrees. Particularity is rendered by suspension to a homological non-reducible distance from the structure of capital itself. As the case of the history of Palestinian political prisoners shows, the real living bodies carry systematization, particularity, and the distance between them at the same moment. They actualize their right to eat, they eat the food given by the colonial prison authorities, and they practice eating in its particularity as a singular but repetitive practice. The collapse of the homological distance, for example, in the case of a hunger strike or when one individual swallows another's right to eat, is directly related to the irresolvable nature of suspension itself. The apparatuses of suspension, then, are not inherent to the processes of production. Rather, they manage the edges of production in a certain way so as to smooth its functionality.

In this section, I have tried to reread the dynamics of the systematization and materiality of the colonial prison by positioning them in their larger context. The common characteristics of the formal social history of capital and the historical differences that are not subsumed by it are articulated in the literature as one way of practicing critical readings of the late colonial contexts. The Israeli colonial prison exhibits some of these common characteristics while bringing us to the point of rethinking some others. In the concluding section, I refer to these particular and unique aspects of the Israeli colonial prison.

3.

Like any other complex socio-historical phenomenon, the colonial prison system in Palestine may be read from different angles. The one offered in this chapter tried to locate the major constitutive split inside the colonial prison complex, that is, systematization and materiality. While the reigning paradigms of thinking the colonial prison are those of systematization, the realities of political imprisonment in Palestine have recurrently shown different formations of hybridity that escape systematization. I argued that the main regenerating site of this phenomenon is the interface between the processes of systematization and materiality. The tracing of materiality through its main formative characteristic of particularity is approached by the mechanisms of suspension and return, which are general modes of operation in the social history of capital and the history that is not subsumed by it. These, though, could have their own unique variety in the colonial context.

In the context of the Israeli colonial prison, the thrust towards total systematization is grounded in fear of the return of particularity.

The recognition that particularity will inevitably return is both a structure of feeling built into the mechanisms of suspension, and a colonial ideological apparatus. The distinction between these two is an analytical one. One could argue that ideological apparatuses are means of coping with irresolvable contradictions in systems of domination. The ideological stitching of these open contradictions is most visible in the over-investment in reproducing the abstract political prisoner via constantly renewed bureaucracies of systematization, for example, the use of sociological and statistical data and analyses in instituting new policies for professionalizing the cadres of the Israel Prisons Authority.[19]

As for the collectivity of the political prisoners, at least in the heyday of its national phase, the formation of the communal apparatuses of systematization had two main interconnected dynamics. In its relation to Palestinian socio-materiality, the thrust for systematization was one-directional from particularities to systematization, that is, from local identities to the national one. In its relations with the colonial authorities, it systematized the return to particularities in order to restructure the power relations inside the colonial prison. These two patterns of systematization trapped the collectivity in the arena of the formal social history of the prison system which is, a priori, controlled by the colonizer and structurally exclusive towards the colonized.

The necessary condition for the human rights organizations is the discursive formation, abstract political prisoners. Regardless of their national background—Palestinian, Israeli, or European— these organizations are built on certain premises that a priori exclude the possibility of a history not subsumed by the notion of abstract human. As a third party, located in between and supposedly beyond the localities of Israeli and Palestinian direct manners of engagement with the conflict, these organizations must—in order to be relevant to both—speak a universal discourse and a locally systematized one. These positions, and their manners of speaking, then, necessitate a certain socioeconomic background of educated middle-class professionals. These constellations of the human rights organizations are part of the maintenance and reproduction of a certain equilibrium point of the colonial condition in Palestine.[20]

To conclude this essay, the reading of the colonial prison system in Palestine through its materiality could open our understanding to hitherto unthought-of aspects of its realities. The implications of such a reading lead us to reposition these realities within their larger context, namely late capitalism/colonialism. What is offered here is an initial reframing that demands more thorough and exhaustive efforts to explore critically what has been taken for granted. Moreover, this reading raises serious doubts concerning the premises underlying such accepted notions as struggle, resistance, and colonizer–colonized dynamics.

NOTES

1. The corpus of literature on the topic of material conditions in the Israeli prisons is enormous. The aim of this essay is not to review it, but rather to explicate the role of these conditions in reproducing the colonial prison. For a review of part of this literature, see E. Nashif, *Palestinian Political Prisoners: Identity and Community*, London: Routledge, 2008, pp. 38–71.
2. More often than not, the crises in relations between the political prisoners and the prison authorities occur when one side changes a basic material condition, such as the quantity of a certain food item or the amount of time for the daily break. Such crises are usually resolved by reaching an agreement on the quantity, quality and management of these material conditions. See also Walid Daka's article in the present volume.
3. The modernization paradigm is the major discursive formation in this regard. Moreover, it is not restricted to the colonizer or the colonized and the mediators between them. Although there is no specific research on the history of imprisonment in Palestine that traces the transitions from the Ottoman to the British Mandate, and then to the Israeli period, two bodies of literature can help to explicate the manner in which the modernization paradigm is applied to the history of the prison system in Palestine. The first is the academic literature on the transitions in various spheres of relations between state and society. Examples of this are: A. Ayalon, *Reading Palestine: Printing and Literacy, 1900-1948*, Austin: University of Texas Press, 2004, and R. El-Eini, "The Impact of British Rule on the Landscape of Mandate Palestine, 1929–1948," Jerusalem: Hebrew University, unpublished doctoral dissertation, 2000. The second body of literature is the discursive practices of both the political prisoners and the prison authorities. Although this is not mainly concerned with the history as such, the modernizing frame could be explained as an organizing principle of the influx of the current events with their relations to the past. For a review of the literature of Palestinian political prisoners, see for example: Nashif, *Palestinian Political Prisoners*, pp. 41–65.
4. El-Eini, "The Impact of British Rule," pp. 31–82.
5. One way to understand systematization is to frame it as part of the decoding/recoding processes of the capitalist writing machine. See G. Deleuze and F. Guattari, *Anti-Oedipus: Capitalism and Schizophrenia*, Minneapolis: University of Minnesota Press, 1983, pp. 139–53.
6. There is by now a developing and vibrant body of literature on the Israeli colonization processes through architecture and spatial formations. For examples of architectural systematizing practices, see Z. Efrat, *The Israeli Project: Building and architecture, 1948–1973*, Tel-Aviv: Tel-Aviv Museum of Art. For recent debates on the theoretical and political levels of these processes, see, for example, A. Ophir, M. Givoni and S. Hanafi, *The Power of Inclusive*

Exclusion: Anatomy of the Israeli rule in the Palestinian occupied territories, New York: Zone Books, 2009.

7. See, for example, the following reports on these two specific prisons, A. Masiqa, "The Offers of Ofer," *Roim Shabas*, Vol. 24, pp. 3–6 (September 2008), and N. Telem, "In the Gilboa They Aspire for the Higher," *Roim Shabas*, Vol. 26, pp. 12–15 (September 2009).

8. Nashif, *Palestinian Political Prisoners*, pp. 72–98; B. Harlow, "Political Detention: Countering the University," *October*, Vol. 53, pp. 40–61 (Summer 1990).

9. Nashif, *Palestinian Political Prisoners*, pp. 41–2.

10. Compare, for example, Hamas' organizational manual for the interrogation phase with that of the PFLP, which was published in the early 1980s. For Hamas: *A Conflict in the Dark: The dynamics of confrontation in the dungeons of interrogation*, "The Occupation's Prisons," Ibn al Yaman Media Center for Security Awareness. For the PFLP: *The Philosophy of Confrontation behind the Bars*, n.p.

11. Nashif, *Palestinian Political Prisoners*.

12. There have been various attempts in the literature to address the issue of materiality, coming from different approaches, but it seems that there is no single acceptable definition of the concept. Here, its fuller exposition will be clearer as the essay unfolds. See, for example, G. Bataille, *Visions of Excess: Selected writings, 1927–1939*, Minneapolis: University of Minnesota Press, 1985; R. Williams, "Problems of Materialism" in his *Culture and Materialism*, London: Verso, 1983, pp. 103–22, and S. Timpanaro, *On Materialism*, London: NLB, 1975.

13. The concept "agent" is used here for lack of a better term. Definitely, materiality is not an agent in the accepted modern sense of the term. As a baseline, one could think of it as an agency without a particular agent/subject. As will be shown later on in this chapter, it is a formative accumulated concrete labor.

14. See, for example, the following: A. Mbembe, *On the Postcolony*, Berkeley: University of California Press, 2001; W. D. Mingolo, *Local Histories/Global Designs: Coloniality, subaltern knowledge, and border thinking*, Princeton, NJ: Princeton University Press, 2000, and B. Cohen, *Colonialism and its Forms of Knowledge: The British in India*, Princeton, NJ: Princeton University Press, 1996.

15. Such as with the following: E. Nashif, *Gradus for Opening the Episteme*, Ramallah: Muwatin, 2010 (in Arabic); D. Chakrabarty, *Provincializing Europe: Postcolonial thought and historical difference*, Princeton, NJ: Princeton University Press, 2000, and Mingolo, *Local Histories/Global Designs*.

16. Chakrabarty, *Provincializing Europe*, p. 56.

17. Ibid., pp. 54–5.

18. Ibid., p. 66.

19. IPS, *Annual Report for 2008*, Media Department, 2009.

20. See, for example, how Negri and Hardt reposition human rights organizations as part of the moral arsenal of the empire: M. Hardt and A. Negri, *Empire*, Cambridge, MA: Harvard University Press, 2000.

3
Who Is a Security Prisoner and Why? An Examination of the Legality of Prison Regulations Governing Security Prisoners

Alon Harel

The Israel Prison Service uses the category of a "security prisoner" as a relevant category in determining rights and privileges of prisoners. The classification of prisoners into "security prisoners" and regular (non-security prisoners) is based on regulations issued by the governor of prisons in accordance with its authority in section 80a(a) to the Prisons Ordinance. This classification has enormous importance for prisoners. Security prisoners are deprived of many of the rights granted to non-security prisoners. For instance, section 19(a) denies security prisoners the right to phone conversations. Section 18 of the regulations governing security prisoners denies them the right to conjugal visits, and they also do not benefit from early release, which is often granted to other prisoners. While this chapter suggests that using classificatory systems to differentiate among prisoners in accordance with the type of crimes committed by them is permissible, it also suggests that the classificatory system used by the IPS is deficient for three reasons: over-broadness, rigidity and over-harshness.

It is evident that prison authorities are entitled to classify prisoners on the basis of their dangerousness and they are also entitled to differentiate the privileges granted to prisoners in order to address security as well as other concerns. But, are they entitled to evaluate dangerousness on the basis of the fact that a prisoner was convicted of a particular offense or belongs to a group which is, as a statistical generalization, particularly dangerous? Can statistical considerations be used to evaluate the dangerousness of prisoners?

This is not an easy question. The legal system in general is suspicious of the use of classifications and it often imposes strict restrictions on the use of such classifications. Evidence law strictly excludes the use of statistical inferences in criminal trials. Yet, in other contexts, the law permits the use of such classifications. The practice of racial profiling is strictly regulated but it is permissible in some contexts. The question of whether the use of classifications which are statistically relevant is permissible or not depends on the context and the severity of the consequences it may have on the victims of such a classification.

I believe that the prison authorities are entitled to use broad (statistically relevant) categories based on the types of offences committed by the prisoner, the age of the prisoner, her motivations and other criteria of this type in order to evaluate the dangerousness of prisoners. After all, dangerousness of a prisoner is often difficult to predict. As I show below, depriving the prison authorities of the power to use such criteria may have undesirable effects not only on society as a whole but also on prisoners themselves. At the same time, such a use ought to be strictly regulated; it ought to be narrowly applied and not deny prisoners their basic rights even when such a denial may contribute to safety and security. Prisoners are entitled to (some degree of) individualized scrutiny of their dangerousness. More specifically, they are entitled that *their specific dangerousness rather than the dangerousness of a typical prisoner belonging to their category* provide the basis for determining their rights and privileges. The classification of a prisoner on the basis of broad categories is permissible, but such a classification ought not to be mechanical or automatic. Precisely as we do not convict (or acquit) a person simply because she belongs to a group, so we are not entitled to deprive a prisoner of privileges simply because she belongs to a collective, even if members of that collective, as a statistical rule, impose grave social risks. A non-differential treatment of prisoners—one that fails to account for their individuality—is incompatible with the fundamental principles of a liberal state, that is, a state which is committed to treating its citizens as individuals rather than as members of collectives or groups.

This analysis raises a challenge for prison authorities. On the one hand, they are required to make the life of prisoners as tolerable as possible. This requires prison authorities to differentiate among prisoners on the basis of their dangerousness in order to grant privileges to those prisoners who are less likely to abuse these privileges. It is permissible, for instance, that prison authorities will strictly scrutinize the decision to grant vacation privileges to sex offenders (and not to other offenders), as sex offenders tend to be recidivists. Israeli courts recognized that the type of offence may be a consideration in determining whether an offender is entitled to a vacation.[1] Depriving sex offenders of vacations because of the high level of recidivism among sex offenders is permissible. If prison authorities are barred from making such differentiations, they would be forced to deprive all prisoners of the privileges which are currently denied only to small subgroups of prisoners. To the extent that security prisoners pose special risks, it is permissible on the part of the prison authorities to deprive them of certain privileges in order to address these risks. On the other hand, the classificatory system used by prison authorities ought not to be too crude, rigidly mechanistic, or harsh. It ought to acknowledge the fact that prisoners are not only members of groups; they are individuals with their own lives, ideologies and worldviews. Furthermore, like all human beings, prisoners change, grow and mature; their lives are subject to changes and transformations and such transformations ought to be reflected in the treatment they receive. This chapter suggests that the current classificatory scheme used by prison authorities fails to fully respect the individuality of prisoners and, consequently, it does not meet the standards prevailing in a liberal society.

The classificatory system used by the prison authorities to deprive security prisoners of privileges is impermissible and illegal for at least three different reasons: its crudeness (over-generalization), rigidity and harshness. First, the classificatory system is over-broad, as it fails to account for relevant important differences among different prisoners whose potential for dangerous activity differs radically. Secondly, it is too rigid. The right to individualized treatment dictates that the classification of a prisoner ought to be subject to periodic evaluation. Third, the classificatory system is too harsh, that is, the scope of privileges denied to security prisoners is too wide and it does not serve the purposes of the classification. Let us examine each one of these issues.

The category of security prisoners is too broad; it fails to account for the relevant differences among different subgroups of security prisoners. As Advocate Baker said:

> [A] 14 years old boy that is suspected of throwing a Molotov bottle (that did not explode) is perceived as equally dangerous to a 40 years old man who was the head of a terrorist organization; members of an Islamic group that are suspected of economic support or relations with hostile Palestinian organizations are perceived as threatening state security and are deprived of the right to see their children precisely as fighters that were caught during battle.[2]

The non-differential treatment of criminals whose dangerousness is very different from each other is a violation of their right to fair and individualized treatment. It seems evident that prisoners who are convicted of murder pose greater risks than prisoners convicted of lesser offenses. It also seems evident that the age of different offenders, their personal status, and so on, may be relevant to evaluating their dangerousness. The category of "security prisoner" fails to account for the important differences in the dangerousness of different prisoners. It is unfair that a member of a gang who was convicted of murder would be entitled to privileges which are denied to security prisoners who are convicted for lesser offences.[3]

The "security prisoner" category is also too rigid. Take, for example, the case of Walid Daka, who was convicted of murder in 1986. During his imprisonment, he got married, completed an undergraduate degree, and also indicated in his behavior and in his written statements that his worldview had radically changed since his conviction. Walid Daka petitioned the court seeking conjugal visits with his wife. Within his court petition he demanded that his classification as a security prisoner ought to be reconsidered in light of the changes in his personal life and in his ideology. The petitioner provided ample evidence indicating the radical ideological and personal changes he had gone through. His petition however was denied in the administrative court of Nazareth. Judge Danny Zarfati maintained:

> ... the presumption of dangerousness of a security prisoner given his deeds and his ideological motivations that brought him into the prison does not require positive proof from time to time ... The opposite is true. The prisoner who wishes to be treated differently has the onus to prove that he is entitled to a different treatment. A different interpretation implies discriminatory treatment of prisoners and disrupting the harmony of the regulations.[4]

This decision is wrong for moral, legal and prudential reasons. Morally speaking, it ignores the fact (that was acknowledged by the Court in the case of Suleman El Abid who was convicted of sex offenses) that criminals' degree of dangerousness can change. Like all human beings, prisoners mature, marry, divorce, transform their ideology and change their political affiliations. It is morally wrong to fail to account for these changes as these changes are relevant to evaluating the dangerousness of a prisoner. Legally speaking, the unwillingness to account for such changes violates the principles embodied in Basic Law: Human Dignity and Freedom. The legal system ought to acknowledge the realities of prisoners' lives and these realities are subject to change and transformation. A periodic examination of the dangerousness of a prisoner is therefore legally required, as it is the only way in which the legal system acknowledges the prisoner as a human being entitled to a dignified existence. Dignified existence requires treatment which is sensitive to the transformations of individuals' character, lifestyle, convictions and identities. This is especially true with respect to prisoners who have spent long years in prison and who have established a family, have completed their studies, or have gone through other major changes in their life. Last, it is prudentially wrong to fail to account for such changes as such rigidity does not provide incentives to prisoners to transform their life, to rehabilitate and to integrate again into society. The rigidity of the classificatory system is incompatible with the right of a prisoner to hope, that is, to maintain the realistic expectation that a better future is possible for them—and to behave accordingly.

It would be perhaps too demanding to recognize hope as a basic human right which ought to be legally protected. Hope seems like a state of mind and individuals typically do not have rights to benefit from certain states of mind. It is not the job of the state to guarantee that people benefit from states of mind. Yet, what I defend here is not the right to hope but the right to the provision of conditions and circumstances which provide prisoners with the realistic prospects of having a better future and I believe that the legal system ought to guarantee such a right.

This is hardly a legal novelty. Some important precedents indicate that legal systems recognize the duty to provide prisoners with realistic prospects for a better future. In 1973, the German Federal Constitutional Court has deduced from the right to human dignity and to development of one's personality, coupled with the constitutional ideal of *Sozialstaat*, a positive constitutional right for offenders to be offered the opportunity to resocialize themselves. In 1977, in the important life imprisonment case, the Court confirmed its earlier decision and required that offenders retain a reasonable possibility of being considered for release.[5] These decisions were based on the view that individuals ought to retain some prospects for a better future and that depriving them of such prospects violates their right to dignity. The same set of values requires that the classificatory system used by prison authorities be flexible rather than rigid and that it does not deprive prisoners of a periodic review of their classification as security prisoners. It is inhumane to deprive prisoners of privileges due to a classification which does not fit the realities of their lives.

The over-harshness of the system refers to the fact that the scope of privileges which are denied to security prisoners is too broad. The regulations concerning security prisoners state that:

> The prisoners who have been convicted or are charged with security offences have, as general rule, a potential to endanger the security of the state and, in particular, to endanger the order and discipline in prisons given the type of offence committed by them or given the offence they are charged with, their past, their motivations and their involvement in activities against the security of the state.[6]

It is this reasoning which justifies, according to the regulation, special restrictions concerning contact with the outside world including vacations, visitation rights, phone conversations and conjugal visits.

This concern regarding contact with the outside world is a genuine concern. Contact with the outside world may provide opportunities for prisoners to abuse their privileges. But can such risks justify the broad scope of the restrictions? Could not the dangers posed by phone conversations of security prisoners be mitigated by permitting phone conversations which are supervised or monitored? Could not visitation rights be allowed subject to the condition that they are videotaped or monitored in other ways? The restrictions imposed by the current classificatory system are too harsh given the purposes that they are designed to achieve. Most importantly, these restrictions violate the principle that legal restrictions ought to be as narrow as possible and that effort ought to be made to guarantee that such restrictions are absolutely necessary to serve the purposes for which they are imposed.

I have suggested that the prison authorities are entitled to take dangerousness into account and they are also entitled to differentiate among different prisoners on the basis of classificatory systems. Furthermore, a classificatory system of prisoners can also use as a proxy for dangerousness the type of crime committed by the prisoner. The category "security prisoner" is also permissible, as security prisoners may be dangerous in ways that other prisoners are not. However, such systems ought to satisfy strict conditions; they ought to be narrowly designed to achieve their purposes. They also ought to recognize the realities of human lives and the individuality of prisoners. The current system used by prison authorities fails to meet these standards. Such a failure on the part of the system raises the suspicion that the system is being used not to address the dangerousness of prisoners but to express special hostility towards criminals who have committed crimes against the security of the state, and, perhaps, is even used to convey racial animosity towards Palestinian prisoners.[7] Needless to say, it is not the job of the prison authorities to express their revulsion of crimes of any sort; that is exclusively the job of the courts.

Admittedly, humane treatment of prisoners has potential dangers. A civilized society, however, cannot violate the basic rights of prisoners even if such a violation is conducive to other social goals. Most importantly, it ought to provide all prisoners (like all human beings) a sense that a better future is possible and that they have something to which they can realistically aspire. The Israeli Basic Law: Human Dignity and Freedom provides the necessary legal tools for courts to guarantee that such aspirations be in fact legally protected. The prison regulations governing the treatment of security prisoners are illegal and ought therefore to be amended.

NOTES

1. See prisoner appeal 6481/01 *El Abid v. Israel Prison Service*, PD 57, 678 (2003).
2. A. Baker, "The Definition of Palestinian Prisoners in Israel as 'Security Prisoners'— Security Semantics for Camouflaging Political Practice," *Adalah's Review*, Vol. 5, Spring 2009, p. 66 (Israel).
3. For more on this, see Yael Berda's chapter in the present volume.
4. Prisoner appeal 609/08 (Nazareth District Court) *Daka v. IPS*, delivered on September 21, 2009.
5. BVerfGE 45, 187 [1977].
6. IPS Rules, rule number 4.05.00.
7. For such accusations, see A. Baker, "The Definition of Palestinian Prisoners in Israeli Prisons as 'Security Prisoners' – Security Semantics for Camouflaging Political Practice," *Adalah's Review*, Vol. 5 (Spring 2009), pp. 65–78. Advocate Baker relied in her accusation on the fact that one of the relevant conditions used by the prison authorities to classify prisoners is their affiliation with illegal organizations. This criterion often applies to Palestinian security prisoners convicted of crimes against the security of the state but (as a general rule) does not apply to Jewish prisoners convicted of similar crimes. While I share most of Advocate Baker's concerns, I am not confident that such a criterion is illegitimate, as it could be argued that a prisoner's affiliations with an illegal organization increase her dangerousness. Information provided by a prisoner could be more easily disseminated when the prisoner is a member of an illegal organization. Furthermore, arguably, it could be more easily used by such an organization for criminal purposes.

4
The Security Risk as a Security Risk: Notes on the Classification Practices of the Israeli Security Services

Yael Berda

"I can't tell you what the current criteria are for people who are denied entry into Israel for security purposes," said Sgt. Liron Alush in an exasperated voice, over the phone. "If the criteria that comprise the profile of a terrorist are known, the [terrorist] organizations will know how to get around them." I tried to explain to her that I had a client from the West Bank, a merchant, who had been classified as a security threat because he fit certain classifications and I was trying to get around the classification, or prove he did not fit the profile, in order for him to enter Israel and continue with his work. The permit regime enforced in the West Bank—monitoring and preventing movement of the Palestinian population within the West Bank and into Israel—has become a complex bureaucratic apparatus for identification, profiling and surveillance of the movements of the Palestinian population.

My client thought that the reason for his denial of entry had something to do with his brother being kept in administrative detention. People who are denied entry by the General Security Service (GSS) do not have access to the reasons that led to their classifications as such, the identity of the classifiers, or the components of the discretion that led to the decision to classify them as "denied entry for security reasons." Nor can the classification, as "denied entry for security reasons," be directly appealed. The legal adviser of Judea and Samaria (the Hebrew names of the West Bank area) is generally the only possible address for inquiries and requests to the GSS to reassess and revoke the classification as a security threat.

The civil administration had written in reply to my letter enquiring about my client's classification that there had been no specific information condemning him as a security threat, and yet, we could not obtain a permit for him to enter Israel for a short and important business trip.[1]

"Look. I don't make the profile. The security apparatuses do, and once they make that profile, it's like cast iron. It won't change until they say that the general profile of people who are security threats changes." Relatively generous with information and accustomed to speaking with international and human rights organizations, Liron Alush explained the most important rule of what I have come to call "security theology": the ultimate belief, by agents in the Israeli bureaucratic apparatus, that when it comes to Palestinians, the security apparatuses are not only well equipped to make classifications about entire populations and construct the elaborate profile of "the terrorist," they also have almost unlimited executive discretion in deciding the content of the category of "security threat."

The category of the security threat is a master category, around which an entire taxonomy and system of classification revolves when it comes to identifying and distinguishing between friend and foe, in Israel's permanent state of emergency. The security threat is thus not only a category, a tool for classifying people; it becomes a paradigm of thinking, a binary schema for seeing the Palestinian population. A person can be either a potential security threat or not a threat. All other possibilities collapse into the master category of the security threat.

I wish to describe the classification system of the GSS that has become known to me through my work as a human rights lawyer in Jerusalem. I explored it further through research I conducted on the bureaucracy of the Occupation, a racialized bureaucracy based on rules, decrees and regulations that vary by race, and separate rules and regulations for the governing of the Jewish vs. the Palestinian population in the Occupied Palestinian Territories (OPT). This bureaucracy controls the management, movement and political economy of the Palestinian population in the West Bank. It is based on a bureaucratic model of colonial administration,[2] which is quite different from the classic Weberian model of bureaucracy whose principles are: speed, precision, knowledge of the files, hierarchy and processing by known rules and regulations. I analyze the contemporary use of security threat classification *vis-à-vis* Palestinians in the OPT wishing to obtain from the military civil administration a permit for movement, and the effects of the classification of Palestinian prisoners as security threats, particularly those that are sentenced in military court or are held in administrative detention. Specifically, I address the security threat classifications governing the lives of "security prisoners" within the Israeli prison system.

CLASSIFICATION OF SECURITY PRISONERS

The categorization of prisoners as "security prisoners" occurs both with regards to residents of the OPT tried in the military court and Palestinians who are Israeli citizens tried in Israeli criminal courts. While some of the classification guidelines of the Israeli Prison Service (IPS) pertain to the classic crimes against the state, such as sedition, spying, or treason, part of the classification is in fact a criminalization of political attitudes, beliefs, or circumstances.

The categorization of prisoners into criminal prisoners and security prisoners is usually done with regards to their identity, their offense and their political affiliation at the time of the sentence. It is an internal administrative decision of the IPS, based on internal regulation 04.05.00 of the IPS.

The categorization is based on several substantial tests regarding the nature of the offense and the motivation of the offender, that is, whether the offense was committed in conjunction with security-related circumstances or for nationalistic reasons. This guideline can also be interpreted as pertaining to the political circumstances of the offense or the political leanings of the accused. If the offense might have served in any way a terrorist organization or a person interested in jeopardizing the state security, the prisoner would be classified as a security prisoner. The nature of the motive is determined on the basis of intelligence provided by the police or the GSS. These intelligence reports are not available to the prisoner or his lawyer, and are hence impossible to contest. If any doubt arises, the default assumption is that the prisoner is a security prisoner.

As a master category, when it comes to Palestinian prisoners, the security threat is a primary status, one which needs to be positively falsified, since in the eyes of Israeli bureaucracy, within every Palestinian who belongs to the suspect population lurks the phantom of the terrorist, whose motives are nationalistic in nature—even if these motives have not yet been manifested, they may at any moment.

A brief look at the offenses regarded as security threats reveals two patterns. The first pattern of classification, the main method of criminalizing political membership, is directed against politically oriented acts on behalf of or for the benefit of organizations; the other towards genuine terrorist activities. Political offenses, even fairly mild ones, like organizing an illegal protest, become security offenses when their motive is deemed nationalistic by the GSS. The last reason for classifying a prisoner as a security prisoner is a colonial legacy of Mandate Palestine: here are violations of the emergency defense regulations of 1945, a set of military decrees, allowing the executive power (usually the army) to suspend the law, including basic civil rights, in order to restore order and security in a state of emergency. These decrees were mainly used during the Mandate against members of the Jewish Etzel and Lehi movements; they specify participation or performing services for an illegal association, carrying weapons, firing a weapon or planting a bomb, holding military training sessions and providing a haven.

THE LORDS OF PROFILING

An essential part of the bureaucratic labyrinth of population management under occupation, the GSS is usually the most efficient and competent when compared to other departments. This state of affairs is not unique to occupation bureaucracies but has been a feature of most regimes which maintained a secret police.[3] Arendt was adamant about the role of the secret service in turning what she called "suspect populations" into "objective enemies" through profiling systems. While suspect populations need to attempt or commit an offense, objective enemies are "carriers of tendencies" and therefore do not need to commit actual crimes. The indication of their danger is their belonging to a certain category of persons. Arendt asserts that the work of the secret service is endless because of the constant need to create more "suspect populations":

"The superfluous-ness of secret services is nothing new, they have always been haunted by the need to prove their usefulness and keep their jobs after their original task had been completed."[4] It is important to put Arendt's analysis in context. She wrote of totalitarian regimes and had in mind the notorious Nazi and Soviet secret services. While we cannot compare these with the Israeli regime, Arendt's analysis does provide us with powerful insights and analytical tools for understanding the process of classification of persons as "security threats."

Ronen Shamir offers a theory of profiling, which is a major component of what he calls a new "global mobility regime," based on a paradigm of suspicion: one in which crime, immigration and terrorism converge to create a distribution of risk management.

This theory explains, in terms of socio-spatial distances in a mobility regime, why certain types of people may be classified as security threats while others may not. At the very least, the mobility regime aims at slowing "suspect populations" down. This allows for practices of surveillance, gathering of intelligence and statistics about the population and its movement. Shamir writes:

The global mobility regime is predicated, first, on the classification of individuals and groups according to principles of perceived threats and risks; Secondly, on an emergent technology of intervention that provides the technical/ statistical means for creating elaborate forms of such social distinctions.[5]

Shamir suggests that the engine of the contemporary mobility regime is a "paradigm of suspicion" that conflates the perceived threats of crime, immigration and terrorism, and that the technology of intervention that enables it is biosocial profiling.

The mechanism of biosocial profiling assigns people into suspect categories, which then translate, through the paradigm of suspicion, into practices and technologies of containment. Shamir uses Jonathan Simon's analysis of policing and governance through models of risk management:

Profiling predicts behavior and regulates mobility by situating subjects in categories of risk. Techniques that "use statistics to represent the distribution of variables in a population," treat individuals "as locations in actuarial tables of variation," and seek to predict behavior and situate subjects "according to the risk they pose."[6]

According to Shamir, the practices of profiling of the mobility regime represent a fusion between insurance-oriented risk-management strategies and a criminal justice-oriented sentencing paradigm: "In the process, profiling shifted from being a method for assigning specific individuals into various categories of risk into an all-encompassing method that targets society as a whole and treats mobility per se as a suspect practice."[7] The profiling practices of the GSS differ between Palestinian residents of the OPT, who are restricted in movement, and Palestinian prisoners who are citizens of Israel. In dealing with Palestinians, the GSS is freed from the distinctions between home and foreign territory. While some scholars believe that following the Oslo Accords the role of the GSS in the OPT has been attenuated, I argue that it has simply changed. From a service based on agents on location, the GSS has become a larger and more bureaucratic organization, which has shifted its mission from collecting relevant information on Palestinian activities to collecting *all* information.[8] The GSS categorizes its actions on the basis of the racial identity of those it pursues. In a sense, the profiling and classification practices remained as bureaucratic colonial legacy, the rule of racial difference.

FROM SUSPECT POPULATION TO OBJECTIVE ENEMY: THE HISTORIC ROLE OF THE SECRET SERVICES

According to Hannah Arendt's succinct analysis of the processes secret services create for population management, suspect populations (usually minorities) are populations viewed by the leadership of the ruling majority as problematic. Their loyalty to the state is questioned, but the suspicion is dormant. At first, this causes the state to deploy more resources in surveillance and information gathering. Adriana Kemp shows the evolution of the suspicion of the Israeli state towards Palestinians, who first became a "trapped minority"[9] and then turned into, in the state's conception, a "dangerous population." A trapped minority is a population trapped between physical state boundaries, the state's apparatus of control, and their ethno-cultural identity. Kemp argues that the transformation of the Palestinian citizens of Israel into a dangerous population is "a result of a coupling between the national goals of the dominant ethnic group and the constant preoccupation of the disciplinary state with population management and surveillance."[10] She shows how using the territorial terminology of "security areas" to refer to areas where the Palestinian citizens of Israel lived under a military government between 1949 and 1966 enabled the formation of the Palestinian minority as a "dangerous population." The legal and physical creation of territorial boundaries, dangerous areas and border zones, designed to combat threats to the security of Israel's Jewish population, serve as a projection on the Palestinian citizens of Israel and as the reason and justification for surveillance.

Returning to Arendt's analysis, we see that "dangerous populations" do not necessarily reflect majority–minority relations, but a sociological category. The category of "objective enemy" refers to an enemy that is not a danger to the state, but that is hostile to the state. To be included in this category, one does not need to do anything criminal or even *think* anything in order to become an enemy. The objective enemy "is defined by the policy of the government and not by his own desire to overthrow it."[11] An objective enemy does not have to be a member of an organization or the instigator of political action in order to become suspect—the suspicion is based on her membership in her ethnic/racial/social group. The shift from "suspect population" to "objective enemy" may coincide with the transformation of the organizational power of the secret service. In terms of administration, when the secret service is in the position of advising the political leadership and decision makers, and then implements their decisions which are based on its own recommendations, its institutional influence is vast because of its clandestine and extra-legal structures. However, in the advising and executive positions, the secret service remains part of a dynamic organizational negotiation and competition between governmental departments and thus it is prevented from gaining full authority and discretion on the subject of categorization of security threats.

In times of crisis and uncertainty, for instance in the period following the outbreak of the second Intifada (the Al-Aqsa uprising) and the crashing of the complex bureaucratic system erected by the Oslo Accords, the GSS gained autonomy, exclusivity and legitimacy over the process of identification, categorization and classification of dangerous persons and security threats. Describing the role of the GSS in the civil administration offices managing the bureaucracy of the occupation in the OPT, Brigadier General (res.) Dov Zedaka explained, in an interview I conducted with him in 2006, how the GSS gained complicity and legitimacy while other administrative bodies or officials held alternative opinions. He described a dramatic shift in the managerial paradigm of the civil administration. From the year 2000 until the end of the Israeli military's Operation "Defensive Shield" in Jenin in 2002, the civil administration turned from an administrative body, focused on civilian as well as military aspects of the occupation, into a security apparatus of control in service of the heads of the military battalions. The agencies shifted their point of view and their practices from a paradigm of management of civilian population—the civil administration's stated purpose and *raison d'être*—to a security paradigm of management, that is, one interested in separating, sifting and identifying threats. This shift was empowered by a collective feeling of the "inability to distinguish between friend and foe."[12] The blur in the agent's ability to distinguish between the categories of friend and foe in the Palestinian administration—people who used to work with the Israeli civil administration in the OPT in the double-headed bureaucracy erected by the Oslo accords—was startling. It motivated a greater demand for profiling and the creation of a plethora of new criteria and stable methods of identification that would enable the administrative apparatus to combat uncertainty by distinguishing between "friend" and "foe." At the time, the master category available was the classification of persons as "security threats" and the profiling component, comprised by the GSS, became the core practice. In Zedaka's discussions with GSS representatives regarding the extent of the restrictive measures imposed on the Palestinian population in the West Bank, he revealed a striking use of pre-emptive guilt by the Service representative in the debate, used toward any agent who questioned or criticized the extent of security measures used against the Palestinian civilian population. For example, when the GSS proposed to augment the age of workers required to obtain labor permits for work within Israel from 30 to 35, any objection would encounter the reprimanding reaction: "If something happens, do you want to take responsibility?"

CREATING THE SECURITY THREAT: HOW THE MECHANISM WORKS

The security threat is a single, master category; all other distinctions and classifications are organized around it. Once this category is introduced on a daily basis into an administrative system, it calls for radical shifts in personal, administrative and regulatory practices. In time, in a similar mechanism to Kemp's description of the construction of dangerous populations through the making of territorial boundaries, the security threat yields a practice that demands the erection of physical barriers such as checkpoints, separation walls and maximum-security facilities. While the category of security threat is always instigated amidst crises, a state of emergency or administrative uncertainty, once the security threat category is set in motion, is institutionalized, ceases to be an exception due to an emergency situation and becomes the only category dominating people's thought and any political debate. This is because of its radical quality and the imminent danger it presupposes.

THE METHOD: RADICAL SIMPLIFICATION, STANDARDIZATION AND HOMOGENIZATION

The construction of the category of the security threat is fairly simple. It first relies on a radical simplification of traits or tendencies. It then creates a standardization key or index, which includes criteria such as age, geographic area, and membership or participation in political and cultural organizations and family relations. This index formulates a template of a security threat, which becomes a default category. The final stage of this procedure is the homogenization of the security threat; a process that at once creates a collective general profile and individualizes any form of political membership.

Like all classification systems, categories become institutionalized and accepted through the rule of experts in their specific domain, along with their set of professional vocabularies and repertoire of practices. The processes of radical simplification, standardization and homogenization are inclusive in the sense that they can be applied to most situations, from the permit regime in the West Bank to the classification of prisoners, and are exclusive in the sense that they can be constructed and applied administratively by the GSS alone, as it is considered the authority over the identification and profiling system. Most experts have their own jargon, their own secrets of the trade and sometimes they portray their professions as exclusive and highly complex, wishing to protect their expertise. However, in order to execute their expertise, the secret services need to collaborate with other organizations, particularly government agencies; hence, they must explain and simplify the content of the categories they use. In the case of the "security threat," the expertise does not need to be simplified, since its very existence reifies and upholds the domain of expertise. It is precisely the secrecy and seriousness of the classification, the fact that no one knows the components of the classification, which render the category uncontested and beyond critique. Over the years, this uncontested domain of expertise has created a knowledge monopoly, which, combined with the monopoly of the GSS on decision making and administrative discretion regarding the profiling indices, has erected an impenetrable wall of taxonomy and classification of the Palestinian population.

INSTITUTIONAL LEGITIMATION OF THE SECURITY THREAT

In the last couple of decades, a constant flow of military and anti-terrorism experts have entered and graduated Israeli universities, colleges and strategic research institutes, merging the security apparatuses with bases of academic power in the field of security studies and public policy. In Israel, as in the US, the field of security studies is expanding. The flow of security experts to and from the university creates an environment which provides academic legitimacy for the practices carried out by the GSS, among them the process of identification and profiling of security threats. This expertise gains legitimacy and justification by its academic location and the invention of the field of knowledge. It is then proliferated and exported to governments and private companies; as the knowledge base widens in scope and detail, technological advancements, such as biometric devices, are put to work, and they, in turn, generate new sets of criteria and constraints. The academic and market-oriented legitimacy for security consultants and their profiling capabilities creates a closed circuit of legitimacy, when political, financial and administrative interests feed each other in a loop, which solidifies the profiling and classification practices into objective and ordinary executive actions. Legitimacy for the construction of the security threat is justified, since it addresses public opinion and targets existing public fear, which is perpetually inflated exponentially to continue and expand the need for generations of new security knowledge and technology. The justification of the "security threat" classification relies on the Jewish Israeli public perception of Palestinian or "Arab" aspirations, the aspirations of an openly hostile population. An interesting example of this mechanism is the Yaffe Center for Strategic Studies,[13] which conducts public opinion polls on national security. These surveys usually address only Israeli Jews as respondents and questions regarding the Palestinian–Israeli conflict are presented as binary options: security or peace. One of many such surveys researching public opinion and national security in Israel is Asher Arian's report "Israeli Public Opinion on National Security 2002."[14] Section C of the report, entitled "Arab Aspirations," reveals the manner in which the category of the security threat is constructed, when respondents are limited to answer the questions by the options given to them. Arian writes:

> Figure 11 charts that in 2002, 42% of the respondents thought that the Arabs wanted to kill a large part of the Jewish population of Israel, and an additional 26% thought that their goal was to conquer the State of Israel, together totaling 68%. In contrast, in 1999 a total of 47% gave those two answers.

The only two other possible views that the survey offered were that the Arabs aspired to recover all the territories lost in 1967 (25 percent in 2002) or recover only some of those territories (7 percent in 2002).

Dov Zedaka's explanation of the process by which the uncertainty in distinguishing between friend and foe and the lack of control of the civil and military administrative bodies during the outbreak of hostilities in 2000 aided the GSS in gaining authority and legitimacy is convincing; yet it is partial. The omnipresence of the category of security threat—the fact that it can appear in any governmental department—is versatile in its usage and employment and can be used by the police or by employment agencies; this helps the process of legitimizing and institutionalizing the category of security threat. The institutionalization renders it an inevitable, acceptable and indispensable part of administrative daily life. However, in order to maintain legitimacy, the contents of the security threat and the details it involves must remain constantly vague and ever-changing.

THE SECURITY THREAT AS A THREAT:
THE DANGERS OF CRIMINALIZING A POPULATION

The most dangerous aspect of the classification of "security threat" or "security prisoner," besides its dehumanizing moral aspects, is the criminalization of political membership, organization, or belief. In a situation of perpetual conflict, when political organization is classified as a danger and attracts threats, sanctions and retaliation from the authority, a political deadlock is created. People refrain from organizing political alternatives, and thus, the only public space available to be truly active politically is through militancy. An arbitrary classification system of political membership as security threat discourages non-violent social action, or any possibility for social organization needed to stop violence. If political membership and participation in a militant faction are rendered the same as non-violent political activity, both yielding the classification as a security threat, people have nothing to lose but their dreams of a different political future. Those who are afraid will be immobilized and paralyzed, retreating from society in general. Those who have less fear can be motivated to become militant. In any case, as soon as the security service and the prison systems create a risk management profiling system that is a zero-sum game, where identity equals risk, there is no point for activists and political leadership to opt for non-violent solutions. It is actually surprising how, under the harsh classification regimes of the security threat, many Palestinians have chosen non-violent political and social action, even though it carries with it similar consequences to the violent actions.

The category of the security threat and its use in dealing with Palestinian prisoners who are citizens of Israel or residents of the OPT is a category that obscures the real problem of Israeli society and government. Security profiling and classification obfuscate the political problem of coping with the political, social and economic problem that the Israeli state has with its Palestinian citizens and the residents of the West Bank and Gaza Strip. The category of the security threat prevents the motivation and generation of political solutions, perpetuating mediocrity and despair on the administrative level, as well as in the general public.

It is through simplification and homogenization of people into a template of a "security threat"—a process of transforming a large part of the Palestinian population into objective enemies on the basis of their identity and political affiliation—that the security threat paradigm creates a security threat. It does so by blocking any form of political alternative, by obscuring the difference between non-violent and violent political action, by deliberately canceling the difference between criminal activity and political activity and by criminalizing membership and identity. The "security threat' classification mechanism is only useful to those organizations and agencies whose power grows with the increase in security threats and the fear from them, not to anyone who seeks security and protection. For the Israeli public, the security threat classification mechanisms pose a ubiquitous and insidious security threat.

NOTES

1. Telephone conversation on November 5, 2005 with Sgt. Liron Alush, the head of the population registry department in the office of the legal adviser to Judea and Samaria in the military civil administration.
2. See Y. Shenhav and Y. Berda, (2009), "The Colonial Foundations of State of Exception: Juxtaposing the Israeli Occupation of Palestinian Territories with Colonial Bureaucratic History," in M. Givoni, S. Hanafi and A. Ophir (eds), *The Power of Exclusive Inclusion: Anatomy of Israeli Rule in the Occupied Palestinian Territories*, Cambridge, MA: Zone Books, MIT Press.
3. H. Arendt (1951), *The Origins of Totalitarianism*, 1st edn, New York: Harcourt, p. 420.
4. Ibid., p. 423.
5. R. Shamir (2005), "Without Borders: Notes on Globalization as a Mobility Regime," *Sociological Theory*, Vol. 23, No. 2, p. 200.
6. J. Simon (2007), *Governing through Crime: How the War on Crime Transformed American Democracy and Created a Culture of Fear*, Oxford: Oxford University Press, p. 771f.
7. Shamir, "Without Borders", p. 211.

8. For this reason, citizens of other countries desiring to enter Israel are interviewed at the borders. They are asked about the phone numbers of their Palestinian relatives in the OPT or in Lebanon, as well as their itineraries in Israel and the West Bank.

9. The term was coined by Danny Rabinowitz (2001) in "The Palestinian citizens of Israel, the concept of trapped minority and the discourse of transnationalism in anthropology," *Ethnic and Racial Studies*, Vol. 24, No. 1, pp. 64–85.

10. A. Kemp (2004), "Dangerous populations: state territoriality and the constitution of national minorities," in J. Midgdal (ed.), *Boundaries and belonging: states and societies in the struggle to shape identities and local practices*, Cambridge: Cambridge University Press.

11. Arendt, *Origins of Totalitarianism*, p. 423.

12. Interview with Brigadier General (res.) Dov Zedaka, former head of the military civil administration in the years 1998–2002 on December 20, 2006, Tel Aviv.

13. Incorporated, since 2006, into the Institute for National Security Studies (INSS) at Tel Aviv University.

14. See A. Arian (2002), "Israeli Public Opinion on National Security 2002," Memorandum No. 61, Yaffe Center for Strategic Studies, Tel Aviv University.

5
Palestinian Women Political Prisoners and the Israeli State

Nahla Abdo

INTRODUCTION

In a security-obsessed state like Israel, whether described as a *Mokhabarat* state[1] or as a "state of exception,"[2] the prison system comes only second—after the military establishment—in exemplifying the true nature of the Israeli state. In such a system, sexism, racism and other forms of subjugation, often camouflaged by the law of the state, are widely unleashed onto the prisoner "other." In this chapter, I would like to shed some light onto an area that remains heavily under-researched: Palestinian women political detainees.

In Israel's settler colonial rule, the simple human right of freedom of expression is often suppressed and confiscated from the colonized/occupied. It is little wonder then that thousands or tens of thousands of men and women are subjected to various terms of political detention/imprisonment. Still, there is one particular form of resistance which subjugates the *Munadelat* (Arabic for female freedom fighters)[3] to particularly harsh terms of detention: participation in the armed struggle. It is this group of Palestinian political detainees which is the focus of this chapter. Data used here is drawn from an extensive fieldwork of interviews, life histories, focus group discussions and a collection of women's narratives conducted during 2007–08 in the West Bank. The majority of these women were detained between the late 1960s and the 1980s. Prison terms among this group of women ranged between three years to up to life sentence. Many of these women were released following the Oslo Accords, through prisoner exchange deals.

A BRIEF HISTORICAL BACKGROUND

Women's participation in the national liberation struggle has and continues to be part and parcel of the overall Palestinian anti-colonial resistance movement. Faced with continued settler colonial regimes since the turn of the twentieth century, witnessing the killing and humiliation of family members, seeing their land confiscated, homes demolished and forced to become refugees, women—like their male counterparts—became part of the anti-colonial liberation struggle. During the revolution of 1936, Palestinian women played an important role in the armed struggle: they hid and transported weapons, and used them in various cases. Yet it was not until the late 1960s with the emergence of the PLO in 1964, and following Israeli occupation of the rest of the Palestinian territories of the West Bank and Gaza in 1967, that women emerged publicly as part of the movement, partaking in all forms of struggle, including military struggle.

In their armed struggle, Palestinian women used weapons against the occupier—they shot and were shot, killed and were killed, placed bombs in army outposts and so on—but in most cases they were captured by the occupying army and ended up spending months or years in Israeli prisons. For some, detention was short-lived, while for others, it was quite long and arduous.

DECONSTRUCTING THE WESTERN CONCEPTION OF PALESTINIAN *MUNADELAT*

It is rather unfortunate that the voices, stories and experiences of Palestinian women freedom fighters in general and political detainees more specifically have hardly, if at all, been given adequate attention by Palestinian or other scholars. Despite the fact that female political detention among Palestinian women has become a social phenomenon, accounting for hundreds of women who spent varying periods in Israeli detention, this issue, especially as it folded historically, has not been given adequate attention. New documentation on this topic began to emerge in the past decade or so. For example, according to the organization Women's Organization for Political Prisoners which works closely with B'Tselem, "the number of Palestinian women arrested since the start of the [first] Intifada is estimated at about 300, 18 of them administrative detainees. At the end of June 1989 there were 32 women prisoners, 2 of them administrative detainees, 13 of them awaiting trial, 17 of them serving sentences following trial."[4] These statistics, however, do not account for all women detainees and definitely not for the wave of female political detainees between the late 1960s and 1980s who are the subject of this chapter.[5] This phenomenon, I argue, has failed to attract any serious scholarship. Ironically, however, the re-emergence of women's military resistance after 2000 has generated a large body of literature, especially by Western feminists. But as will be seen shortly, this literature is de-historicized and de-contextualized.

Since 2002, a large number of Western Orientalist literature emerged to deal with the female military resistance dubbed "suicide bombers." Notable here is the work of Andrea Dworkin, Barbara Victor and Mia Bloom among others.[6] While none of these authors concerned herself with contextualizing the phenomenon historically or contemporarily, or cared about the actual experiential lives of these women, all shared a similar perception of these women: *Munadelat* were constructed as "terrorists," "murderers" and most importantly, "fallen women," described invariably as women who undertook "suicide bombing" to cleanse their name and the name of their family from the shame they had allegedly brought to their families. On this, Dworkin has the following to say: 'These women idealists who crave committing a pure act [which] will wipe away the stigma of being female ... After all those women were sexually abused by their men and threatened to be killed by them.'[7] "Blood for honour," feminist Orientalists allege, meant that women are willing to trade their death for "restoring lost family honour." Of course, the Arab family in this literature is pejoratively conceptualized as the prime oppressor of its female members. I must note here that I use the phrase female "suicide bombers" in this chapter because of my conviction that the initial emergence of this phenomenon is well suited within my larger context of women freedom fighters, who have been prevalent in Palestinian national resistance since the 1960s.[8]

This literature falls largely within the notion of "culture talk," which focuses on cultural symbols, such as family, patriarchy and religion. In some way this is also a form of what Richard Falk terms "the politics of deflection": by focusing on the messenger rather than the message—on the individual woman, her psychological state, behavior, gender status and sexuality, undermining her lived circumstances—such writings have distorted not only the rationale behind the legitimate anti-colonial struggle, but also managed to rid history of its relevance and deflect attention from the heart of the issue: the legitimate resistance of the occupied/colonized against the occupier/colonizer. Elsewhere, I provide a detailed critical analysis of these Orientalist writings.[9] For the purpose of this chapter, I will contextualize the national struggle by placing it within Palestinian national culture. This contextualization will help to reassess the ideological fallacy of Western Orientalist writings.

To begin with, the term "suicide bomber" is an alien invention imposed on Palestinian culture, which is rich in resistance and anti-colonial artefacts (for example, songs, idioms, poetry, and so on). Throughout the Palestinian struggle for liberation, Arabic terms used to describe the resistance have strongly corresponded to particular historical junctures within which resistance occurred. For example, during the 1920s–40s, terms like *Thawrah* (Arabic for revolution) and *Thuwwar* (revolutionaries) were common descriptions for anti-colonial resistance. In the 1960s–80s, the term *fidaeyyah* joined Palestinian resistance culture and came to describe women willing to sacrifice themselves for the nation/cause. During the first Intifada, terms like *Asserah*, *Um al-Aseera* (mother of female political detainee) and *Shaheedah* (female martyrs) were added to this political culture's vocabulary. Nothing but positive qualities, it must be emphasized, has in fact been attached to all these terms. Yet throughout all the phases of resistance, *Nidal* (freedom fighting) or *Munadelah* (female freedom fighter) were used to describe women's militant resistance.

While such terminology remains alive in Palestinian popular culture, it was not so for much of the intellectual feminist elites. The hegemony of ideological globalization, along with the submissive "peace process" brought about by Oslo, have affected a new ideology: one that advocates "dialogue," "peaceful resistance" and "non-violent resistance," prioritizing these over other means of resistance. This new ideology is directed towards legitimizing state and imperialist terror, while considering anti-colonial resistance as unlawful forms of "terror." It is in this context that Israel declared the Gaza Strip an "enemy state," legitimizing Israel's untold and horrifying destruction of Gaza. These are also the conditions which allowed Western Orientalist feminists to turn the *Munadelat* into "suicide bombers," deflecting attention from the true terror of the state to that of individuals.

FAMILY, SEXUALITY AND WOMEN'S POLITICAL DETENTION

To reject the culturalist and racist writings of Western authors who emphasize the role of family, religion and sexuality in their discussion of Palestinian *Munadelat* by no means suggests that these issues are of no import to Palestinian culture. What Western authors ignore is that these same concepts are used by the Israeli prison system as basic tools for torturing women: these are primary colonial tools of torture used to force confessions from the detainees.[10] Before discussing this further, it is important to emphasize that the claim that Palestinian *Munadelat* use militant forms of resistance because they broke away from family values/traditions and because of their oppressed sexual and gender status is rather baseless. My data strongly demonstrate the fallacy of this racist construction of women, as none of the women interviewed even recognized themselves in such a discourse. In fact, all women interviewed—17 of them from varying places including Ramallah, Jenin, Nablus, Gaza, Jerusalem and Tulkarm—spoke highly of their parents and other family members; they recounted the love and special attention they received, and described the trust and confidence they enjoyed within the family and community.[11]

Moreover, except for one woman whose financial situation stood against her further education, all women interviewed had received higher education before and during their involvement in the resistance movement. Some had left their villages and lived in Ramallah to enroll in the only Palestinian Teachers' College; others traveled to Beirut, Syria and other Arab countries to attend university. Also, in contradistinction to existing Western racial constructs of Palestinian women, all the women interviewed were secular and defined their political affiliation as on the left. None was religious and most belonged to Marxist-Leninist wings of the PLO.[12]

These women, unlike what we are led to believe, were not forced by the male leadership to join the national liberation movement. They were not silent victims of Palestinian patriarchy or male dictates, being family members or political leaders. As most of the women admit, their parents were supportive of them in every way, though they never fathomed the idea that their daughters would be imprisoned. Still, women chose their own paths out of their own free will and conscious decision, without informing their parents. It is true that their parents were angry at such decisions, but both daughters and parents, especially mothers, reconciled and reconnected as soon as they were detained, resuming a respectful relationship after release. The decision to join the military resistance, as several women said, made them well aware of and ready to pay the heavy price, including risking their lives and accepting all the consequences, which in this case ended up being confined in prison for many years. In my article "Palestinian *Munadelat*: Between Western Representation and Lived Reality,"[13] I provide a full account of how Palestinian women joined the resistance, and the relationship they had within their families before, during and after release. This analysis defies the Western feminist conception of Palestinian *Munadelat* and shows its fallacy. The following pages provide the context within which concepts of family and sexuality are used in Israel's racist prison institution.

SEXISM AND RACISM IN THE ISRAELI PRISON SERVICE

The institution of prison in Israel, in so far as Palestinian political detainees are concerned, mirrors the state's racist/Orientalist and sexist ideology and construction of the Arab-Palestinian "other." This system constructs an *a priori* image of Palestinian women as "docile," "subservient," "obedient," "religious," and most of all fearful of any relationship or act which concerns their body or sexuality. This *a priori* construct functions as the baseline for the institution's means of torture against Palestinian women. Prison's racism, it is also maintained, is extended to Israel's "other Jews"— Mizrahi (Arab) Jews (prison interrogators/officials)—a population which until the early 1990s constituted the majority of the Jewish population of Israel.

It is not surprising therefore that the role of the "bad cop"—the interrogator who beats, whips, slaps and threatens to rape women, such as in the cases of Rasmiya Oudeh and Aishah Oudeh—could be a Mizrahi Jew. He is described as an Arabic-speaking man with an Arabic name, familiar with Arab culture and knowing all the slurs and sexual curses in Arabic. He is also described by his victims as "big with a huge belly," with a "thick black moustache," or "short and fat," yet, mostly "scary." For example, Haleema, who was detained in 1987 and was sentenced for five years, was interrogated/tortured by a man called Shawqy. She described him as "terrifying" and likened him to "Farid Shawqi,", an Egyptian actor known in the Arab world as *"wahsh al-Shashah al-Arabiyyah"* (the beast of the Arab big screen). Two other interrogators mentioned during the research were "Abu Hani" and "Abu-Nimr." It might be noted here that perhaps none of these are the men's true names, since Jewish (Arab) immigrants/settlers were forced to change their names into specific Jewish names to integrate into the Jewish society/state.

Most women interviewed were subjected to varying forms of torture, ill-treatment and reprisal against members of their families. Some women had their family homes demolished immediately upon or soon after their detention; in the case of others, family members were dragged to the prison, and placed in close range to the detainee's cell for her to watch or hear. For example, "Aishah"—who was detained in 1969, sentenced to a life imprisonment and released in 1985, in the "Nawras Exchange Deal"—did not have any brothers, so the Israeli Prison Service (IPS) dragged her innocent cousin to prison and tortured him while she stood and watched. During another episode of interrogation/torture, she heard a prison officer who spoke in a loud voice ordering men from the next room to "bring Aishah's mother and sister-in-law and hang them from their breasts so she could hear their scream."

Sexual-psychological means, such as spreading lies about female behavior in prison, were also used. "Nahed" from the Green Line, who was detained in 1979 for a rather short period (12 days), reported that a female Jewish-Mizrahi prostitute (or who looked like a prostitute) was sent to speak to Nahed's father, who had been denied the right to see his daughter; the "prostitute" told him stories about her close relationship with his daughter. However, after her release and when told these stories, Nahed replied that she had spent all her time alone confined to a filthy cell and had not seen a single woman throughout her detention. Bringing prostitutes and female drug addicts to meet up with women political detainees, as my interviewees confessed, was a common practice.

Physically, Palestinian female detainees are also subjected to all forms of torture during interrogation, including beating, shaking, suspension, segregation and forced nakedness. "Aishah," "Ameenah," "Alia" and "Iman" talked about their experiences of *shabeh*, which is a tool of mental and physical torture: the detainee is stood against a wall with hands tied to the wall and feet tied together or chained to a chair. This process can last for several hours or for overnight, causing tremendous pain and harm to the neck and back.[14]

Some of the women have also been subjected to the experience of *kees*, where the whole body is covered with a dark bag that reeks of a foul, lingering smell. "Alia," for example, described the stench as that of defecation, while "Ameenah" and "Haleemah" believed it is the odor of stinky urine: "It is as if someone ate a kilo of asparagus," "Ameenah" muttered. Lawyer Walid Fahoum, also interviewed, has corroborated the use of such methods of colonial torture used against Palestinian political detainees.

Yet, what most women found specifically ruthless is the way interrogators use women's bodies and sexuality to force a confession out of them. The experience of "Aishah" who spent 45 days under interrogation is worth detailing here. Like other stories relayed, "Aishah" was quite concerned with the foul language used by her interrogator, especially terms like *sharmouta* (Arabic for "whore"), *qahbah* (Arabic for "slut"). Despite their political activism, most women continued to adhere to traditional norms and values surrounding sexual conduct. In her book *In My Own Eyes*, Felicia Langer provides chilling accounts of sexual torture of women political detainees she herself witnessed as a defense lawyer.[15]

The following is "Aishah"'s experience of torture. It is adapted from my research on Palestinian *Munadelat*: "When I asked the interrogator why he is slapping me he responded 'because you are sharmouta.' 'I am not', I replied. 'What are you then? Tell us how many men did you fuck?' Unable to use the same language, I responded, 'I did not sleep with any man and my personal life is none of your business.'"[16]

In almost all consequent episodes of interrogation-cum-torture or "*jura'at taa'dheeb*" as "Aishah" insisted on referring to them, the prison officials insisted on calling her *sharmouta* and *qahba* and one official demanded she repeat "I am *sharmouta*" ten times.

After a long and arduous session of torture as she refused to talk and adamantly refused to say what they demanded of her, "Aishah" was subjected to a horrifying experience of an actual threat of rape. One day she was dragged to a room with a "big" man pacing the room. She described what followed:

> The man leaned on the table, put one hand there and the other on his waist and started to check me out from head to toe, he then ordered me to sit down ... then said: "You are sharmouta and you know it." I answered "I am not sharmouta". He said back: "the difference between the ordinary sharmouta and yourself is that you are sharmouta with brain ... I order you to say: 'I am sharmouta' ten times ... and you have to obey." "You cannot force me". "I will show you!" He sat on the table, surrounded me with both of his legs, pulled my hair back and started slapping me on the face ... He would only stop to remind me of what he wants me to say. After a while he stepped down, approached me and repeated: "how many men did you fuck?" I answered "none!" He said: "you want to convince me you are still a virgin?" His eyes became red and scared the hell out of me ...
>
> I was then dragged to a room where a man with a short, thick black moustache and a huge belly stood. Moments later a tall

blond female guard with army uniform joined in. The man stared at me and said: "take off your clothes!"

I shrank, crossed my arms and put them on my chest to protect my body, the same moment he ordered other men who came to the room to undress me. I resisted with all my force but was unable to prevent them. He pulled my arms behind my back and cuffed them with a sharp chain and pushed me on the floor naked ... He then came closer to me, pushed his two knees against my belly ... using a stick, he pushed my legs apart and put them under his knees. The woman put her foot on my head so I wouldn't move ... he started pressing on my chest with his huge disgusting hands, then he began to push the stick into my vagina. I resisted so hard as never ever before ... that moment I felt stronger than ever before ... Minutes later and after pouring a lot of cold water on my body, one held me from one arm and the other from one leg and started to wipe the floor with my body ... then they dragged my body outside the room, parading me in front of a row of young Palestinian men who were lined up against the wall ... .[17]

While "Aishah" underwent a horrifying experience of attempted rape, Rasmiya Odeh's tale of rape was strongly documented by defense lawyer Felicia Langer and the London *Sunday Times* report of June 19, 1977 which concluded that "torture of Arab prisoners is so widespread and systematic that it cannot be dismissed as 'rough cops' exceeding orders. It appears to be sanctioned as deliberate policy."[18]

In Rasmiya Odeh's case, her father was brought to prison and was ordered to rape his daughter. When he refused, prison officials forced a stick into Rasmiya's vagina and left her to bleed, while her father lay unconscious on the floor. Although my case study documents Israel's colonial methods of torture used in its prisons during the late 1960s and late 1980s, torture of political detainees to date, as local and international human rights bodies suggest, still exists.

CONCLUSION

Palestinian women political detainees, this chapter has argued, have been, at least, doubly victimized: first through their distorted representation by Western Orientalist feminists, and secondly, as *Munadelat* who faced untold forms of torture by the settler colonial state and its prison institution. On the one hand, they were represented as silent victims of their "culture" and traditions, unable to make independent decisions, especially those related to their body and sexuality. On the other hand, the chapter demonstrated how Israeli's prison used the same factors believed by Western Orientalist feminists to be the primary oppressors of women: culture, family and sexuality as a means of torture and control. In all of this, Palestinian women *Munadelat*, as my data show, were anything but their Western constructed image. They also proved to have agency and resist their colonizers and victimizers as well.

NOTES

1. I. Pappe (2008), "The Mukhabarat State of Israel: A State of Oppression is not a State of Exception" in R. Lentin (ed.), *Thinking Palestine*, London: Zed Books, pp. 148–70.
2. G. Agamben (2005), *State of Exception*, Chicago, IL: University of Chicago Press.
3. It should be noted here that the term "*Munadelat*" was the description all my interviewees insisted on using to characterize their activities.
4. For more on this see, Information Sheet: Update August 1, 1989. According to Palestinian Society Prisoners Club (Nadi El-Aseer), 900 female political prisoners were arrested since the year 2000. As of January 2011, 37 women political prisoners were still in Israeli jails. Addameer Prisoner Support and Human Rights Association states that up to March 2010, 34 Palestinian women political prisoners were in Israeli jails.
5. For further detail, see N. Abdo (2008), "Palestinian *Munadelat*: Between Western Representation and Lived Reality," in Lentin (ed.), *Thinking Palestine*, pp. 173–89.
6. A. Dworkin (2002), "The Women Suicide Bombers," *Feminista*, Vol. 5, No. 1, pp. 19–28; B. Victor, (2003), *Army of Roses: Inside the World of Palestinian Women Suicide Bombers*, New York: Barnes and Noble; M. Bloom (2005), *Dying to Kill*. New York: Columbia University Press.
7. Dworkin, "The Women Suicide Bombers," p. 5.
8. For more on the context of these women, see D. Naaman (2007), "Brides of Palestine/Angels of Death: Media, Gender, and Performance in the Case of the Palestinian Female Suicide Bombers," *Signs*, Vol. 32, No. 4, pp. 933–56.
9. Abdo, "Palestinian *Munadelat*."
10. On April 16, 2008, five human rights organizations filed a petition to the High Court of Justice (HCJ) against the GSS, the Israel Police and the Attorney General demanding that the use of family members as means of exhorting pressure on suspects during interrogations by state authorities be absolutely prohibited. The Petition was filed by an attorney from the Israel Public Committee against Torture (PCATI). Israel's Supreme Court dismissed the petition after the Attorney General stated to the Court that using family members as an interrogation method is prohibited. See HC 3533/08, *Sweiti, et al. v. GSS*, not published, decision delivered on September 9, 2009.
11. For further details, see Abdo, "Palestinian *Munadelat*."

12. It might be noted here that this historic account of the female secular resistance might not fit today's profile of political detainees, most of whom are religious and members of Hamas.

13. Abdo, "Palestinian *Munadelat*."

14. See also Bana Shoughry-Badarne and Avigdor Feldman's chapters in this volume.

15. F. Langer (1975), *With My Own Eyes: Israel and the occupied territories, 1967–1973*. London: Ithaca Press.

16. Abdo, "Palestinian *Munadelat*," pp. 181–3.

17. Ibid.

18. "Israel and Torture," *Sunday Times*, June 19, 1977; F. Langer, *With My Own Eyes*, London: Ithaca Press, 1975.

6
Prison Policy and Political Imprisonment in Northern Ireland and Israel

Alina Korn

Like Northern Ireland, Israel imprisons people for committing politically motivated offenses, defining them as terrorists, and, like Northern Ireland, Israel does not formally acknowledge holding "political prisoners" within its prison system. According to the Israel Prison Service (IPS), people arrested on suspicion of, or convicted and sentenced to imprisonment for offenses against the security of the state are classified as security prisoners for administrative purposes, but the IPS has never classified any prisoner as a political prisoner. In practice, however, though neither has ever acknowledged holding any "political prisoners," in both jurisdictions there has been a legal or practical *de facto* recognition of the political status of paramilitary prisoners. Moreover, the similar legal structure has made it possible in both countries to use different legal procedure from the ordinary criminal one against people who have committed politically motivated offenses. And in both cases, after their trial, prisoners have gained recognition of a status that separated them from ordinary prisoners.

In Northern Ireland, people accused of terrorist offenses, where violence was used for political ends, were tried in special no-jury courts; in administrative terms they have been held separately according to their organizational affiliation, with an explicit recognition of paramilitary command structures. Although originally envisaged as a temporary measure, the special courts system became a permanent institution in Northern Ireland's criminal justice system, trying thousands of people and sending many of them to serve long sentences in prison.

In Israel, almost half of all the prisoners held by the Israeli prison system are Palestinians who have been sent to prison by the military courts in the Occupied Palestinian Territories (OPT). These military courts have been given wide, extra-territorial jurisdiction which enables them to try any person—whether a resident of the territories or not—and any offense: whether committed in or outside the territories. In fact, Israel has established in the territories a double legal system, which enables it to subject the Palestinian inhabitants to a different legal system from the one applied to Israeli citizens, including the Jewish residents of the settlements.[1]

In an attempt to describe the horror of the Israeli prison system, I wish to refer first to the Northern Irish context. This comparison makes sense not only because of the similarity, but also since a large part of the legal and institutional measures used by the State of Israel are clearly a British legacy: from the emergency legislation and the administrative detention, through the changes in ordinary judicial proceedings, to the structure of the prison system. Despite many similarities, however, an examination of the authorities' attitudes towards paramilitary prisoners in Northern Ireland can also point out the differences. Such an examination will show that the meaning of imprisoning the Palestinians and the roles this imprisonment plays in the conflict in our region are different from those played by the prisons in the Northern Ireland conflict.

PRISON POLICY IN NORTHERN IRELAND

Between the years 1969–76, the British policy in Northern Ireland was of reactive containment, due to the need of the British authorities to react to the loss of control by the local Unionist government. Troops were deployed as a temporary measure to support Northern Ireland's security forces and help prison staff in guarding the prisons. In this context, harsh steps were taken against terrorist suspects, including the use of internment, in order to quickly contain the high levels of violence, while trying to reach a political solution. In early 1972, Billy McKee, a senior leader of the IRA in Belfast, led 40 Republican prisoners on a hunger strike demanding recognition of their political status. On the verge of McKee's dying of hunger, the IRA prisoners were granted what was euphemistically called "Special Category Status," understood by everyone as political status. *De facto* prisoners in this category were granted a prisoner-of-war status, obtaining similar conditions to those of the internees. These conditions included segregated accommodations and living in Nissen huts compounds (cages) in Long Kesh Prison. During the period of the Special Category Status, the prisoners effectively controlled large areas within the cages, gaining various concessions relating to their imprisonment.[2]

During 1974, the policy regarding paramilitary prisoners was changed. Now the emphasis shifted to establishing law and order through criminalization of the insurgents. It was part of a wider political and military strategy designed to deny any acknowledgment of the political character of the conflict. Terrorist violence was defined as a law-and-order problem rather than a political one, and terrorist suspects were processed by the Diplock system. Lord Diplock was appointed to find a legal solution to the detention without trial of hundreds of Republicans. His recommendations legally established the distinction between "ordinary" criminality and "scheduled" offenses, committed as part of a series of terrorist crimes. Diplock empowered the state to treat paramilitaries differently, deviating from the legal procedures applied in the case of ordinary crimes.[3] From 1973 on, anyone accused of scheduled offenses in Northern Ireland was tried by a single judge, in a special juryless court, using amended rules of evidence.

As of March 1976, it was decided—following the recommendations of Lord Gardiner's report in 1975—to revoke the Special Category Status, and to treat paramilitary convicted prisoners as ordinary criminal prisoners (ODCs—Ordinary Decent Criminals), regardless of their paramilitary connections or their political motivation. The construction of the new Maze Prison (formerly Long Kesh), completed in 1977, alongside the Special Category Status compounds, was meant to enable holding high-risk prisoners in cellular conditions, as part of the implementation of the policy of phasing out the Special Category Status.

The prisoners' refusal to wear prison uniform and to do prison work were two central elements of their protest. In effect, the enforcement of the regulations regarding uniforms and work became a focus of the political and ideological struggle between the prison authorities and the prisoners, and it was accompanied by great brutality on the part of prison officers.[4] Hundreds of prisoners who refused to wear the uniforms and conform to the new prison regime joined the protest and went "on the blanket." The refusal to wear the uniform led to the refusal to wash, known as the "dirty protest"; eventually, the great hunger strike led by Bobby Sands started in April 1981. Ten Republican prisoners died during the summer of that year. Although officially the Conservative government and the Secretary of State for Northern Ireland declared that there has not been and will not be any concession to the IRA, the reality seemed to be different: the strikers' basic demands were accepted immediately after the strike ended. From the beginning of 1982 on, the prisoners at the Maze enjoyed the equivalent of the Special Category Status. The regime within the prison changed significantly from what was customary between 1976–81, and IRA convicted prisoners were in fact granted freedom of movement within the prison.[5]

The hunger strikes made the managerial and staff level in the Northern Ireland prison service realize that it was impossible to forcefully impose symbols of criminal incarceration upon paramilitary prisoners. The post-strikes approach—from 1981 until the early release in 2000—was termed "managerialism." As in the period up until 1976, managerialism saw the prisons as the sites for holding combatants rather than the battleground upon which their struggle could be beaten. On the other hand, the treatment of paramilitary prisoners and the consideration of the political motivation of the various factions were presented as a technical issue rather than ideological. The engagement with them was understood within a paradigm of effective and good management and was characterized by pragmatism—a willingness to maintain a narrow dialogue, focused upon the trivial details of prison life, rather than the grand questions of political status.[6]

RISE IN IMPRISONMENT RATES

As a result of the prolonged conflict, the law enforcement and prison systems in Northern Ireland grew rapidly, making it possible to hold large numbers of detainees and paramilitary prisoners sentenced to long terms of imprisonment.

Over 2,000 suspects were interned between 1971 and 1975, and about 10,000 defendants were brought to trial in the Diplock special courts between 1973 and the 1994 ceasefires.[7] As a result, the prison population in Northern Ireland grew dramatically after the outbreak of violence, from a rate of about 600 prisoners in 1969 to almost 3,000 prisoners by 1979. It stabilized from the 1980s to the late 1990s, between 1,600 and 1,900 prisoners, and has reduced significantly since 1998, following the release of the paramilitary prisoners as part of the Good Friday Agreement. Following the sharp rise in the prison population, the prison staff in Northern Ireland also rose dramatically: from 292 in 1969 to 2,184 in 1976. In the 1980s and early 1990s, the number stabilized at over 3,000.

With the occupation of the West Bank and Gaza territories in 1967, the IPS took over the Jordanian prisons in the West Bank and the Egyptian prisons in Gaza.[8] The empty facilities quickly filled up with thousands of Palestinians arrested by the IDF. Tens of thousands of Palestinians accused of committing security offenses, ordinary criminal offenses, and traffic offenses are tried in the system of military courts in the OPT. Indeed, in the first two decades of the Occupation, the Palestinians formed between 45 and 60 percent of the overall prison population in Israel. In those years, between 75 and 82 percent of all Palestinian prisoners were serving relatively long-term sentences for offenses against the security of the state.[9]

Until the middle of the 1980s, over 3,000 Palestinians were held in IPS facilities, and between the years 1986 and 1992, the number of incarcerated Palestinians was over 4,000.[10] After the signing of the Oslo Agreements in 1993 and the establishment of the Palestinian Authority, the number of Palestinian prisoners in Israeli prisons gradually decreased, and in 2000 there were 1,759 Palestinian prisoners in IPS custody—the lowest number ever recorded. This trend was reversed after the outbreak of the Al Aqsa Intifada in September 2000. Since then, the number of Palestinian prisoners has risen. From 2005, the number of Palestinian prisoners classified as security prisoners passed the 5,000 mark. In 2006, it reached the highest record, standing at 9,516 (about 46.1 percent of the overall prison population in Israel), and in 2010, Palestinian prisoners classified as security prisoners numbered 6,620.[11] The prison staff has also expanded over the years, rising from 3,784 staff members in 2000 to 8,447 in 2010.

In the first years of the Occupation, the majority of the Palestinians classified as security prisoners were imprisoned in incarceration facilities in the OPT, and only a minority were held in prisons within Israel, mixed with the criminal prisoners. A separation between the populations was instated in 1970. Since then, Palestinian security prisoners are held in separate prisons or segregated wings.[12] In the early 1970s, the prisoners' leadership in the security prisons consolidated and they began to organize. The prisoners conducted a continued struggle not only to improve their imprisonment conditions, but also to achieve a level of "internal autonomy," to reduce the involvement of the IPS in the running of their lives, and to gain a status that is currently *de facto* the status of political prisoners.[13]

Despite the similarity, it seems that the IPS's policy towards the Palestinian prisoners cannot be properly understood by applying the managerial models of the prison service in Northern Ireland.

Since the British saw the prison as a central arena in which to fight Irish nationalism, the paramilitary prisoners' struggle gained over-prominence. The demand to recognize the political status and later the struggle to retrieve the Special Category Status emerged against the authorities' attempts to criminalize the paramilitary prisoners, and to scatter them in the criminal wings. The political prisoners' demands and their heroic struggles emerged against this background. Unlike in Northern Ireland, Israel has never presumed to subject the Palestinian political prisoners to a unified prison policy, nor has it implemented a policy of criminalization in an attempt to conform and integrate them with the ordinary prisoners. From a very early stage, Palestinian prisoners were classified differently, separated from the criminal prisoners, and held in separate wings or different prisons. The racist and discriminatory treatment of the Palestinian prisoners, and their group characterization as dangerous terrorists, made it possible to subject them to sweeping severe restrictions. However, it was precisely this characterization that led to the *de facto* recognition of their status and their collective identity.

The IPS policy regarding the Palestinian political prisoners should be understood against the background of the wider processes of Israeli control of the Palestinians within and outside the prison. The prison system plays an important role, not so much as a means of fighting terrorists, but rather as part of the normalization of the incarceration regime imposed on ever-growing parts of the Palestinian population. The large differences in the rates of detention and imprisonment of the Palestinians compared to those rates among the paramilitary prisoners in Northern Ireland should be looked at with regards to these processes of the confinement of the Palestinian people.

Since the occupation of the territories in 1967, thousands of Palestinians have been detained every year. The Israeli General Security Service (GSS) interrogates approximately half of the detainees. The investigation lasts about a month and in most cases ends with a confession and an incrimination of other suspects. About half of the detainees are not interrogated by the GSS. Their investigation is passed on to the police, together with a summary of the incriminating testimonies against them.[14] According to estimates by the Palestinian Authority's Ministry of Prisoners Affairs, since 1967 about half a million Palestinians have passed through the gates of the Israeli prisons. It is difficult to find a family in the OPT who has not had one of its sons detained or imprisoned.

As already mentioned, most of the Palestinian prisoners and detainees in the Israeli prisons are classified as security prisoners. The security classification enables the IPS to separate the thousands of incarcerated Palestinians from ordinary criminal prisoners and subject them to a harsher regime within prison and severe restrictions with regards to their contact with the outside.[15] As for Palestinian criminal prisoners, although theoretically the severe restrictions derived from the security classification do not apply to them, they do not enjoy similar conditions to those of the rest of the criminal prisoners; many of them are convicted (in addition to the criminal offenses) of residing in Israel illegally, and they are deprived of various educational, therapeutic and occupational opportunities.

IPS POLICY AND THE PALESTINIAN SECURITY PRISONERS

IPS policy towards Palestinian security prisoners has been influenced by political developments as well as changes in personnel such as changing ministers and commissioners. Until the beginning of the 1990s, there was no unified policy.[16] The policy was pragmatic and tended towards liberalization. Talks were held with the prisoners, and the prisoners' leadership gained formal and informal recognition. Imprisonment conditions were improved and the autonomy within the prison was expanded, to a large extent thanks to a continuing struggle and the holding of general, coordinated hunger strikes by all the imprisoned Palestinian organizations.

The security prisoners' first hunger strike took place in 1970. Most of the security prisoners were held in extremely poor conditions in prisons within the OPT. The strike lasted seven days and in its wake Red Cross representatives were allowed to visit the prisons regularly.[17] In 1972, the prisoners in Ashkelon Prison (Shikma) started a hunger strike demanding the return of basic rights and living conditions. One of its leaders died during the strike. This strike was a breakthrough that marked the beginning of a struggle for more rights, and it led to an improvement in the imprisonment conditions.[18]

Throughout the 1970s and 1980s, several strikes were called, demanding an improvement in conditions, an end to prisoners' beatings and the recognition of their representatives. Following a strike that started in 1986, there was a change in the IPS approach and it started holding negotiations with the prisoners' spokespeople. A hardening of IPS policy was evident in 1991 with the appointment of Gabi Amir as Commissioner of IPS. He introduced a harsh policy and took measures to reduce prisoners' freedoms. In reaction, the prisoners in all the security prisons started a termless hunger strike, demanding, among other things, the abolition of solitary confinement cells. Lasting 18 days, the strike ended with the intervention of the political echelon, and in its wake, the prisoners' conditions were improved and their authority to run their lives in the wing was recognized. In 2000, a short time before Orit Adato came into office, the prisoners in all the security prisons began a hunger strike in protest of worsening prison conditions, that included the cessation of family visits, solitary confinements and beatings. Following the strike, a committee was set up (the Freinbuch Committee), which recommended unified rules for treating the security prisoner population. Between 2000 and 2003, Orit Adato served as IPS Commissioner. She introduced a relatively liberal policy and during her tenure the prisoners obtained various improvements in their living conditions.[19]

Until the end of 2003, the frameworks traditionally used to organize the lives of the prisoners and regulate their relationships with the staff and prison management were more or less preserved. As of 2003, however, under Commissioner Ya'akov Ganot, a harsh policy was reintroduced, and the restrictions on the living conditions of the security prisoners were toughened. In August 2004, about a year after the appointment of Ganot, and in reaction to the hardening of the policy, the security prisoners began a general hunger strike. The hunger strike lasted 19 days and ended gradually. The IPS prepared itself effectively and succeeded in crushing the prisoners' leadership, isolating the striking wings and bringing the strike to an end in an isolated and chaotic manner, with no plan or agreement.[20]

Ganot's appointment as Commissioner of the IPS at the end of 2003 marked not only the shift towards a harsher policy and a stricter adherence to orders and procedures, but also a matching-up of IPS policy with the new blueprints for ruling the Palestinian population. Ganot received full backing from the government to expand the IPS's incarceration capacity and to adapt it to its new functions, which went beyond the traditional roles of incarcerating prisoners.

The Oslo Agreements left Israel with security, administrative and territorial control of various parts of the Palestinian territories, enabling it to continue its settlement policy. Through a system of bypass roads and four main blocs of settlements, the West Bank has been divided into three parts and split up into smaller population reserves, in parallel to the complete fracturing and fencing of the Gaza Strip. Since the start of the second Intifada, the West Bank has been under total closure and severe restrictions have been imposed on the movement of Palestinians inside the West Bank by means of hundreds of manned checkpoints and roadblocks. The gradually completed "Separation Wall," the barriers and other physical obstacles encircle Palestinian towns and villages, cutting them off from the rest of the population and enclosing some of them within internal enclaves cut off from one another.[21]

In parallel to the splitting up and the fragmentation of the West Bank into small territorial entities, similar steps have been taken within the prisons. During the 2004 hunger strike, the prisoners' leaders were already separated from the rest of the prisoners and held in two isolated wings. After the strike, the splitting up of prisoners increased, and their separation in different prisons and in isolated wings in the same prison, according to geographical divisions and considerations, deepened. Not only are the prisoners assigned to prisons according to a regional division, they are also divided into different wings within the same prison according to blocs and smaller sub-areas, in a way which parallels the splitting up of the Palestinian space and Israel's division of the Occupied Territories into isolated areas.[22]

This division is presented as a response to the prisoners' and their families' demands that they be held in prisons close to their places of residence in order to make it easier for families to visit. In fact, it allows the authorities to expand their spatial control over the prisoners both inside and outside the prison, to split the prisoners up, to revive oppositions and to foment disputes based on geographical and local affiliation at the expense of national solidarity or organizational affiliation. The IPS moves prisoners between prisons and wings in order to influence the election of representatives to the committees representing the prisoners, and in order to ensure that the primary commitment is to the regional representative rather than based on political or ideological considerations. In this way, the prisoners' struggle to improve their living conditions and to promote their rights, is reduced into particular and isolated demands, such as the residents of a certain area seeking to increase the number of visitors and prolong visiting hours. These demands join to other requirements of the residents of the area, such as to remove a checkpoint or other restrictions imposed on them.[23]

EARLY RELEASE OF POLITICAL PRISONERS AND THE GOOD FRIDAY AGREEMENT

In contrast to its non-compromising rhetoric, Britain has often found it expedient to release Irish political criminals before they served their full sentence or even a substantial part of it. Political realism led British politicians to recognize that continued incarceration of "patriots" was an obstacle and did not serve political stability.[24]

In Northern Ireland, the process of early release of life-sentence prisoners within the criminal justice system has gained the support of policy makers, professionals and parts of the public because it was perceived as effective. Life-sentence prisoners in Northern Ireland, most of them convicted of terrorist-related murders, serve an average of approximately 15 years—considerably less than their counterparts in Britain or in Israel. Since 1985, with the conflict ongoing, more than 450 prisoners sentenced to life imprisonment were released, with only one of them reconvicted for a terrorist offense.[25]

The demand to release prisoners who have committed politically motivated offenses was raised by both the Republican and Loyalist groups following the ceasefires in 1994. The Irish government quickly recognized the political importance of the prisoners issue, and started to release prisoners within months after the 1994 ceasefire.[26] Although the releases stopped as a result of the collapse of the IRA ceasefire in February 1996, they were reintroduced a few weeks after the announcement of the restoration of that ceasefire in July 1997.[27]

A change in Britain's policy concerning the prisoners issue came with the election of the Labour government, who understood that the solution to the prisoners problem and a quick release of prisoners were key to achieving an agreement. Apart from a small number of dissidents opposed to the peace process, almost all the paramilitary prisoners were released under the terms of the Good Friday Agreement. British politicians, including the secretary of state, directly negotiated with paramilitary prisoners while they were serving their sentence, and prisoners were released in order to take part in the negotiations and in their organizations' meetings on the outside. In fact, the release of paramilitary prisoners and their reintegration into the outside society were at the center of the efforts to resolve the political conflict in Ireland.

When Tony Blair became prime minister, he was determined to give Sinn Féin another opportunity to join the Northern Ireland peace talks that had started in June 1996, and from which it had been excluded because of the IRA's failure to keep the ceasefire. On July 19, after intense discussions, the IRA restored the complete cessation of their military operations. In the Good Friday Agreement, signed in April 1998, it was agreed that all the prisoners belonging to the organizations that had signed the agreement would be released within two years. A month after the signing of the agreement, the British and Irish governments released a large number of Republican prisoners allowing them to participate in the *Ard Fheis* (party conference) of Sinn Féin in order to secure support for the agreement. In August 1998, a release commission began discussing prisoners' individual applications for early release, and the massive release began a month later. In August 2000, the last political prisoners entitled to early release under the Good Friday Agreement were released, bringing the sum of all the released prisoners to 433.[28] The notorious Maze Prison was closed.

THE RELEASE OF PALESTINIAN POLITICAL PRISONERS

The release of prisoners, found in Northern Ireland to be of major significance for the reconciliation process and the progress of the agreement, has not materialized in our region and has been systematically undermined by the Israeli governments. On September 1993, the PLO and Israel signed the Oslo Agreement which was supposed to begin a peace process. Although the prisoners issue was not discussed directly within the articles of the agreement, various statements by the Israeli government suggested that there would be a massive release of Palestinian prisoners under certain conditions.[29] The Cairo agreement, signed on May 1994, stipulated the release or handing over to the Palestinian Authority of 5,000 prisoners. By the end of July, 4,500 prisoners were in fact released, and eventually, 550 "released" prisoners were restricted to the boundaries of the town of Jericho.[30] The Second Oslo Agreement of 1995, signed by Yitzhak Rabin and Yasir Arafat in Washington, outlined the procedures for an additional future release of convicted prisoners and administrative detainees. However, Rabin's assassination and the continuing escalation of violence disrupted the release process. At the beginning of 1996, the Israeli government unilaterally froze all talks relating to prisoner release.

Although thousands of Palestinian prisoners have been released in the post-Oslo area, as part of the political agreement or as part of confidence-building measures, Israel continues to arrest thousands of Palestinians each month. Israel has refused to release, as part of the agreements, hundreds of Palestinians imprisoned before the Oslo Agreements and convicted of murdering and injuring Jews, and it persists in refusing to release dozens who have been sentenced to life imprisonment and have already spent 25 and 30 years in prison. All of them are older people, some very ill.

CONCLUSION

Two things should be learned from the British experience throughout the conflict in Northern Ireland. First, during the 1980s and 1990s, when the conflict was at its peak, at the height of the terrorist attacks and despite internal criticism, prisoners sentenced to and serving time for murder and terrorist offenses were released and went out on leave regularly. Throughout the conflict the British acted pragmatically; they realized that in the special circumstances of Northern Ireland, prisoner release could be highly beneficial.

Secondly, the decision to release prisoners who committed politically motivated offenses was a turning point in the conflict in Northern Ireland. The disagreements and arguments about methods and release procedures should not obscure the political rationale that led to the decision to begin this process. The lesson that can be learned for our region is that whatever procedures are selected, they should be followed out of a clear commitment of the governments that the prisoners would be released within a determined period of time as part of the process of resolving the conflict.

NOTES

1. For more details, see Sharon Weil's chapter in this volume.
2. See K. McEvoy (2001), *Paramilitary Imprisonment in Northern Ireland: Resistance, management, and release*, Oxford: Oxford University Press.
3. See J. Moore (1997), "Paramilitary prisoners and the peace process in Northern Ireland," in A. O'Day (ed.), *Political violence in Northern Ireland: Conflict and conflict resolution*, London: Praeger, pp. 81–93.
4. See L. McKeown (2001), *Out of time: Irish Republican prisoners, Long Kesh, 1972–2000*, Belfast: BTP Publications.
5. Moore, "Paramilitary prisoners."
6. McEvoy, *Paramilitary Imprisonment in Northern Ireland.*
7. Unless otherwise stated, all data relating to imprisonment in Northern Ireland are taken from McEvoy, *Paramilitary Imprisonment in Northern Ireland.*
8. S. Malka (2005), "Security Prisoners in Israel—A Historical Survey," *A View of the Prison*, pp. 7–12. (in Hebrew)
9. For more details see A. Korn (2003), "Rates of incarceration and main trends in Israeli prisons," *Criminal Justice* Vol. 3, No. 1, pp. 29–55.
10. The data published by the IPS concerning the rates of incarceration of the Palestinians do not include the Palestinians held at military facilities. In certain

periods during the conflict—for example, at the first Intifada—the number of Palestinians detained and imprisoned in various army prisons was higher than those held in civil custody.

11. Drawn from IPS website, 18 August 2010.
12. See R. Shaked (2008), "Security Prisoners in Israeli Prisons," *Ro'im Shabas*, Vol. 23, pp. 26–9 (in Hebrew).
13. See S. Malka, S. (2005), "The Hunger Strike 2004—'A Hot Summer,'" *A View of the Prison*, pp. 27–34 (in Hebrew); Shaked, "Security Prisoners in Israeli Prisons."
14. Amos Harel, "The New Headache of IDF in the Territories," *Ha'aretz*, May 2, 2008.
15. Arab citizens of Israel classified as security prisoners are also subjected to harsh restrictions similar to those imposed on the Palestinian residents of the OPT. In January 2009, there were about 370 Israeli Arab citizens classified as security prisoners. A small number of Jewish prisoners are classified by the IPS as security prisoners, but they are not subjected to the harsh conditions reserved for the Palestinians, and enjoy all the privileges granted to the rest of the prisoners. See A. Baker (2009), "Prisoners and Detainees in the Israeli Prisons," *Adalah's Electronic Newsletter*, No. 59 (in Hebrew).
16. Malka, "Security Prisoners in Israel."
17. Shaked, "Security Prisoners in Israeli Prisons."
18. Malka, "The Hunger Strike 2004."
19. Malka, "Security Prisoners in Israel."
20. See Walid Daka's chapter in this volume.
21. For further discussion, see A. Korn (2008), "The ghettoization of the Palestinians," in R. Lentin (ed.), *Thinking Palestine*, London: Zed Books, pp. 116–30.
22. See Walid Daka's chapter in this volume.
23. Ibid.
24. Moore, "Paramilitary prisoners."
25. See K. McEvoy (1998), "Prisoner release and conflict resolution: International lessons for Northern Ireland," *International Criminal Justice Review*, Vol. 8, pp. 33–60.
26. About a year after the IRA ceasefire, the British government restored the remission rate of 50 percent for those convicted of paramilitary offenses which had applied up until 1989 and was reduced to 33 percent.
27. McEvoy, *Paramilitary Imprisonment in Northern Ireland*.
28. Ibid.
29. Only people who were arrested before 13 September 1993 and were not members of political parties opposed to the agreement were eligible for release; the release of prisoners was conditional to the Palestinians declaring amnesty for collaborators and to progress being made on the issue of missing Israeli soldiers: see "Prisoner release and conflict resolution".
30. The release was conditional upon signing an individual declaration pledging to support the peace process, although these conditions were not agreed on in Cairo. Most of the parties opposed to the agreement refused to allow their imprisoned members to sign the declaration. However, at the beginning of June, a few Hamas members signed the declaration. Instead of being released, they were transferred to another prison: see ibid.

Part II
Arrest, Interrogation, Trial, Release

7
The Arrest and Persecution of Elected Political Leaders—Interview with Sheikh Muhammad Abu Tir

Interviewed by Abeer Baker and Anat Matar

General elections for the Palestinian Legislative Council (PLC) were held on January 25, 2006. Palestinian voters in the Gaza Strip and the West Bank, including East Jerusalem, were eligible to run for office. The results brought victory for Hamas, with 74 seats to the ruling Fatah party's 45, providing the former with a decisive majority of the 132 available seats and the authority to form a majority government on its own. It should be noted that already on September 26, 2005 the Israeli occupation forces had detained 450 members of the Hamas party, most of whom were involved in the coming elections either through active campaigning, or through taking part in the municipal elections in the various West Bank cities.

On June 25, 2006, Palestinian militant groups in Gaza took Corporal Gilad Shalit hostage. A couple of days later, Israel launched a series of military operations which left hundreds of Gaza residents dead and the territory besieged. Reprisals and collective punishment against civilians extended to the West Bank as well. The Israeli government announced that Palestinian members of Parliament and cabinet ministers had no immunity, threatening to detain them as a bargaining chip towards the release of the Israeli soldier imprisoned in the Gaza Strip. And indeed, on June 29, 2006, the Israeli Army conducted widescale detention operations against scores of Hamas supporters, including cabinet ministers and members of the PLC elected on the platform of the pro-Hamas "Change and Reform" List. Eight Palestinian government ministers and 26 PLC members were detained, in addition to other Hamas leaders.

Sheikh Abu Tir is a resident of East Jerusalem who lives in the Umm Tuba neighborhood, a neglected Palestinian area adjacent to the Har Choma settlement. The personal status of Abu Tir, like that of all Palestinian residents of Jerusalem, is highly complex.

East Jerusalem has been occupied territory since 1967, defining all those living there as protected civilians entitled to all the protective measures granted this status under international humanitarian law. However, following the end of the 1967 war, Israel annexed parts of East Jerusalem, subjecting them to domestic, Israeli law. The Palestinian residents were issued permits allowing permanent residence in Israel, which ostensibly provided them with protective means approximating those at the disposal of Israeli citizens, with the exception of the right to vote and the right to be elected to Israel's legislature.

Since the 1993 Oslo Accords, however, Israel has recognized that East Jerusalem, despite its legalized annexation, is at the heart of the conflict, acknowledging that its residents are part and parcel of the Palestinian people living in the West Bank and the Gaza Strip. Accordingly, Israel agreed to allow the Palestinian residents of East Jerusalem full participation in elections for the PLC and for the Chair of the Palestinian Authority, as both voters and candidates.

In 2006, along with three friends from East Jerusalem, Sheikh Mohammad Abu Tir ran for a seat in the PLC on behalf of the "Change and Reform" list. Their subsequent victory in the elections has taken an extremely heavy toll: their Israeli residency was revoked by Israel's Interior Minister on the grounds of "lack of loyalty"; they were detained, sentenced to three-and-a-half years' imprisonment and, finally, issued a deportation order prohibiting them from the entire area of Israel, including East Jerusalem, viewed by Israel as part of its domestic territory.

We met Sheikh Abu Tir, widely known for his red, hennaed beard, on June 14 2010, at his home, only days before an Israeli court rejected his petition to freeze the deportation order against him pending a High Court of Justice (HCJ) ruling on his previous petition to retract the arbitrary administration decision revoking his residency. On June 25, Abu Tir was detained on charges of illegal sojournment in his own home, the home in East Jerusalem in which he and his ancestors have lived for generations. He refused a bargain that would have gained his release in return for his pledge to leave Jerusalem, preferring to remain in detention and to have his day in court. It was our distinct impression, in the course of this interview, that Abu Tir sincerely hopes to conclude his long chapter of repeated imprisonment, turning to parliamentary political action to influence public opinion. Unfortunately, this hope has been nipped in the bud. Abu Tir's case constitutes a distinct example of Israel's arbitrary uses of power to silence voices of dissent and non-violent resistance through groundless detention, abduction, imprisonment and deportation. As of March 2011, he is still in prison.

Could you provide some context for this interview and tell us about yourself?

I was born in 1951. I was born here, in East Jerusalem, in Umm Tuba. My family has lived here for many generations. I graduated from the "Al-Aqsa" Sharia high school in 1971, qualifying me for study at the Sharia colleges of Jordan and Egypt. However, my political activism kept me from further studies. I'm quite widely known and popular among Palestinians both locally, in the West Bank and Gaza Strip, and on an international Palestinian level. I gained the epithet "sheikh" while I was still in junior high [school]. By now I'm considered one of the prominent theorists of the Hamas movement in terms of its politics, its doctrine and its international ties and image.

Over half of your life has been spent in Israeli prisons.

True. I've been detained seven times in the course of my life and spent over 30 years in prison. The first time was in 1974 on returning from Syria and Beirut. The military court in Lod [Lydda] sentenced me to 16 years' imprisonment for training with the Fatah movement. My sentence was reduced to 13 years and I was released in 1985. Then, in 1989, I was detained again on charges of membership in a military organization and dealing in arms, and sentenced to 13 months in prison. Soon after my release in 1990, I was rearrested. This time, the format was so-called administrative detention, without charges or due process of any kind. I was in prison for six months as an administrative detainee. In 1992, I was sentenced to six years' imprisonment for possession of, and dealing with, arms for Hamas. Then again, quite shortly after my release, in 1998, I was detained for a fifth time and sentenced to seven years in prison, for terrorist activity and membership in the "Izz ad-Din al-Qassam Brigades." My sixth incarceration began at the end of June 2006 following my election to the Palestinian Parliament (in January 2006), as a member of the "Change and Reform" list. The military court sentenced me to 40 months' imprisonment for membership in Hamas and I remained in prison until my recent release in May 2010.

Your first periods in prison were for membership in the Fatah movement, then, and now you're one of the prominent members of Hamas. Can you explain the shift?

My decision to terminate my membership in the Fatah crystallized while I was in prison in 1976. I didn't like the way Fatah members— or members of the other organizations—conducted themselves morally. This had various facets. The people of the Marxist contingent declared total war on religion and tried to impose their views by force. The same was true of the nationalist contingent. It went against my most basic intuitions. I couldn't countenance these assaults on religion any longer and decided to leave Fatah. The people of Fatah had in fact misled us into believing that Fatah included a religious caucus, when no such organized group existed. The remarks they made about us, as people with an affinity for religion, and similar responses we heard from members of the Popular Front were in fact what led to our conclusion that we indeed constituted a group united by shared characteristics which, in turn, distinguished us from Fatah and the Popular Front. Before then, the religious groups were not at all united or organized as a political bloc.

In Nafha Prison, I met Sheikh Ahmed Yassin. This was in 1984. The prison manager in the Ashkelon [Asqalan] Prison decided to punish me after a sermon of mine at one of the Friday prayer sessions that seriously angered them and they had me transferred to Nafha. Shortly after my transfer, Sheikh Ahmed Yassin arrived there. My gradually deepening bonds with Sheikh Yassin and his influence strengthened my connections with Islam and with the religious political school. After my release from prison, Sheikh Yassin came to visit me twice, here in my home. When the first Intifada broke out, the Hamas movement became more prominent as did my own involvement with the organization.

Your most recent imprisonment was different from all the previous ones. This was a case of purely political grounds; the charges followed directly from your candidacy and victory in the elections. Can you describe the process that led to these elections and when your participation morphed into "a breach of law"?

During my previous prison term [1998–2005], there were discussions of the question of elections for a Palestinian Parliament. The issue was whether or not to enter the race as representatives of the Hamas resistance movement or as part of a separate, independent movement. We decided to run independently as the "Change and Reform" list. It was Abu Mazen [Mahmoud Abbas] who pushed us to take part in elections for the legislature and for municipal government. The people of Fatah expressly asked us to participate. Israel, on the other hand, objected to holding elections. It opposed Hamas' participation altogether and in particular, the participation of East Jerusalem residents, like myself. Later, however, Israel succumbed to international pressure and especially that of America.

The elections were not conducted in secret. Our campaign was totally public. It was the Israeli police force that brought us the polling booths from the West Bank. Everything was conducted under police supervision. Following our victory, it was clear to us that they'd wanted us as false witnesses: they wanted to demonstrate that elections had been held while denying their outcome. Apparently, an attempt was made to "swallow" us in terms of the elections process. But the outcome shocked them. It wasn't at all what they had intended. So following our victory in the elections, the East Jerusalem Parliament members representing our bloc were given a choice: either resign from the legislative council or your right of residency in East Jerusalem will be revoked and your "blue ID card"—identifying you as residing within Israel—will be confiscated. This is based on Israel's annexation of East Jerusalem, which it does not hold to be occupied territory. In many areas, Israeli law grants us rights equal to those of the rest of Israel's residents. In practice, however, a very deep chasm divides the Jewish neighborhoods of East Jerusalem from the Palestinian ones. In actuality, government policy towards East Jerusalem is marred by systematic and intentional discrimination. This is highly visible in the field of urban planning and development and in the disgraceful level of state and municipal services we receive despite being fully entitled to both. It is also very evident, of course, in the area of residents' status and protection.

When given the above choice, we were allowed a month to decide whether we wished to resign or lose our rights of residency. Then, quite suddenly, in the course of that month, our residency rights were revoked and we were detained. With me, from East Jerusalem, three other men were detained: Khaled abu 'Arfa [Minister of Jerusalem Affairs], Ahmad 'Atun [a member of the legislative council] and Muhammad Tutah [a member of the legislative council].

Do you recall the details of how the detainment occurred in this most recent case?

On June 29, 2006, I arrived back home in the evening and asked my wife to lock up the house. I had a sense that something might happen. It's worth noting that the times were tense: the Israeli Army had already attacked Gaza the previous day. At 1 a.m., the security forces knocked at my door. They entered, conducted a search of the house, created total bedlam in our home and confiscated books, notebooks, journals and other things. They entered the bedroom. One obnoxious policeman tried to seize the Parker pens I had there. Some of the policemen were familiar faces and I asked one of them, "Where are we headed?" He answered, "The top guns have gone berserk. We don't know where!" I was taken to Ofer Prison. During the interrogation, I learned that my "crime" was membership in Hamas. I explained that I had run on behalf of an independent party, not Hamas. I told them, "You allowed us to run, didn't you? I'm not crazy enough to get out of prison in 2005 and get sent straight back in 2006! I'm sixty and I'm already too old for this."

The way you've described it, one might think this was the first time you were detained …

I spent thirty years in Israeli prisons without ever having fired a single shot—but this detention and imprisonment was particularly pointless, superfluous. That really hurt. In the many days I've spent in prison, over different periods of my life, major personal events have come and gone, which has been deeply painful. My mother, my father, my sister and my uncle passed away; my daughters married; my son-in-law passed away, leaving my daughter a widow; my grandchildren were born and grew to adulthood, completing their academic degrees while I was away from home. Now, at least, I want to be there with them. What is happening to us is cruel, this whole imprisonment—baseless. No rhyme or reason. This is unjust.

What do you see as the true objective of the imprisonment? Revenge for taking Gilad Shalit prisoner several days earlier? A way to pave the way for your deportation?

I don't think the motive has any direct connection with the soldier Gilad Shalit. In my view, the imprisonment was a way to block our political work. All my previous detentions and prison terms involved the GSS [General Security Service] while they had no part whatsoever in this case. It was a totally political, top-down decision. Following our election to office on January 26, 2006, we began working very diligently. We treated the fact that we had been elected with great seriousness. This was what we had striven for. But we met with restrictions immediately, well before the detention. I was personally held up for long hours at checkpoints every time I entered Ramallah. We could tell they simply didn't want us to put our time to effective use. They wasted and robbed our time at checkpoints, roadblocks and questionings. I'm not referring to Israel exclusively. This was the Palestinian Authority too. Now, in hindsight, we see clearly that allowing our participation in the elections wasn't intended to allow our views visibility or legitimacy but, rather, in order to co-opt and silence us. We were meant to listen, to take orders and not to exert any influence whatsoever. But the public sounded its voice, much to the dismay of Israel and of the Palestinian Authority. We were legally and rightfully elected to office as Parliament members and, as it turns out, that entitled us to nothing, not even fundamental parliamentary impunity. What is granted to members of parliaments the world over is denied us. We're not even protected from criminal charges for our very membership in a party that was legally elected to office! Can you imagine a situation inside Israel where a party is legally approved before the elections, after which a representative of that party is elected to office and then, following his election, charged for the very fact of being elected? No court would allow such a surreal process! But for us, impunity is only before God. Clearly, detention is the easy way to remove us, to weaken us and to neutralize our formidable influence. The reasons behind this detention and imprisonment were purely political and the only thing capable of ending it was, accordingly, political, a political decision. A single phone call from Abu Mazen to Condoleeza Rice and we were out. But he did it because he too wanted us exiled. Not a single person from the Palestinian Authority phoned me following my release.

What do you think of the response of the international community to your latest imprisonment?

Here and there, various supporters published statements, including one from the Inter-Parliamentary Union, but all in all it has been far from enough. There has not been sufficient support for us.

You're carrying with you, in your shirt pocket, a document ordering you to leave East Jerusalem within days. In other words, you've been deported. What will you do? Where will you go?

I won't budge of my own accord even after my temporary resident's permit expires. It's crystal clear that banishing us from Jerusalem is an attempt to banish our influence. We're exiled due to our participation in a democratic political process. We haven't broken a single law. We didn't operate in secret. We cooperated and found ourselves, at the end, in prison and exiled from our homes. They don't want the Palestinians to hold any political power in East Jerusalem. What they want here is a drug-and-violence-ridden population that they can marginalize and control. In the past, deportations from Jerusalem were based on what the authorities termed the deportee's "center of life"; now the background is political views. My family has lived here for five hundred years. I'm slated for deportation at any moment. First, they issued demolition orders against my home, the home I grew up in and live in today with my family. Now there's an easier way: rather than disappear the house, they disappear the head of the family. I petitioned the High Court for an injunction freezing my deportation pending the fundamental court ruling on the issue of my revoked residency. I'll hope for the best.

8
My Arrests, My Interrogations

Osama Barham

One day in 1979, while I was on my way home with my father, one of the Occupation patrols stopped us and asked for our IDs. My father took out his ID card, but I didn't have one as I was still under 16. One of the soldiers kicked me with his foot, which was dangling down from the jeep. My father held up his ID card, trying to convince them that I was still a minor. The lieutenant threw the card to the ground. My father, God rest his soul, was a high school principal, and the soldiers had insulted him in front of his students, some of whom were at the scene. That night I decided to avenge the insult by raising a large Palestinian flag. As it was hard to find pieces of material in all the colors of the flag, I had to rip up one of my mother's blouses to complete it. The Occupation forces took down the flag the next morning. I felt then that I had avenged my father.

That incident marked the beginning of my political activism. From then on, I began to participate in demonstrations and became a leading activist. I worked in various groups and organized marches on national days.

I was arrested a total of eight times, for 18 days at a time, following the flag incident. The Occupation forces arrested the political activists, afraid they would stage mass demonstrations to mark national occasions such as Land Day, or to commemorate the establishment of the various Palestinian national factions. During that period the soldiers would gather 20 young men together in a room no bigger than 20 square meters and beat us up. We were unable to sleep because the room was so cramped, but also because we could hear the screams of our comrades who were being beaten.

1981–82

One night in 1981, a large number of Occupation soldiers raided our house at 2 o'clock in the morning. They surrounded the house then barged into the room where I was sleeping, dragging my father with them. I woke up to one of the soldiers shoving me hard with his foot, while the other soldiers aimed their guns at me. They led me out with my hands and feet cuffed with metal chains and blindfolded. I fought a little with one of the soldiers because he had shoved and hit my brother. Once inside the military jeep that took me to the Central Jenin Prison, also known as "The Slaughterhouse," the soldiers began kicking me so hard that at a certain point I stopped feeling the impact of their boots. We arrived at Jenin Prison, where they had an interrogation division. A secret service agent greeted us, introducing himself under a false name. He escorted me into a small room, removed my blindfold and told me in Arabic, "Come here. Let's finish the story." I asked him, "What story? I swear to God, there isn't really any story." He then opened the drawer of the desk in front of him and said, "Let's put God in this drawer." That's when I knew that I was in for a rough interrogation session. He later claimed that the biggest and hardest men of the resistance had been crushed by his beatings.

He began beating the front of my neck until I lost the ability to speak. He yelled, "I've heard a lot about you. And it's personal between us. My professional career is tied to you. And if you don't confess here and now, I'll retire." I said, "So retire right now." He went berserk, pummeling me with his fists and kicking me, and only stopped when the other agents restrained him. Once he had calmed down, he resumed the beating. After several kicks to the stomach, I fell to the ground. I started to vomit blood. The interrogator throttled me. I was transferred to a hospital in Haifa. They examined me and apparently decided I was fit to take a second round of interrogation.

The second round was with an interrogator who took the role of a caring, educated person who was opposed to abuse. I remember that our conversation was vague, lacking in any specific accusations, since the goal of the interrogation was to gather information about our political activities. After several hours with the "soft" interrogator, he suddenly switched and began to threaten me and to use harsh forms of torture against me. He took a chair and pressed it between my legs so that the pressure was concentrated on my testicles. He forced me to sit on my feet and pushed me backwards, putting all his weight on the chair. He held me in this excruciating position for half an hour, which felt like an entire day. My legs turned green and I was in horrendous pain. Later during the interrogation, he asked me to sit in the same position again but I refused, since taking the beatings was less painful. A second round of beating of every possible kind began. The ordeal continued until noon the next day. Then they put me in a windowless cell no bigger than one square meter. It was pitch black and I could see nothing. On the evening of the second day, they replayed the same scenario of beatings and threats, following which an officer hung me by my arms from a pole until I felt they had dislocated my shoulders. It lasted for twelve hours. Usually this type of treatment would take place at night so the questioning could start in the morning when the prisoner was completely exhausted. The interrogation lasted for 48 days, during which I was transferred to the hospital on three occasions. Then I was released.

After I finished high school, I enrolled on a journalism and media course. One day an intelligence officer sent a request to talk to me. As soon as I arrived at the interrogation center in Tulkarm—infamous for the two young men who had been martyred during their questioning there—a solider appeared and tied me up. I was then transferred to the Far'a military camp where the interrogators wore military uniforms. Eight interrogators entered the room in which I was being held. They had taken on crude Arab names like "Abu Jabal" ("Father of the Mountain") and "Abu Khanjar" ("Father of the Dagger"). They asked me what college I attended and what my field of studies was, even though they knew all that information perfectly well. When I told them that I was a journalism and media student, they immediately began to rain blows down on every part of my body. The beating lasted long after I'd fallen to the ground. I couldn't stand on my feet. During the beating they asked me, "So you want to write about Far'a Prison, you bastard?" They asked because the press and human rights organizations had written extensively about the prison, particularly after a prisoner lost his life during questioning and their harsh methods of interrogation—such as shoving prisoners' heads down the toilets—had been exposed. I was released after being subjected to brutal sessions of military interrogation over 32 days. I had lost 18 kilograms. My father didn't even recognize me and started crying when he saw me.

THE MOST BRUTAL TORTURE SESSIONS

I was arrested again eight months later. I was picked up at my house at 1 o'clock in the morning. After surrounding the house, the Occupation forces climbed up to the roof and the surrounding trees. A few ran up to the house and shouted for me to come out. I walked out of the house with my father and they asked me to raise my hands, warning that if I lowered them I would be responsible for what happened next. They ordered me to walk straight ahead. After I had taken a few steps forward, they told me to lie on the ground on my stomach under a tree. At that moment, a number of soldiers pounced on me, binding my hands and feet behind my back. They lifted me up and rubbed my face in a mound of white sand. One of the soldiers stepped on my back and I was left lying there in the sand. They ordered my father to get everyone out of the house, including my mother and my younger sisters. They screamed at him to open all the doors and windows. Their hysterical yelling terrified my sisters and mother. They asked my father to run in front of them to shield them, and continued to push him around until they had finished searching the entire house.

Next, they smashed everything up with axes, ripped up the floor tiles, wrecked the furniture and slashed open the couches and beds with knives. After more than an hour of this, they took me away with them. I asked them if I could put on a pair of sandals. They said no. I asked to say goodbye to my mother and sisters. They said no. They took me to the Tulkarm interrogation center. This round of interrogation was more brutal than any of the previous rounds.

I arrived at the interrogation center at night. An interrogator greeted me and said that he had wanted to get to know me for some time since he had heard so much about me. He said that we were going to end my case, whatever it took. He took me into the interrogation room and sat me down on a small chair that was no higher than 20 cm above the ground, with a back that was also 20 cm, which meant that you could not actually rest your back on it. He left and returned with a cup of coffee and ordered me to drink it. I told him that I didn't drink coffee. He asked whether he should bring me tea or something else. I told him that I didn't want to drink anything. He left and came back with two crackers and asked me to eat one, but I refused. "You don't eat from Jews?" he asked. I told him that wasn't the reason, but didn't say why I had refused, which was because I feared that they'd prevent me from using the toilet. It was well-known that interrogators would barter with detainees for a confession over permission to use the toilet.

Afterwards, another interrogator appeared and introduced himself as "Tzadok." In all coolness, he informed me that he had been responsible for the death of a personal colleague of mine several days earlier during his interrogation.

Tzadok told me, "Tonight I'm going to stay up with you and either end your case or your life." I told him that my name was

Osama Barham, and that if he could get my name out of me again, I would confess to anything he wanted. The challenge infuriated him and he hit me repeatedly with incredible force. I stared back at him with steely determination the entire time. He shouted at me to give him my name, but I refused to answer him. I pretended not to hear him. He screamed louder still until other interrogators came from their own interrogation rooms to interrupt the beating, sensing that he might kill me. Another agent sat with me and tried to calm me down. I felt a strange and ferocious sense of determination. An hour later, Tzadok came back and sat me down on a chair bolted to the ground. He bound me to the chair and pressed down on my handcuffs, inflicting excruciating pain. He then threw a bucket of icy water all over me and switched on a large ceiling fan, in addition to the air conditioner, which he had set at an extremely low temperature. I felt frozen, like a plank of wood. He left the room.

It was as if my body had shrunk from the cold. I raised my leg up as far as I could to try to reach the controls on the air conditioner in order to raise the temperature. After several attempts I managed it. When he returned an hour later, he found the room warm, and realized that I had changed the setting to warm air. He asked me whether I had raised the temperature, to which I replied that since he could see my footprints on the button, he didn't need to ask. He immediately started beating me and screaming at me, before trying to strangle me. Other interrogators intervened after hearing his hysterical yelling. They whispered something in his ear and that was the last time I saw him.

*   *   *

The intelligence services arrested all my friends and close acquaintances. I was transferred to the Jenin interrogation center. There, one young guy confessed that we were putting together a cell to resist the Occupation. The interrogations were so brutal that one of my friends lost his mind for two whole years. Another friend's ear, as was my brother's, was split open, from the blows to the head they received during their questioning. I began to cough up blood constantly and developed an ulcer.

In 1984, I was convicted of having affiliations with an illegal organization (Fatah al-Intifada) and for possession of weapons. I was sentenced to seven years and released in 1992.

1993: BACK TO TORTURE

I was arrested again in 1993. The Occupation forces raided my house at 3 o'clock in the morning. I saw the soldiers surrounding the house, and hiding behind the walls and in the trees. I saw them climb up onto the roof of my house and my brother's house, which was adjacent to mine. After they had the houses surrounded, they began to make a huge racket. They raided the house of one of the neighbors, no more than a dozen meters away, and yelled, "Where's Osama's house?" That is when I understood what they were trying to do: trick me into trying to escape to give them the opportunity to kill me. I called back to them that Osama's house was right here, and they came closer. They asked me to come out, which I did, along with my father. They asked my father to stop where he was, and for me to come forward alone. Their weapons were mounted with laser scopes, and their red dots covered my entire body. They pointed their weapons at my head and ordered me to lie down on the ground. They tied me up and told me to strip to my underwear. They crowded all the family into one room, then led them outside and told them to lie down on the ground on their stomachs. Next they conducted an inch-by-inch search of the house, smashed up the furniture with axes and ripped up all the beds.

They led me to the interrogation center in Tulkarm, and here a new phase of unimaginably intense suffering began. First, they put me into a room with a blackboard. An interrogator entered the room and wrote out the following four lines: "organizing and organizing others, weapons, explosives, communications from abroad." Then he told me, "Take five minutes to think about it. I need an answer for each of these issues." I responded that I didn't need five minutes because I had no answers to any of them. He asked, "Is that your final answer?" "Yes," I replied. Then he threatened, "Since you reject dialogue and easy treatment, I'm going to bring in someone who knows how to deal with you." A man entered with a pompous air and told me, "I've set aside fourteen days for you. They brought me here and cut my vacation short, so I have a personal beef with you." He continued, "They call me in when there's a stubborn case, so I'll consider yours either my personal success or failure."

"Go ahead, talk," he said. "Welcome," I replied. He suddenly hit me in the head with a closed fist. I dropped to the floor with my hands and feet shackled. He began to hurl insults at me, and I insulted him back. He warned, "Don't make that mistake," to which I said, "You stop first." He actually did stop insulting me, but instead grabbed my neck and choked me so violently that I almost lost consciousness. Next, he pulled out my chest hair, leaving me with large bald patches. I didn't give him any indication that I was in pain, but on the contrary showed only indifference. He pinched my chest and nipples roughly, but despite the intense pain I continued to appear unmoved. He called in another interrogator and told him, "This one can't feel the pinching." So they both pinched my skin, one on each side. I didn't move an inch and challenged them to do their worst. They went crazy, grabbing and squeezing both sides of my neck, causing it to turn black and blue and my chest to become inflamed. Then they started to yank out my moustache, ripping out large patches, and still I showed no sign of pain. They beat me to get a scream or some other reaction out of me, but I was determined not to show the pain. It was only when they dealt some particularly cruel blows to my stomach and genitals that I screamed out loud and fell to the ground.

I woke up to find my whole body drenched. It seems that I had lost consciousness and they had thrown water over me in an attempt to revive me, after which a doctor had told them to take me to hospital. They drove me in a police car to the Tel Hashomer hospital, where a doctor apparently told them to stop the beating for two days. Two days later, the interrogators told me that the hospital report had stated that I'd been acting and was able to withstand the beatings. During the two days in which they didn't beat me, they sat me down on a low chair that was bolted to the ground and placed a filthy, stinking bag on my head. My hands and feet were tied down, and I was denied sleep for hours on end as the interrogation went on. The interrogation continued, but the torture took another form.

An older, stern-eyed interrogator arrived. He sat on the chair in front of me and more than ten other interrogators joined us. He told them not to ask me anything related to the purpose of my questioning. They asked me political and historical questions. He looked at me as if he were studying my personality. After an hour he said in a low voice, "You, Osama, are with us for 90 days, as prescribed by law. After that we'll request another 90 days from the High Court. You'll be with us either until you're finished or we're finished. We're stronger. We're a nation. You're done for sure." And he left.

The torture was relentless. The interrogation would continue for days on end without breaks even for meals. The officers would take turns. After pushing me to the brink of exhaustion, they employed the "shaking method." The interrogator would stand on a chair, grab me by the chest and shake me with intense force and speed, squeezing down on my spine. People subjected to this brutal method of torture can be paralyzed, as a number of prisoners were before the Israeli High Court banned its use.

The shaking went on for a protracted period of time, and I did all I could to resist. But I could not persevere much longer as a fierce pain had developed at the base of my neck. It went on until the following morning, when even the interrogator seemed exhausted. I was put in a cell for two days. I began to feel an intense pain in my hips, made worse by the kidney stones I'd been suffering from even prior to my arrest. My kidneys had apparently become infected from the pressure caused by the shaking and my attempts to resist. The pain was indescribable. I told the interrogator about the pain in my kidneys and my swollen left hip. However, instead of calling a doctor, he took me into the interrogation room and tried to extract a confession out of me in exchange for medical treatment. He placed a canvas bag over my head, blocking my vision, and pressed my right side with the inflamed kidney up against the corner of a metal filing cabinet. I screamed. He relieved the pressure slightly and then began to direct questions at me. Then he hit my genitals hard. My automatic reaction was to raise my legs up in defense. I couldn't see him, but my knee came into contact with his stomach and he started yelling. He tore the bag off my head, said "You just hit me," and called for another interrogator.

They both beat me for nearly half an hour and then told me that they were going to take me to court for assaulting an interrogator. That evening they took me to court under tight security. We entered the military court and the Military Prosecutor claimed that I had attacked an interrogator. At that point, I took off my shirt to reveal the marks of torture, the heavy bruises I had developed from the pinching and the places where my chest hair had been ripped out. It was a gory sight. I told the judge exactly what had happened. The judge decided to forbid the use of physical violence against me. After the hearing, I returned to the interrogation triumphant.

The interrogators now resorted to a new method of torture. They turned on a radio with large speakers used as amplifiers at large public gatherings. The sound was deafening and I was afraid that my eardrums would burst. I understood that this was the method they would use on me from now on. I could see the interrogator from a small hole in the bag they had put over my head. I moved my leg as if I were dancing to the song blasting out from the speaker.

Surprised, the interrogator asked, "Are you enjoying yourself Osama?" I replied that I was because I hadn't listened to music in a long time. He asked if I was being serious. I said yes, and asked if I was listening to a song in Hebrew. He told me that yes, it was an Israeli song. I said that I was overjoyed. My answer made the interrogator wonder if I had lost my mind, and so he took me into another room and asked me several questions to ascertain my psychological state. When he confirmed that I hadn't gone insane, he sat me back down in my spot next to the speaker, then snapped off the music, told me that I was going to rot in jail until I was withered and old, and left.

ADMINISTRATIVE DETENTION

I was held in prison cells for 34 days. I was later transferred to Far'a Prison, where they told me that the court had sentenced me to six months' administrative detention. The administrative detention order was renewed 14 times, and I was held for a total of six-and-a-half years, without trial and with no idea of what the allegations against me were. I had become the most senior Palestinian administrative detainee. I was released following an intervention by human rights groups, led by the organization Open Doors. Dr. Anat Matar from Open Doors introduced my case to Advocate David Libay, an eminent member of the Labor Party. After Labor won the elections and Yossi Beilin became the Minister of Justice, I was offered a deal, according to which I would be banned from entering any area within the Green Line following my release and would not engage in any political activity. With that, the nightmare of administrative detention had finally drawn to an end after 78 months. It was November 17, 1999. I abided by the agreement but was aware that the intelligence services were following me. I knew that they would do anything to demonstrate that I had broken the agreement in order to detain me again.

THE ATTEMPTS OF THE ISRAELI SECURITY FORCES TO ASSASSINATE ME

On the night of December 13, 2000, the Israeli security forces attempted to assassinate me. Several days earlier, in my private office, I had tried to call a lawyer friend from Nazareth, inside the Green Line. Someone answered who I took to be a friend of the lawyer. He encouraged me to visit them in Nazareth, to which I replied that I was not permitted to enter the 1948 (Israeli) areas. I realized that I was talking to a member of the Israeli intelligence services. He insisted on giving me his phone number. I later discovered that the intelligence services had bugged the office phone and were monitoring all my ingoing and outgoing calls.

I told the journalist Amira Hass what had happened. She took the number the intelligence officer had given me—he had called himself "Chaim"—and tried to contact him, but he hung up on her. I realized that they were not going to leave me alone and started to get depressed. I stopped leaving Nablus except on the days when I was required to sign military forms under my restrictive conditions of release. I was very careful, afraid that they would exploit any opportunity to detain me again. I didn't answer phone calls from anyone I didn't know, but began to receive more and more calls from unknown individuals.

The second Intifada was just beginning and the situation was escalating. Israel had tightened its detention policy and I became even more cautious.

Sa'ad al-Kharouf was one of my closest friends. He made a point of not letting me out of his sight and spent hours with me, especially after he heard about the attempts of the intelligence services to provoke me into making a mistake. Sa'ad had studied in Germany and worked as a mechanical engineer. He owned a clothing store which was well known in the city. I often sat in the store and helped him to sell clothes.

One night, Sa'ad called me at quarter to midnight and asked me to go with him to see a friend whose car had broken down in Boreen, a village close to Nablus. I asked Sa'ad to come to pick me up. When he arrived at my house, I went out to greet him with Khalil, my brother-in law, who was staying with us that night. Sa'ad suggested that Khalil go with him instead of me, fearing that the intelligence services would harass me for going out late at night.

Sa'ad and Khalil went out to bring back the friend whose car had broken down. After some time had passed, I called Sa'ad to ask him why they were taking so long as it wasn't far. He said that they were still on the road. I called him again, twice, a few minutes later to make sure they were alright but got no reply. When I called him for a third time, someone answered in Hebrew. I asked him about Sa'ad but the line went dead. I called his phone repeatedly but got no answer. We became frantic with worry and contacted all the nearby hospitals in case they had been in an accident. But the hospitals had no information about them. We called a friend who works at the Red Cross and asked him for any news about accidents or injuries. He told us that three people had been martyred and a number of others injured in the area Sa'ad and Khalil had been heading to. They had been taken to a hospital in Ramallah, since Israel had denied them access to the hospitals in Nablus. I called Na'el, a relative of mine, and asked him to check with a hospital in Ramallah whether Sa'ad and Khalil were there. Na'el told me that they hadn't yet identified the injured at the hospital. I thought that Sa'ad and Khalil had been detained for entering a tense security zone, since it was common for the Occupation forces to detain anyone they found in a dangerous area.

I would listen to the Israeli news at midnight each night to hear updates about the security situation, since it was the beginning of the Intifada. There was a news program in Hebrew on the Reshet Bet radio station that reported on the news of the past 24 hours. At midnight, I turned on the radio as usual and listened in shock to the first headline: the military had foiled a major military operation and killed a leader of the Islamic Jihad, along with a companion. I immediately understood that Sa'ad and Khalil had fallen into a trap set up by the intelligence services. It was Khalil's bad luck that he had been with Sa'ad and not me, as the intelligence had planned.

I told Israeli lawyer Tamar Pelleg-Sryck and Dr. Anat Matar what had been reported on the radio. I told them that I was at home with my family and that I hadn't been killed or involved in the incident. I also got in touch with Israeli Member of Knesset Zehava Gal'on, who had been the director of human rights organization B'Tselem before becoming a Member of Knesset for the Meretz political party. I had great respect for her.

After the military learned that I wasn't in the vehicle they targeted, Israel told the Palestinian security forces that I was planning to launch a large military operation. I was the last to hear about it. My friends advised me to go into hiding, fearing that they would target me again. And that is what I did the day after Sa'ad's funeral.

I then knew for certain that Sa'ad had been killed in an Israeli setup. Khalil had been badly wounded and had to stay in an Israeli hospital for three months, during which time he was questioned by the intelligence services. Khalil told me what had happened. He said, "We were heading to where Sa'ad's friend told us his car had broken down. When we got there, in Boreen, Sa'ad's friend's car was parked at the side of the road. We pulled up alongside it and got out of the car. As soon as our feet touched the ground, they sprayed us with bullets. The firing lasted for several minutes. Sa'ad screamed and fell onto the hood of the car. I was also hit several times. I lost one of my kidneys and part of my stomach, and was shot in the legs. I was bleeding internally and blood was pouring from my mouth. I hid behind a car wheel and when the shooting stopped shouted out, 'Why are you trying to kill us?!' One of the intelligence officers asked me who I was and I told him that I was Khalil al-Ardah from Arraba. He asked, 'Aren't you Osama Barham?' When I told him that I was Osama's brother-in-law, he asked me why I had come instead of Osama."

Two days after the incident, the person who had called Sa'ad and asked for his help with his car turned himself in to the Palestinian security forces and told them what had happened. He had been arrested in Haifa, from where soldiers and intelligence officials had accompanied him to Jalame Prison and forced him to call Sa'ad's mobile phone at 2 o'clock in the afternoon to tell him that he had products to deliver to him. Then he was forced to call Sa'ad again late at night to tell him that his car had broken down near Boreen. The intelligence had taken the young man's car and set the trap for Sa'ad and myself, unaware that Khalil was in the car and not me. That is why they reported that they had killed me and Sa'ad and fabricated the story that we had been on our way to carry out a major military operation.

HIDING AND RENEWED DETENTION

After Sa'ad's assassination, I went into hiding in Ramallah for three years. I assumed the name "Muwafaq" and didn't leave the house for whole months at a time. I couldn't see any of my relatives, including my son Laith. After around a year, I was able to bring my wife and son to my hideout. We had a daughter there who we named Haneen. My son thought that Muwafaq was my real name and would call me it in front of other people. He didn't find out my real name until years later.

On October 23, 2003, I was out buying clothes for my children in a store on the outskirts of Ramallah. Eid was approaching and my mother was supposed to come to visit us. She hadn't seen me for three years. She hadn't even heard our voices for fear that the phones were tapped and our location would be exposed. Five minutes after entering the clothing store with my wife and two children, three men with Arab features entered and took out their guns, aiming them at my head, and ordered me to go with them to a vehicle waiting outside. They tied me up with cords, forced me to lie down on the floor of the car and drove away. I was transferred to the Bet El military camp.

A helicopter landed in the camp from which a man exited and greeted me with, "Osama Barham, hello!" I responded that my name was Muwafaq Amer. He replied, "Osama or Muwafaq, what's important is that you're in our hands now. You should thank God that you didn't get into your car, or you'd be going crazy about your wife and kids right now." He was insinuating that if they hadn't been able to arrest me at the store, they would have attacked the car.

I was then transferred to the al-Moscobiyya interrogation center in Jerusalem [also known as the Russian Compound]. On my arrival, a high-ranking intelligence official who identified himself as the head of the entire interrogation center said, "Osama, you can bet that this time you're ours and you're going to confess everything." I asked them why they had tried to kill me. He didn't answer me but called over the other interrogators, introducing me as "Osama the Engineer" and "Professor Osama." A soldier who was transferring prisoners from one cell to another and heard that I was Professor Osama asked me, "Professor of what?" I answered him sarcastically, "nuclear physics," and, to my surprise, he believed me! For the entire duration of my stay, he called me the nuclear physics professor and would only cuff me right outside the interrogation room. It seems that he had respect for science.

This time the head of interrogation said to me, "Osama, I challenge you to give a confession." I told him that I was ready to be challenged because I had nothing to hide. They questioned me for two weeks, without using violence, but prevented me from sleeping the whole time.

Immediately after my arrest, I was informed by one of the interrogators that a friend of mine, Bader Salman, had been killed in an explosion at his house. The interrogator showed me a report in an Israeli newspaper about his death and told me, "I have other bad news to tell you. Your wife and little children were also killed. They were near Bader's house." He took the newspaper away and continued the interrogation as if nothing had happened. I was held for 35 days after being told this terrible news, isolated and prohibited from seeing anyone, even my lawyer. I couldn't sleep from the grief and sorrow. The minute I was allowed to meet my lawyer, Ahlam Haddad, I asked her what had happened to my family and how they had been killed. She replied, "I've just spoken to your wife. Your family's fine. Nothing has happened to them." I realized then that it had been the interrogator's cruel attempt to break my spirit. I saw my children only 20 months later, although my wife—who was banned from entering Israel—could not visit me until a full two years after my arrest.

After that I was held in an interrogation cell for two months without being questioned. Although their evidence was thin, the court found me guilty of being a member of an illegal organization and in possession of lethal weapons. I was sentenced to five years' imprisonment. I finished serving my sentence in June 2008.

9
Colonel and Major

Avigdor Feldman

Colonel and Major Steve and Mason
Old masters of torture
White whiskers
Cheeks pinker after gallons of Gin
Belly sloping under a sweaty Khaki shirt
Cork hat tilted to the center of the head

Colonel and Major Johnny and Sheriff
Beating hand spotted brown with age
Beating hand as confident and steady as ever
Palm open—a slap
Palm closed—a fist to the belly
Palm rolled up—a blow to the head
Two palms strike and tear
Cymbals in your ears!

Colonel Motti and Major Danny
Are back with the old instruments of their craft
The slanting chair
The low chair borrowed from a nearby kindergarten
The stinking cap
A set of exercises copied from a 19th Century German book
"A healthy body, a fine soul"

Colonel Owl and Major Kitten
Red meaty tongue oiling dry lips
With greasy sentences of poisonous honey:
"Being asked how he was the subject answered that he never felt
    better"
"The subject was offered a rest in his cell but preferred to go on
    chatting with us"
"The subject expressed his gratitude for our hospitality"

"We asked the subject to be serious"
"To be reliable"
"To be one of us"
"The subject lowered his head"

"The subject asked to tell the whole truth"
"The subject asked for a pen and a pencil"
"The subject wrote"
"The subject listed names"
"The subject drew some pictures"
"The subject closed his eyes"
"We kissed the subject on his lips"
"The subject passed on to a better world"
We hereby sign our names
In the margins of the confession
Colonel and Major

10
Welcome to Shin Bet Country[1]

Avigdor Feldman

Welcome to Shin Bet country. You are the only passenger arriving on this night flight. Four men entered your home: three policemen and one Shin Bet officer. No one introduced you to him, but you recognize in him the ambassador of an unknown land, in which you have been chosen to travel. This is a guide to the country and its customs.

PARASITES

You are under arrest. The policemen show you the warrant. It was issued at the request of a police officer and signed by a judge. But the Shin Bet are the ones who are really interested in you. In the first days of your trip, you will see few policemen, if any. Only once you have passed your initiation and are deemed ready for confession will you see a police officer. He will take down your confession; he has no idea what you have done or how you have been interrogated.

Until 2002, the year that the "Shin Bet Law" passed in the Knesset, the Shin Bet had been an unseen parasite on the back of the justice system. The demand for a law that would smoke the Shin Bet out of its closet resulted in a law that empowered it with authorities stretching far beyond those of the police. And still it is the Shin Bet custom to hide among the folds of a state attorney's gown; the keen-eyed would indeed notice a tiny lump protruding on the nape of the police representative asking to detain a suspect due to "violation of security regulations." From this lump, the Shin Bet representative whispers into the policeman's ear the familiar text. Now the Shin Bet is free to order secret bugging, invade private properties as well as search them without the owner's attendance. In order to enact its power in these forms, it no longer needs the police.

DRESS

Even in this darkest of hours, the discerning tourist would do well to study the language of body and dress. The Shin Bet man wears civilian clothes, like an undercover policeman. But the beat cops wear jeans, Nike sneakers, T-shirts tagged "property of the Central Prison." The Shin Bet wear the uniform of the civil servant. You, the tourist, would do best to leave your special apparel at home. You will have no need of it, as you will soon be presented with your very own black bag.

TRAVEL DOCUMENTS

You do not need a visa. The ambassadors already have all you will require for entry to Shin Bet country. These are the various kinds of files on you, all numbered and computerized. Some data had been collected through surveillance, detective work and tailing you. The Shin Bet collects and holds these data, since it is exempt from the Law on the Protection of Privacy: "the Security Service shall not be held responsible for infraction [of privacy] which has been undertaken reasonably in the performance of its duties and in the service thereof." Data is collected through wiretapping. The head of an investigation unit in the Shin Bet is authorized to order a short-term wiretap; a permanent wiretap may be ordered by the Minister (not by a judge—as per ordinary offenses), if he thinks you are endangering national security. If the Minister did not think that, you would not be here. Other information is obtained through informants. They used to be called rats, but I think that terminology is obsolete.

TRAVEL GEAR

Do not take a suitcase. You will be provided with a box, that is, not you but your shadow—the protagonist of the material which the Shin Bet has been collecting on you. During your trip, you will find out that in this place, your shadow has an independent existence. Your shadow travels in a cardboard box marked with the trademark of the Tnuva Company. The boxes are an integral part of the Shin Bet experience, and are brought to every one of your court appearances. The boxes contain the confidential material about you which is presented to the judge. You will not see it, now or ever. As the Shin Bet would have it, this is Pandora's Box. You think a lot about the box; as far as you're concerned, it still holds the produce it held before it was chosen as the abode of your shadow. For you, it is Bandora's Box.[2]

CONFIDENTIAL MATERIAL

Secrets are to the Shin Bet as the two-way radio is to the Shin Bet officer. In Shin Bet country, doors are locked. During arrest, expulsion, and home demolition procedures, the judge will be presented with materials unavailable to you or your lawyer. The judge must be convinced that the evidence before him is real and not fabricated, that confessions were extracted legitimately and without torture. The judge is convinced. If you're lucky, later he will claim to have been misled. Sometimes the Shin Bet does not trust the court, and part of the material will be hidden even from the eyes of the court by order of the Minister of Defense, who decides when its disclosure may be detrimental to national security. Only a Supreme Court judge may banish the demon of confidentiality from the box. The Supreme Court judge decides based on materials presented him by Shin Bet officers without you or your lawyer being present. The Shin Bet men will convince the judge that exposing the material will damage national security. He may also one day claim to have been misled.

YOUR TRAVEL COMPANION: YOUR LAWYER

On your lonesome nocturnal travels through Shin Bet country, you have requested a lawyer to accompany you, to lift your spirits, to tell you that not all is lost, that justice will be done, to furnish you with chocolates and not-too-serious novels. By law, the Shin Bet man in charge of the investigation may prevent you from seeing your lawyer for up to seven days. The head of his unit may extend the period by another eight days. Then there are judges agreeing for a continuation of this prevention. All in all, you will not see your lawyer for 15 days or more. After these days, your trip in Shin Bet country will be over. Your confession will have been taken down, your scratches healed, your sleep-deprived eyes will have finally shut.

The lawyer you will see at the end of this period will not be one of your choosing. By order, you may be represented only by a lawyer authorized to appear in all military proceedings. There are very few

Arab lawyers with such authorization, and very few lawyers with any interest in dressing your wounds.

SONGBIRD, THE

One day a strange tourist appears in Shin Bet country. He shakes your hand, says "Dr. Livingstone, I presume." He is dressed like you and speaks your language. You talk with him. Then he goes off, sails set for parts unknown. You will not see him again until your trial. He will appear under an assumed name, and even if your trial is public (not a likely occurrence), his name will remain unknown. He will say that you confessed to him. The natives of Shin Bet country call him "the Songbird" because he can sing.

BLACK BAG

While traveling, why not try blending in with the locals? If you can, dress as they do. In Shin Bet country, it is customary to wear a black plastic bag over your head all day and all night—and when in Rome … The bag smells of urine and covers your shoulders as well. There is no point in bringing a lavender-scented bag from home.

FRUIT

In Shin Bet country, your diet will consist mainly of the fruits of the imagination (or more precisely, the fruits of the imagination will consume you.) How so? The black bag, while tangible, foul-smelling and revolting, is not believed to exist by the court, which considers it a fruit of the imagination. You, who have partaken of this fruit of the imagination, will never forget the taste. The fruits of the imagination may one day turn into a thin gruel known as "minor details which do not compromise a confession." The black bag is a good example. For many years, the Shin Bet denied its existence. Its representatives denied stocking such an item, labeled it an invention, and avowed that it was never placed on detainees' heads for hours and days. Later—this humble historian of Shin Bet country does not have in his possession the ruling containing the change—it was admitted that the black bag does exist and is used to prevent detainees from identifying each other. According to the Shin Bet, it is used only for short periods, while the detainee waits in the corridor for his turn to be investigated. In this case, the court ruled that the black bag was a minor detail which does not compromise the confession.

SANDWICH, THE

Another fruit of the imagination is the sandwich. The seasoned lawyer can pick up its scent during the cross-examination of the Shin Bet man in court. When the lawyer asks, "Did you, in the course of the investigation, place your foot on the testicles of the detainee, and when the desired reply was not forthcoming, did you proceed to place pressure on them?," the Shin Bet man's eyes open wide in uncomprehending amazement, and—here it comes—he replies: "Nothing of the sort ever happened! On the contrary, the accused felt hungry during the investigation, and since the hour was late and the mess hall closed, I went out and bought him a sandwich." "Are you referring to that pita pocket with hummus and salad?" asks the lawyer wearily. "Right," answers the Shin Bet man in every case, and adds that the pita was bought with his own money.

Interestingly enough, it appears that the sandwich which the Shin Bet feeds the court is a universal form of nourishment. In the book *A Dry White Season* by the South African André Brink, a Security Service investigation is described:

> According to Capt. Stoltz, the deceased had declined to cooperate, although in every case he was treated with kindness and courtesy. In reply to Advocate Leo's question, Capt. Stoltz affirmed that the deceased had never been assaulted in his presence. Throughout his detention, the investigators had bought food for the deceased from their own private funds.

TRAVEL LOG

Unlike the police, the Shin Bet is not required to supply a meticulous documentation of the course of interrogation. A brief, curtly phrased document termed in Shin Bet jargon "Letter of Agreement" will do. The "Letter of Agreement" combines laconic statements extracted from the suspect with laconic epigrams contributed by the interrogator, typically ranging from "It's a shame to prolong the interrogation," "We know everything anyhow," to "Be a man" and "Be brave." The interrogee's speech is grinded into clipped Shin Bet language paced by the imaginary metronome which endows the exchange between interrogator and interrogee with a *staccato* that begs for a wild, jittery operatic adaptation—something along the lines of Alban Berg's *Wozzeck*, in the course of which the text gradually dwindles into a series of hoarse barks.

LODGINGS

Where will you live during your travels? The Shin Bet runs wards in various prisons. Interrogations take place in these wards, which are entirely under the control of the Shin Bet (unless you happen to be a Circassian officer, in which case you may be interrogated in a suite at the Dan Carmel Hotel). The wards do not keep any real records of inmates. Thus, it is impossible to find out in retrospect whether you were held in a cell or in the yard.

YARD, THE

The location most often used to be described in courtrooms by detainees from Shin Bet country is neither the beaches nor the snowy peaks, but a mid-sized yard in one or another of the prisons in which the Shin Bet maintains a ward. From these testimonies, one may reproduce, in a detailed manner worthy of the most tedious *nouveau roman*, every inch of the yard in which a detainee has stood, waiting to be interrogated, for a day or a week, usually in light clothing, as the fruit of the imagination—the black bag—rots upon his head. The court has yet to accept as fact the existence of a yard in which detainees are kept standing, deprived of sleep in order to extract confessions from them.

SHOWER

The bed in your cell will remain impeccably made, its sheets taut and the maid left unemployed as you remain in the yard. The shower, on the other hand, will be used, especially the cold water facilities and especially in winter. The cold shower has also been decreed a fruit of the imagination: "An impudent invention," as the court ruled in one case.

LOST CONTINENT, THE

The shower, the yard, the sleep deprivation, the threats, these have all up to now been a lost continent, an Atlantis slumbering underneath the waves of Shin Bet testimony, even as evidence on them was given at public trials. The Nafso affair has dredged them all up above the waterline. Nafso's evidence is no different from that of hundreds of others given in the Supreme Court, military tribunals, district courts, and the courts in the Occupied Palestinian Territories. The courts never believed it. The special military court, which included a district judge as well as senior military judges, did not believe Nafso either. Would the HCJ have believed him? Past experience shows that despite the similar claims made in the past, no court has ever ruled invalid a confession obtained through a Shin Bet investigation.

AFTERWORD

The HCJ has abolished the established use of torture, but many recent signs show that the lost kingdom of the Shin Bet is rising once again from the depths. The "Shin Bet Law" has been enacted, but the service is still parasitic upon other authorities: the police, the Israeli Prison Service and the Attorney-General's prosecutors.

NOTES

1. Shin Bet is an abbreviation for the General Secret Service; the name is obsolete in Hebrew (the service is nowadays usually referred to as *ha-shabak*), but still current in English.
2. *Bandora*—Arabic for "tomato."

11

A Decade after the High Court of Justice "Torture" Ruling, What's Changed?

Bana Shoughry-Badarne

September 6, 1999 was a very special day for the human rights community in Israel. After decades of authorized use of torture by Israel's General Security Service (GSS), the Israeli High Court of Justice (HCJ) declared an absolute prohibition on the use of "brutal or inhuman means in the course of an investigation."[1] Therefore, the court decided that, as a general rule, the use of shaking, painful waiting positions (*Shabeh*), the "frog crouch" and excessive tightening of handcuffs are illegal. More important, the court ruled that "the 'necessity' defense does not constitute a source of authority, which would allow GSS investigators to make use [*sic*] physical means during the course of interrogations."[2] However, the court indicated that GSS interrogators who use physical pressure in extreme circumstances (such as a ticking bomb) might not be held criminally liable as they may rely on the "necessity" defense.[3]

Hereinafter, my review of the implementation of the court's ruling during the last decade, as documented systematically in hundreds of sworn affidavits collected by lawyers of the Public Committee against Torture in Israel (PCATI) in the last decade, will reveal that while fewer detainees face torture today, the treatment of all Palestinian political ("security") detainees by GSS interrogators is still humiliating, inhumane, and often cruel.

THE PROHIBITION OF TORTURE AND INHUMAN TREATMENT

The customary prohibition of torture and other cruel, inhumane or degrading treatment (hereinafter: ill-treatment) constitutes a central layer of international human rights law and international humanitarian law. It is also enshrined in international law treaties that the state of Israel has signed and ratified, such as the Fourth

Geneva Convention,[4] the International Convention on Civil and Political Rights (ICCPR)[5] and the Convention against Torture and other Cruel Inhuman or Degrading Treatment or Punishment (CAT).[6] Furthermore, the prohibition of torture and other ill-treatment is customary, absolute, non-derogable and binds all states at all times.

The definition of "torture," under article 1 of CAT, is based on four cumulative elements:

(1) The element of intention: the act (causing suffering and pain to the victim) was purposefully committed;

(2) the pain and suffering requirement: the act causes the victim severe pain and suffering, whether physical or psychological.

(3) The purpose requirement: the act was committed in pursuit of a certain goal, including to secure information or a confession from the victim, punishment, intimidation, or discrimination.

(4) An official involvement: the act was committed by persons in authority and, or at least, with the consent or deliberate disregard of the authorities.

The United Nations Committee against Torture has interpreted the involvement and participation of individuals in torture in a broad manner. This interpretation includes any form of participation in the act of torture, including experience, solicitation, providing a superior instruction, tacit consent and concealment.[7] Acts which don't fulfill all the above listed four requirements constitute "ill-treatment."

TORTURE IN ISRAEL SINCE THE HCJ "TORTURE" RULING

It is extremely difficult to provide statistical data on the percentage of torture victims among GSS interrogees, because such information is classified. In addition, Palestinian political ("security") detainees are usually cut off from the outside world during their interrogation; they are almost always prevented from meeting with a lawyer. Nonetheless, following primary information that a person was tortured or ill-treated, a PCATI lawyer visits the alleged victim in jail, usually more than once, and collects a sworn affidavit with the details of the prisoner's complaint. PCATI's lawyers document dozens of complaints against torture every year, but many victims never complain, especially because the complaint is examined by the same authority that allegedly abused and continues to abuse them.

Consistent allegations made by Palestinian detainees in detailed affidavits to PCATI's lawyers and other human rights organizations have described the use of interrogation methods which clearly constitute at least ill-treatment and often torture. In several cases, these allegations have been substantiated by internal GSS memoranda, by testimony of GSS interrogators in court and by medical evidence.[8]

The series of humiliations, abuse and victimization of Palestinian residents of the Occupied Palestinian Territories (OPT) begins at the moment of arrest, through the use of painful plastic handcuffs, beatings and humiliation.[9] On the way to the interrogation room, prisoners are subjected to strip searches, in a humiliating manner that many times does not respect their privacy, especially for female prisoners. At the beginning of the interrogation, the interrogators usually present the prisoner with a page describing his or her rights and obligations, and emphasize especially to the interrogee that these rights, including use of the shower and the bathroom, are completely dependent on the will of the interrogator. Prevention of the prisoner's right to meet with an attorney until the end of the interrogation and admission of culpability is routine, and many prisoners report that the GSS interrogators present meeting with an attorney as possible only after the interrogation has been completed.

Routinely, while at the interrogation room, interrogees are held in painful handcuffed positions for hours. A few report painful handcuffing in the cell as well.[10] PCATI's petition against systematic use of painful shackling in the course of the interrogation was rejected, *inter alia*, on the basis of the state's statement that "as a general rule there is no permission to use shackling as a means of interrogation."[11]

In the interrogation room, prisoners are subjected to cruel and humiliating treatment characterized by, *inter alia*, cursing, yelling, spitting, degradation, threats—especially threats to arrest female family members and threats of home demolition. Kicks and punches are not rare. Interrogees retrospectively report that they were interrogated in their cells by prisoners working for the GSS, and some were subjected by them to harsh physical violence in addition to psychological threats.

Between interrogation sessions, Palestinian political ("security") detainees are usually held in solitary confinement in small filthy cells, in a separate wing of the prison facility where deliberately degrading conditions prevail. There are no beds and a hole is provided for sanitary needs instead of toilets. An opportunity to shower and shave is considered a privilege. In many cases, detainees complain of cold, dampness, a shortage in undergarments and soap, in addition to small amounts and poor quality of food. Detainees are held in difficult conditions of sensory deprivation through, among other things, sleep deprivation due to long and not necessarily regular hours in the interrogation room, as well as lack of natural light or access to a clock. Artificial light is on constantly for 24 hours a day.[12] Thus the interrogee loses all contact not only with the world outside the interrogation room, but also any ability to judge the passing of time. Add to all the above cases of conditioning of medical treatment upon revealing of information. Independent prison monitors on behalf of the Public Defender's Office and the Bar Association prison monitors are not allowed into these cells because of "concern that defense lawyers would be exposed to confidential interrogation methods."[13]

Approximately 15 percent of the complaints filed by PCATI leave no doubt that the explicit use of psychological and physical torture during GSS interrogation is still practiced and authorized. The methods that I shall describe in what follows were taken from 20 complaints filed by PCATI to which the authorities' response did not deny the facts described in the complaint. Despite this, the complaints were rejected and the Attorney General decided not to order a criminal investigation by the Department of Investigations of Police Officers (DIP), probably because the authorities applied the necessity defense at an early stage of an internal inquiry.[14]

It is important to emphasize that each of the torture victims faced five to eleven acts of torture, carried out repetitively by two to eight interrogators over a significant period of time (three to seven days). Some of the victims reported that at the beginning of their interrogation, GSS interrogators displayed a piece of paper, written in Hebrew, supposedly a permission from the court to initiate an unimpeded interrogation, and used consistent fixed terminology for the different "interrogation exercises." The victim's complaints show systematic performance, undoubtedly not the violent act of a single interrogator—a "rotten apple"—as an immediate reaction to a supposedly urgent need for information. These methods are often accompanied by threats that failure to pass on information will lead to paralysis. Indeed, some interrogees were injured or hurt and sometimes were brought to the hospital as a result of the torture to which they were subjected, and returned to the interrogation room after their initial medical treatment.[15]

Hereinafter, I point out interrogation methods which specifically stand out as torture, as described in many complaints filed by PCATI and which were not contradicted by the answers received from the Officer in Charge of GSS Interrogee Complaints.

Threat or declaration of "military interrogation"

Until 2007, at the beginning of the interrogation, the interrogator used to tell the interrogee that he or she had been classified as a "ticking bomb" and/or they will be subjected to a "military interrogation." This frightening phrase was commonly used, accompanied by a symbolic act such as transfer to an adjacent room, or changing the prisoner into Prison Service clothing. Interrogees were informed that a court approved the "military interrogation." At the end of the "military interrogation," interrogators switch to the above-mentioned "lighter" interrogation methods, often threatening that if interrogees stopped cooperating they would be returned to a "military interrogation." Due to a multiplicity of such complaints, we were informed in February 2007 that the use of the term would be stopped, yet recently we received new complaints in this vein.

Painful "banana" and "half-banana" positions

This position is used by at least two interrogators, who seat the interrogee, with his hands and feet cuffed, on a backless chair or with the backrest to the side and not supporting his back. While in this position, the interrogator holds the interrogee's cuffed legs or steps on them. The interrogator commands the interrogee to bend backwards so that his head would reach as close as possible to the floor; a second interrogator "assists" him with shoving and pulling. In the half-banana position, the interrogee is forced to bend backwards at a 45-degree angle and to stick to this position. The use of painful positions is done in a series, each time for several minutes with a break of a minute or two in between. Several times the use of these positions was accompanied by punches and slaps, spitting, shouting in the ear, or pulling on the handcuffs when the interrogee would not carry out the instructions, or if his body betrayed him and he fell or tried to sit up. Some victims reported that their eyes were covered and they were suddenly and sharply slapped in the face, nose and ears while blindfolded. All the victims reported their head falling to the floor, and some lost consciousness, waking up to find a medic awakening them or finding themselves in the shower where water was being used to awaken them. The victims reported that these positions caused severe back pain and a feeling that their back is being broken. Indeed, the interrogators often threatened to break their backs. There are also reports of harsh pains in the chest, stomach and head, usually thanks to the loss of balance and repeated falls to the floor, or due to the blows.

Frog crouch

The interrogee is required to squat while leaning only on their feet or toes. This position is also carried out repeatedly over time, and sometimes accompanied by pushes and blows. Interrogees reported harsh pains and shaking of the body as a result of interrogation in this position.

Distorted standing positions

The interrogee is forced to stand with their back to the wall, knees bent either at 90 or 45 degrees, sometimes while standing on the toes rather than on the feet. In this position, we have reports of the uses of blows, slaps and punches. Some were "shaken" from this position and many reported falling.

Shaking

Since the HCJ ruling, we have received very limited number of complaints on use of this method, generally during which an interrogator is being shaken by the shoulders or by the shirt.

"High handcuffing"

There is nonconventional use of handcuffs, such that, in addition to being handcuffed next to the wrist, the interrogators add another set of handcuffs higher up the arm, usually in the area of the elbow. After the cuffing, the interrogators pull the cuffs in different directions, or fasten them in "creative" ways, causing severe pain. Most of the prisoners tortured in this way reported that the cuffs were placed above cotton, a sock, or an elastic bandage. Others suffered bleeding as a result of this cuffing. Another method of nonconventional cuffing is the fastening of the legs of the interrogee to a metal triangle where the legs of the chair meet; pressure on the legs, whether intended, or as a result of bending of the back leads to a deep wound, which caused one prisoner a grave infection.

The use of family members as a mean of interrogation

Threats of arresting family members, especially female, and threats of demolishing the interrogee's or their parents' home were reported by many interrogees. Some reported being informed that their pregnant wives would be brought to give birth in the interrogation room. One was informed that his wife was arrested, interrogated and tortured, and as a result lost the fetus. Others reported being informed that their sister would be arrested and raped, or that their sick and elderly parents would be, or already were, arrested. In addition to these threats, PCATI revealed the use of false arrests aiming to convince the interrogee that the threat was indeed being carried out. Thus, for instance, one prisoner was brought to the interrogation room to witness his mother crying, under interrogation, and another was shown his parents in a faked interrogation in a way that brought him to attempt suicide.[16] PCATI filed a petition to the HCJ against the use and threats to use family members as a method of interrogation. The petition was rejected on September 9, 2009, as the court was satisfied with the Attorney General's declaration that the guidelines on the subject would be made more specific, meaning that use of family members as a means of interrogation was forbidden. Nevertheless, complaints against threats to harm interrogees' family members continue to arrive.[17]

During the last two years we have encountered few complaints of the use of brutal physical torture—especially the painful banana position, the frog crouch, and the "high handcuffing"—though this by no means ensures that these methods are not in use. This gloomy picture shows that the HCJ "Torture" ruling indeed caused a change in the regular use of harsh physical torture. Nevertheless, the interrogation authorities simply switched to methods that leave scars primarily on the soul rather than the body. We, at PCATI, believe that the authority to use torture within the GSS still exists, because the torture occurs in an institutionalized and built-in manner. Despite the difficulties in collecting evidence as to the behavior of the GSS—a result of the cloak of secrecy provided for it by the law—testimonies in our hands suggest that apparently torture is still carried out with authorized permission, and the torturing interrogators receive permission beforehand through a special permission procedure. A contempt of court motion, filed in 2008, failed to make a difference. The HCJ judges ruled on July 6, 2009 that the "Torture" ruling is declaratory and thus is not enforceable through contempt of court process.

There is no doubt that beside the ongoing use of torture and ill-treatment in the GSS interrogations, a shelter of impunity has been given to GSS interrogators during the last decade by the State's

Attorney Generals; despite more than 600 complaints, not even one criminal investigation was opened.[18]

NOTES

1. HCJ 5100/94 *Public Committee against Torture in Israel v. The State of Israel*, Piskei Din 53(4) 817, para. 23. See also: HCJ 7195/08 *Abu Rahme v. Chief Military Advocate General*, unpublished ruling, July 1, 2009, para. 42 (in Hebrew).
2. HCJ 5100/94, para. 36
3. Ibid., para. 34; following the court ruling Attorney General (AG) Elyakim Rubinstein issued "GSS Investigations and the Necessity Defence—Framework for Exercising the Attorney General's Discretion setting criteria for refraining from prosecution of GSS interrogators under the necessity defence." For a critical analysis of the court ruling and the AG criteria, see *Accountability Denied: The Absence of Investigation and Punishment of Torture in Israel*, Public Committee against Torture in Israel, Jerusalem, December 2009, researched and edited by Atty. Irit Ballas, Atty. Avi Berg, Mr. Carmi Lecker, Dr. Ishai Menuchin and Atty. Bana Shoughry-Badarne.
4. Articles 3, 27, 31 and 33.
5. Articles 7 and 10.
6. Articles 2 and 16.
7. M. Nowak and E. McArthur (2008), *The United Nations Convention Against Torture – A Commentary*, Oxford: Oxford University Press, pp. 247–8; United Nations Committee Against Torture: Consideration of reports submitted by States parties under Article 19 of the Convention, Conclusions and Recommendations of the Committee Against Torture, United States of America. New York: UN Committee against Torture, UN Doc. CAT/C/USA/CO/2, 2006, at 29.
8. Y. Ginbar, *Back to a Routine of Torture: Torture and Ill-treatment of Palestinian Detainees during Arrest, Detention and Interrogation, September 2002–April 2003*, Jerusalem: Public Committee Against Torture in Israel, June 2003; N. Hoffstadter, *Ticking Bombs—Testimonies of Torture Victims in Israel*, Jerusalem: Public Committee Against Torture in Israel, May 2007; Y. Lein, *Absolute Prohibition: The Torture and Ill-Treatment of Palestinian Detainees*, Jerusalem: B'Tselem and HaMoked—Center for the Defense of the Individual, May 2007, pp. 63–70; A. Linder, *"Family Matters"—Using Family Members to Pressure Detainees*, Jerusalem: PCATI, March 2008; S. Elkhatib-Ayoub, *Shackling as a Form of Torture and Abuse*, Jerusalem: PCATI, June 2009; Y. Ginbar, E. Abram, B. Shoughry-Badarne, C. Leker, T. Atamleh-Mohana and S. Elkhatib-Ayoub, *Implementation of the UN Convention against Torture and Other Cruel, Inhuman or Degrading Treatment or Punishment by Israel—Alternative reports submitted to the UN Committee against Torture*, Jerusalem: PCATI and OMCT, June 2009; M. Bader and A. Baker, *Exposed— The Treatment of Palestinian Detainees during Operation "Cast Lead,"* Jerusalem: PCATI and Adalah: The Legal Center for Arab Minority Rights in Israel, June 2010 .
9. N. Hoffstadter, *No Defense: Soldier Violence against Palestinian Detainees*, Jerusalem: PCATI, June 2008.
10. Elkhatib-Ayoub, *Shackling as a Form of Torture and Abuse.*

11. HCJ 5553/09 *Public Committee against Torture in Israel v. the Prime Minister*, unpublished ruling, 26.4.2010.

12. Lein, *Absolute Prohibition*, pp. 46–53; Bader and Baker, *Exposed*, pp. 14–23.

13. Letter from Shay Nitzan, Senior Deputy of State Attorney for Special Affairs to the Association for Civil Rights in Israel, January 22, 2010.

14. It is important to pay special attention to the fact that complaints of torture by GSS agents are investigated in-house, because the Attorney General invariably refers such complaints to the GSS's "Inspector of Interrogees' Complaints." The inspector is a salaried, high-ranking employee of the GSS with previous experience in the service; he therefore cannot possibly be described either as "independent and impartial," or as capable of investigating "allegations of violations promptly, thoroughly and effectively." For a detailed analysis of this issue see Ballas et al., *Accountability Denied*.

15. See, for example, Osama Barham's chapter in the present volume.

16. See Linder, *"Family Matters."*

17. HCJ 3533/08 *Suweiti v. the GSS*, unpublished ruling from September 9, 2009, para. 4.

18. See Ballas et al., *Accountability Denied*.

12
The Mysteries of Administrative Detention

Tamar Pelleg-Sryck

This article focuses on administrative detention as practiced by Israel against residents of the West Bank since its occupation in June 1967. The cumulative number of administrative detainees arrested during different periods of time since 1967 amounts to many tens of thousands. The number peaked during the first Intifada. According to the information in a letter dated September 2, 1988, written by Yitzhak Rabin, then defense minister, to Deddi Zucker, then Knesset member, between December 1987 and August 1988, the number of detainees reached 2,466. Later, in a letter of July 12, 1993, the deputy chief of staff informed the Constitution, Law and Justice Committee of the Knesset that the number of those administratively detained reached about 12,100. He added that the most noticeable were the first three years of the Intifada, 1988–90, when 10,000 were detained administratively. In the three years that followed, 1991–93, the number decreased dramatically to 2,100. This substantial decrease was due to the Oslo Accords (1993), the letter explained. In 1999, the number of the administrative detainees reached an all-time low, a single digit number. It then went up to 1,000 in 2002 following the Israeli Army's invasion of the West Bank's major cities, during which the Army caused large-scale damage to property and conducted extensive arrests. On July 31, 2010, due to the security coordination between Israel and the Palestinian Authority, there remained 199 administrative detainees held in Israel.

The fluctuating number of detainees is a by-product of the needs of the occupier, which, according to its terminology, are "security needs." These needs change from time to time, according to the circumstances and Israel's policies. Administrative detention is a flexible and convenient tool, due to the ease in invoking (and revoking) it, which requires the mere signature of a military commander asserting that he has examined the "security material" and was thus convinced that the step "is necessitated by security considerations." This authority is granted to the military commander according to the military law applicable in the West Bank, which itself is of his own making.[1]

The procedure of administrative detention, in all its phases, is conducted under a veil of utter secrecy and in violation of the right of the detainee to defense. It enables a person to be held in detention without evidence and without trial, on the basis of classified intelligence alleging that he constitutes a security risk.[2] The nature of the allegations is known only to the actors involved: the General Security Service (GSS) who supplies the "security material," the military commander who signs the detention order, the military prosecutor who is the advisor and representative of the military commander and the military judge who is expected to apply his "judicial review" to the order. This hermetically closed circle, which does not leave even a shred of transparency, does not allow the detainee to defend himself, absolves the prosecutor from the burden of proof and prevents the judge from writing a reasoned decision. This is how administrative detention orders are issued. The maximum period of each single order cannot exceed six months, but the overall detention period can be extended indefinitely. The law did not see fit to limit the total maximum period for which a person can be held in administrative detention.[3]

In these circumstances, anything is possible: any arbitrariness, any extraneous consideration, any prohibited purpose. One can never know why a person was detained and why he was released. One can only guess. As a result, the work of the defense attorney consists in the art of speculation and guess and in the attorney's ability to convince the judge to examine the classified material in the light of his claims.

The military legislation grants the judge, who is an army officer with a legal background, the right "to approve the detention order, to cancel it or to shorten the period of detention."[4] As a rule, the judges tend to approve the detention orders. In certain cases, at the end of one year of administrative detention or more, the judge would reduce the period of detention to four or three months instead of six. This reduction is "insubstantial," as it leaves the military commander the authority to extend the order when it expires. The decision for a "substantial reduction" of the period of detention, which cannot be altered by the military commander unless new and weighty intelligence material has accumulated against the detainee, is a rare phenomenon.[5]

ADMINISTRATIVE DETENTION AS A FORM OF TORTURE

As mentioned above, Israeli military law does not limit the total period of the administrative detention that the military commander is authorized to impose. Any order may be extended "on the eve of its expiration."[6] An administrative detainee cannot possibly know how many years he or she will spend in prison. The period of detention will be revealed to them only *post factum*, when they are released. This is the law and this is the reality. It is a reality that the administrative detainee tries to ignore. And this is the torture inherent in administrative detention: to hope for release towards the end of the order, to suffer disappointment when it is renewed, to nurse new hopes for a forthcoming judicial review, to be disappointed, and to sink into despair mixed with rage, to recover and hope for release. Again and again and again.[7]

In December 1996, I.S., then an administrative detainee held in the Israeli prison of Megiddo, wrote in a letter to the Nigerian writer and intellectual Wole Soyinka, who himself had experienced detention in his native country and wrote about it in *The Man Died* (1972):

> If I am to describe what we are, I would say we're political hostages, upon which psychological torture is inflicted. We can never know when we are going home. This cruel game of "yes hope/no hope" I once described as a mixture of Russian roulette, "she loves me/loves me not", and (these are also your words) a variant of that familiar theme: "Abandon hope all who enter here".

In an essay written in jail and published by the Israeli daily *Ha'aretz* shortly before his release in 1997, I.S. quoted Jacobo Timmerman, "who knows something about life and imprisonment under the military junta in Argentina": "Thinking in terms of a prolonged span of time is extremely useful when there is no fixed sentence, for it annihilates hope, and hope is synonymous with anxiety and anguish." I. S. comments:

> If Timmerman's advice is not adhered to:
>   We might be tempted to drift to hope (and that is bad).
>   We might be tempted to reply knowingly to our children when they ask—in the tortuously innocent way children excel

at—"Father, when are you coming home?" One of us might say, "in a month's time". He will become a liar in the eyes of his children (and that is *very* bad).

A prisoner's wife might be so overcome by hope, that she might clean the house every time one of her husband's "theoretical" dates of release approaches ... Her foolishness might also be so great, so as to drive her to go and wait for the husband by the checkpoint ... .[8]

In short, "hope is synonymous with anxiety and anguish. It is bad. It should not be tried, neither at home, nor at prison. Hope should be annihilated."

I can attest to the fact that during all my years representing administrative detainees, beginning in 1988, I never met a single detainee who was cured of cyclical hope, or who gave up the belief that the High Court of Justice (HCJ) would release him and this despite the fact that the proportion of petitioners released by HCJ decision never even reached 1 percent. Nor do I know a single woman who abandoned her expectations that her detained husband would be released by the end of the term.

BETWEEN ADMINISTRATIVE DETENTION AND CRIMINAL PROCEDURE

By power of military legislation, the occupation authorities have additional means to counter a danger that a person poses to security—as they see it. The military prosecution is authorized to charge a person before a military court and obliged to do so whenever evidence acceptable in the court has been or can be made available. It is the right of the individual not to be subject to the harsh measure of administrative detention if accusations can be brought against him in criminal proceedings, which make defense possible.

The authority of the HCJ, which is binding on military judges, states that where a threat posed by an individual's activities can be prevented by criminal procedures, administrative detention should not be invoked:

The [administrative] detention is intended to prevent and to thwart a security danger resulting from acts that the detainee is liable to commit, where it is not reasonably possible to prevent them by taking regular legal measures (a criminal proceeding) or by an administrative measure less severe in its results.[9]

Moreover, the use of criminal procedure cannot be renounced solely due to the difficulties caused by the sensitivity of the information, its sources, or the means of its acquisition. A thorough and comprehensive investigation should be carried out even in such cases, while aspiring to base charges on open, evidential material, admissible in court.[10]

This jurisprudential practice has been stretched thin over the years. The brakes originally intended to safeguard human rights lost their strength. Military judges do not condition the authorization of the orders by the existence of a proper investigation. In their decisions, they accept the prosecution's arguments that an investigation cannot be effective while only open evidence is used and full investigation is not possible because of the "sensitivity of the information," and "the fear of exposing sources," and that the administrative detention order was lawfully issued even though the detainee had been only ostensibly interrogated or not at all.

Furthermore, administrative detention orders were issued against the accused when the prosecution's request to detain them until the end of judicial proceedings had been rejected, so that they were scheduled to be released on bail. Even these orders have been approved by military judges. Presently, there is a specific provision authorizing the judge to postpone the execution of his decision of the release on bail if the prosecutor requests "to bring the case before the military commander ... to consider issuance of an administrative detention" so that the release be prevented.[11] In the wake of this development in criminal procedure, judges began to approve administrative detention orders accepting the prosecution's futuristic argument that "it was obvious," even though admissible evidence exists that the person's indictment will be followed by release on bail. And if this were not enough, administrative detention orders have been issued in recent years against persons who had completed their prison sentence, on the very day of their release.

Regarding the interaction between administrative detention procedures and detention as part of criminal procedure, the HCJ ruled that if the court decided to release the accused, the military commander was not empowered to detain him administratively on the basis of the same charges as a different material is needed for the purpose.[12] The HCJ deviated from this resolution in a 2007 decision, stating that estimation of the future danger of the detainee could be based on the activity for which he had been convicted.[13]

The precept that administrative detention is a preventive future-oriented measure in contrast to the criminal procedure, which is inherently punitive and focuses on offenses committed in the past, is becoming a dead letter. The prosecution's argument that these are two different, separate and unrelated procedures, each standing on its own, has been accepted by the military judges. The meaning of this argument, and necessarily also its purpose, is that the prosecution and the GSS are allowed to choose which of the two procedures (or both together) to adopt at their own discretion, with no regard for any legal principle. Until about two years ago, administrative detention of someone who at the same time was being tried for criminal activity awakened a shock amongst human rights activists in Israel. At present, no one raises an eyebrow about the existence of parallel proceedings of this kind. They have become commonplace and occur every time the prosecution deems them necessary.

As is evident, the rules and practice of administrative detention in the West Bank are constantly moving further and further away from the principles of the Fourth Geneva Convention, which allow this practice only within very restricted limits. The relevant provisions of the ICCPR are being disregarded.

"ALTERNATIVE MEASURES"

The military commander is empowered to issue administrative "restriction and surveillance orders," such as house arrests, or restrictions of a person's movements to a certain area. These orders have been referred to by the courts as "alternative measures," being less severe than administrative detention.[14]

The HCJ has repeatedly ruled that administrative detention is subject to the principle of proportionality.[15] This means that before a detention order is issued, the authorities should examine whether it is possible to use alternative means that would violate the basic rights of an individual in a less offensive manner, and only if these steps are evaluated as inadequate for preventing the threat, should administrative detention be used and be considered lawful.

From this ruling of the HCJ, not much was left in the Occupied Palestinian Territories (OPT). The instances of release of an administrative detainee to house or town arrest can be counted on the fingers of one hand. The position of the military and the GSS has been that Israeli control of the territories is not sufficient for the required surveillance. This argument was raised during the first and the second Intifada, as well as following the Oslo Accords.

The possibility of using alternative measures has surfaced lately. It appears that following the political-security changes in the region, the Palestinian Authority in the West Bank has taken upon itself the task of safeguarding political security in coordination with Israeli security authorities according to common guidelines and conceptions. Information about the arrests of Hamas and Islamic Jihad activists by Palestinian security forces, which rule the area harshly, have been published in the Israeli media.[16] There are known cases of administrative detainees who were released from detention in Israel only to be arrested in their homes or on their way home by the Palestinian security forces.

I have used these incidents and articles during a recent judicial review of an extension order for the detention of Kh.G. from the Jenin area, who has been in detention since March 2008. I argued that due to the remarkable changes that have occurred in the West Bank and in its cities located in Area A and particularly in the city of Jenin, the circumstances have been created that permit and even obligate the release of my client to his home where he will be under close supervision of the Palestinian security. The judge listened attentively to my assertions, which were recorded in the minutes. Unsurprisingly, in his decision there was no mention of the law concerning the use of alternative means, although it was at the heart of the defense. Unsurprisingly—as most judges neither raise nor respond to legal arguments. The judge based his decision, as noted therein, on classified intelligence material which was handed to him along with classified "clarifications." Not a scrap of the evidence was revealed to us. Without attributing to Kh.G. any violent activity, he considered him dangerous to the extent that justifies continuation of the administrative detention due to his high standing in the Islamic Jihad, his organizational activity, and international connections. However, he gave us hope and signaled the authorities by shortening the detention order (insubstantially) from three to two months due to expire on July 15, 2010 and concluded:

> The time has not yet arrived to determine that the administrative detention has reached a breaking point at which its continuation is not proportional any longer, although it is definitely possible that, in absence of new information reinforcing the danger emanating from the detainee, this point may be close and visible.

Our guess was that the detention would not be extended. We decided to refrain from filing an appeal not to encourage the prosecution to file theirs and possibly win. For some weeks, Kh.G. remained in a state of helpless suspense. On the morning of July 15, he was set free and reached his home late at night without being intercepted by the Palestinian security.

ILLEGAL USE OF ADMINISTRATIVE DETENTION: RECRUITMENT OF COLLABORATORS

From the days of Mandatory Palestine and continuing up to today, the recruitment of Palestinians for collaboration with the Israeli intelligence authorities has been used as a means for supervising and controlling Palestinian society. Administrative detention is an effective tool used to persuade a person living under the yoke of occupation that collaboration is worthwhile. Many administrative detainees at some stage of their detention are brought in front of a GSS official who proposes to them that they become collaborators. Usually, these are very young men or those who are highly respected by their community. In return, they are offered different kinds of rewards. Knowing their special weaknesses, the GSS official offers them, for example, in addition to the shortening of their detention period, a salary following their release, or an entry permit into Israel for work purposes, university studies, or medical treatment. Most of them, even those who have gathered the courage to reject the proposal, are afraid to discuss it with their lawyers. Fewer are those who are willing to confront the GSS by bringing the matter before the judge. Here are two examples from my own experience.

A.S. was arrested for the first time in October 2004 when he was a high school student aged 17. While in prison, he passed his matriculation exams and upon his release in July 2006, he registered for university studies. Three months later, he was arrested anew and was called in for two meetings with a GSS official who offered him work as a collaborator. If he did not accept the offer, he was told, he would be returned to administrative detention. A.S. did not hesitate to report the incident to me and to testify about the GSS official's offer in the course of a judicial review procedure which took place on October 31, 2006. His hope to convince the judge that the refusal to collaborate was in fact the reason for the administrative detention and that he would be released on the spot was destroyed when the judge approved the detention order. We submitted an appeal. In his testimony before the judge of appeals on December 3, 2006, A.S. described in detail the meetings with the GSS official known as "Captain Riad":

> At the end of the meeting he told me that we were now friends, and I agreed. He tried to convince me to work with him and I told him that I had been in prison for 22 months and I wanted to return to my life and to live it and that I had registered for the university and he knew that. He told me about my mother's illness and that it is a dangerous disease. He knew that she was ill with cancer and said that he and I will help her together. He said that if I collaborate with him, he will help my mother and will transfer her to Tel Aviv for treatment and that he will give me money. He said that people who work with him are very satisfied. And I did not agree. He gave me a week to think about it and put me in prison in the meantime.

At the second meeting with the GSS man A.S. said that he had not changed his mind. Only then an administrative detention order was issued against him. The decision of the judge was rendered a week later. Based on the classified material, she held that "security of the region and of the public necessitate the detention."

We had no choice but to address the HCJ. Our petition was not heard as scheduled on January 8, 2007. It was not heard at all. The respondent, GSS, through the state attorney's office, suggested that we forego the hearing in return for the release of the petitioner on January 17, 2007. I gladly agreed. The offer provided further proof that A.S.'s administrative detention was meant solely to "convince" him to act as a collaborator, an issue that the GSS did not want to be raised in front of the HCJ.

Another case occurred in 2010. T.N., aged 32, was administratively detained two months after his release from jail, having served a sentence for possession of "means for combat" and activity in the Popular Front for the Liberation of Palestine. The first attempt to recruit him, as he testified during the judicial review of his administrative detention order, was made by "Captain Haggai," the area chief of the GSS, before the release on October 15, 2009. The "captain" understood that his attempt succeeded, therefore T.N. was released. A couple of months later, when the mistake surfaced, T.N. was returned to administrative detention. At the judicial review of the extension order, that took place on March 11, 2010, T.N. described another meeting with the same "Haggai," on February 3, 2010:

... I was in a meeting with him from 9 in the morning until 3 in the afternoon. We spoke about peace and my village; we have problems with the Palestinian security. Every half hour he would tell me that he wants to help me on condition that we would have telephone conversations, he will call and I will answer, and these calls will be secret. In addition, we will have meetings that will also be secret. Then I told him that this is the work of collaborators. He began exerting pressure on me and said that I have a family and children and that I am building a house and if I do not collaborate I will ruin my life, and reminded me that my wife is about to give birth. He claimed that he wants to help me while I was helping him. I told him that if the issue is that there is material against me and meetings have to take place then there is no problem, but why should the meetings be secret? Then he said that the meetings will take place wherever I wanted: in Jenin, in Jordan, in Israel, in Iran. I told him that this is work for collaborators and that I am not interested.

Similarly to the case of A.S., the judges did not give due consideration to the detainee's testimony about the attempts to recruit him for collaboration. Our request to obtain the notes of the GSS man from the meetings, that he was obliged to keep, was once again rejected. The judge chose to place his trust in the classified material. He held that during the two months of freedom, T.N. had reverted to his dangerous activities. "A grave and imminent threat emanates from this activity to the security of the area and from here arises the obligation to detain him," wrote the judge in his decision and added: "I would like to highlight that his administrative detention is based solely on the evaluation of the danger from this activity, with no connection to the content of the questioning of the respondent at the GSS." He confirmed the administrative detention order for the full length of the five months.

I based my appeal on legal argument that I thought was sufficient to invalidate the administrative detention order that had been issued on extraneous considerations. I referred the judge to a HCJ ruling and Articles 31 and 51 of the Fourth Geneva Convention and to Article 23 of the Hague Regulations that state unequivocally (in the terms used by Article 51): "The Occupying Power may not compel protected persons to serve in its armed or auxiliary forces." In the landmark judgment of the High Court of Justice[17], in reference to the above mentioned articles, recruitment of collaborators was explicitly mentioned. The judges stressed the danger that threatens the protected person who had been induced to become a collaborator and the fact that in most cases there will not be a genuine consent of a protected person to become one.

The military judge rejected our argument that T.N. was administratively detained due to his refusal to assist the GSS, and held that the reason for his detention was his "security activities." Nevertheless, as if contradicting himself, he ruled that the present administrative detention order should not be further extended. He added that his decision is a "substantive" one. T.N. was released on the day his detention order expired.

AFTERWORD

The official Israeli version is that "the use of administrative detention is a result of security constraints and is carried out for preventive purposes within the framework of the ongoing battle against terror when there is no other way to counter the threats to security."[18] In practice, "support of terror" and "threats to security" are ascribed to administrative detainees for various reasons.[19] These terms are not defined. Nonetheless, without any legal back-up, "terror organization" serves as a synonym for "unauthorized organization." Over the years of occupation, dozens and perhaps hundreds of organizations have been termed "unauthorized." Many of them conduct political, social, educational, health and charity activities that may and should be considered humanitarian and/ or human rights ones. Only some of the political organizations have a "military wing" and only a tiny number of their members belong to a military wing. However, it is enough for any "body of persons" whatsoever to have any connection whatsoever with any unauthorized organization whatsoever, for its activity to constitute a violation of the law and a "threat to security," and generate an indictment or an order for administrative detention.

This is the background of a preponderant majority of administrative detainees. During judicial review, we—the detainee and the lawyer—are told that he or she is dangerous because he or she is a "terror supporter." Less often the rationale given for detention is that the detainee is a "senior activist" in some organization; much less frequent is the allegation with a "military action."

The allegations as recorded in the detention orders of detainees I represented from 2002 through 2008 show that the percentage of "military activity" did not exceed 20 percent even in the difficult year of 2002, and it declined in 2008 to 9 percent. It should be remembered that the intelligence information that forms the basis of the allegations is always classified. It represents at the most the opinion of the GSS and sometimes not even that. The reasons for administrative detention cannot be known and scrutinized.

And so we return to the problem from which we began: confidentiality granted to the intelligence information which constitutes *conditio sine qua non* for administrative detention is detrimental not only to the detainee who cannot defend him- or herself. It also makes impossible to conduct an independent research on the subject.

NOTES

1. See sections 284–5 of the Order Concerning Security Provisions [consolidated version] (Judea and Samaria) (No. 1651) 2009 (henceforth "Security Provisions Order"). The consolidated version came into effect on May 5, 2010.
2. Sections 290 and 291 of the "Security Provisions Order" provide the legal basis for the departure from the precepts of the rules of evidence applicable during trial, first and foremost, the principle of disclosure. In a long line of decisions, the judges of the HCJ have given it their unreserved approval. See, for example, ADA [Administrative Detention Appeal] 1/80 *Kahane v. Minister of Defense,* IsrSC 35(2) 253(1980).
3. In the past, and particularly during the first Intifada, I represented detainees who were held administratively for seven years; in 2009, as far as I know, the maximum period of an administrative detention did not exceed five years.
4. Section 287 of the "Security Provisions Order."
5. HCJ 2320/98, *Al-'Amleh v. the Commander of IDF in the West Bank*, Piskei Din 52 (3).
6. Section 285(b) of the "Security Provisions Order."
7. This ignorance of the term of detention that awaits him and the inability to defend himself may amount, particularly with progression of time, to *severe mental torture* as defined in article 1 of the of the UN Convention against Torture and Other Cruel, Inhuman or Degrading. The point of affinity of administrative detention to torture was made regarding Israel and the OPT by the UN Human Rights Committee in 1998 and in 2003.
8. I.S., "Of Hope and Its Trammels, Talking Birds and Security Threats," *Ha'aretz* literary supplement, June 6, 1997 (trans. I. Hammerman, in Hebrew).
9. HCJ 253/88, *Sajadiya v. Minister of Defense*, Piskei Din 42 (3) 801, 821.
10. See ADA 1/88 *Igbareah v. The state of Israel*, IsrSC 342(1) 840 and the references contained in it; HCJ 554/81, *Branssa v. OC Central Command*, IsrSC 36(4) 247; HCJ 4400/98, *Barham v. Judge Colonel Sheffi*, IsrSC 52(5) 337.
11. Section 41(b) of the "Security Provisions Order."
12. See ADA 1/82 *Qawasmeh v. Minister of Defense,* IsrSC 31(1), 666; HCJ 6843/93 *Katamash v. Commander of Military Forces in the West Bank*, unpublished, April 18, 1994.
13. HCJ 2233/07 *Anon v. Commander of IDF Forces,* unpublished ruling, March 29, 2007.
14. Sections 295–8 of the "Security Provisions Order."

15. For example, *Ajuri v. Commander of IDF Forces in the West Bank*, IsrSC 56(6) 352, pp. 23–6; ADA 4/94, *Ben Horin v. State of Israel*, Piskei Din 48 (5), 529, 334, 336, 337; HCJ 1052/05 *Federman v. OC Central Command*, Piskei Din 2005(1)2166.

16. See, for example, Matti Steinberg, *Ha'aretz*, December 13, 2009; Gideon Levy, *Ha'aretz*, May 15, 2010; Avi Yissaharov and Amos Harel, *Ha'aretz*, May 26, 2010.

17. HCJ 3799/02 *Adalah v. IDF Commander*, 23.6.2005, reviewed in 2005 (2), IsrLR 206. Article 31 of the Fourth Geneva Convention says: "No physical or moral coercion shall be exercised against protected persons, in particular to obtain information from them or from third parties." Article 147 includes "compelling a protected person to serve in the forces of the hostile power" among the "Grave Breaches" of the Convention.

18. See *Without Trial: Administrative Detention of Palestinians by Israel and the Internment of Unlawful Combatants Law*, B'Tselem and HaMoked report, October 2009.

19. See Yael Berda's chapter in this volume.

13
Reframing the Legality of the Israeli Military Courts in the West Bank: Military Occupation or Apartheid?

Sharon Weill[1]

The law inevitably creates a great danger of arbitrary power—the rule of law is designed to minimize the danger created by the law itself.[2]

INTRODUCTION

Two persons commit a crime in a given place. General principles, such as the rule of law and the equality of persons before the law, require that both criminals would be subjected to the same criminal legal system.[3] That this system should impose a single body of law to define the criminal code, the rules of procedure, the regulations on police enforcement and the prosecution's policy. In addition, the tribunal that has jurisdiction to try these two offenders should impose a uniform level of punishment.

However, when the place of infraction is the West Bank, these basic principles do not apply. The entire criminal legal system—its legislation, policies and tribunals—depends on the nationality of the perpetrator and of the victim.

Take the case of a Jewish perpetrator. If a Jewish Israeli citizen commits an offense in the West Bank, although it is beyond the territorial sovereignty of the State of Israel, it is the Israeli criminal legal system that is applicable: the accused will be tried in Israel, according to the Israeli criminal code and rule of procedure, and will be entitled to the right of due process according to Israeli constitutional law.[4] To borrow Justice Barak's metaphor, while being in the Occupied Palestinian Territories (OPT), Israeli citizens carry in their backpack Israeli criminal law. Whereas, in the case of Palestinian perpetrators, if the offense was qualified by the army as a security crime or as any other crime that should be under its jurisdiction (including car theft, drugs and traffic offenses), the offender will be judged by the military legal system, in which military courts constitute the institutions of justice and military orders provide the criminal legislation and rules of due process.[5]

Thus, on the same territories, two populations are subjected to two different criminal legal systems: one civilian and the other military. This legal separation was installed through a sophisticated series of legislations and policy, routinely updated following the political changes. The present article aims at portraying this legal separation and exposing the role of the military courts in this mechanism.

A PRELIMINARY COMMENT ON THE APPLICABLE LAW IN THE WEST BANK

The West Bank is defined by international law as an *occupied territory*.[6] Consequently, the applicable law over the West Bank is the law of military occupation, which is a branch of international humanitarian law (IHL).[7] While IHL is completely silent on whether the occupation is legal and whether/when it should end, it provides a legal framework to regulate and administrate the Occupied Territories for the duration it lasts. During this period, the occupant does not enjoy sovereign rights over the territories it occupies. At the same time, it is responsible for administrating the local life of the population under its control, and for providing security. For this purpose, the military government centralizes in its hands all governmental powers—the legislative, judiciary and enforcement authorities.

When the law of military occupation was designed, occupation was perceived as a short and transitional legal status.[8] Yet, contemporary occupations have changed their nature, and have well demonstrated that *"rien ne dure comme le provisoire."*[9] A significant number of post-World War II occupations lasted over two decades, and the longest occupation—the Israeli occupation of the Palestinian territories—entered its fifth decade. Still, because of the legal distinction between *jus ad bellum* and *jus in bello*,[10] almost all international lawyers, academics and practitioners have focused on IHL violations, that is, on regulating the administration of the Occupation. Oddly enough, the preliminary question of the legality of the Occupation itself was left to the political front, although it involves major legal questions such as the right of self-determination, the prohibition of overtaking territory by force, and so on. As a result, as far as international law has been concerned, the exclusive reference to IHL left the Palestinian land and people to become existentially *occupied*.

The law of military occupation, drafted by nations, is an *ad hoc* law that primarily protects the interests of an alien army, which governs a territory and its population beyond its territorial jurisdiction, while observing basic humanitarian standards. It is not constitutional law, nor a synonym for good governance. Granting all the governmental authorities (legislative, judicial and executive) yielded to the military commander, it rather resembles military dictatorship. By no means is it a legal framework designed to govern a people for over two generations. True, as long as the occupation lasts, the occupying forces must respect IHL provisions. Yet, continuing to frame the legal analysis within IHL alone helps in maintaining the occupation, by emphasizing its regulation rather than the need to end the alien military rule over a people deprived of the right to self-determination and civil rights.

An analysis of the military courts' legality under international law is a good example for illustrating this claim. Framing this question only within IHL would imply that the establishment of the military court and its authority to try civilians in occupied territories are in principle legal, although its practice in the OPT involves grave violations of the right to due process[11] that may amount to war crimes and overstepping a given authority.[12] An analysis which stops here virtually suggests that the military system could improve itself, as it has already done.[13] Yet, the control of a civil population through a military judicial system, impartial by definition, and the attack on the liberty of a huge number of persons under a legal guise, would probably remain the same, because the law of military occupation allows administrative detention and criminal proceedings of security offences at military courts. Therefore, the legality of the military courts should not be examined only in light of IHL, which only aims at better regulating their function. A more accurate analysis requires an investigation into the entire legal environment in which the military courts operate and their role within it.

THE AUTHORITY TO ESTABLISH MILITARY COURTS IN OCCUPIED TERRITORIES ACCORDING TO IHL

As the occupying power is not the sovereign of the territory, it is forbidden from extending its own legal system to the occupied territories, and the local legal system continues to apply as it was prior to the occupation.[14] However, under certain circumstances, designed mainly for security reasons, the occupying power has the authority to promulgate new criminal provisions.[15] These offenses should be under the jurisdiction of military courts "properly constituted, non-political, and located in the occupied territories."[16]

The authority granted by the Fourth Geneva Convention to try civilians in military courts is in fact an exception to the rules of IHRL, which state that in general, military courts should not try civilians, because they do not comply with the obligation of independency and impartiality.[17]

As the judges are members of the armed forces and are subject to military discipline, under which they are evaluated for promotion, it is highly questionable whether they can be independent as required by IHRL and the doctrine of separation of powers. It therefore seems that by definition military courts cannot reach the level of independency required.[18] Thus, the authorization granted by IHL to judge civilians in military courts is strictly limited to the explicit exceptions provided by the Fourth Geneva Convention and these should be given very limited interpretation. In all other situations, the general rule of human rights law applies: civilians should not be tried in military courts. It is hence highly questionable if the military courts are entitled to judge traffic offenses and drug/car smuggling crimes, as they routinely do.

CARRYING OUT THE LEGAL SEPARATION

The law of military occupation provided the legal basis to submit the Palestinian residents of the OPT under a military rule and to establish military courts. However, these courts' jurisdiction has been constantly expanded or restricted according to the nationality of the perpetrator, in order to guarantee, on the one hand, Israel's judicial domination over the civilian Palestinian population, and, on the other, the expansion of the Israeli colonialism in the West Bank, that required the application of another legal regime— Israeli law—to the Jewish population, through its extraterritorial application on the basis of personal jurisdiction.[19] Together, these two legal systems—one military, the other civil, applicable to two national populations living in the same area—form the Israeli apartheid in the OPT. The system of separation of populations has been created not only by breaching the explicit provisions of IHL, but through severe violation of fundamental principles of public international law that prohibit colonialism, apartheid and systematic discrimination.[20]

Here is how Judge Menachem Liberman describes the situation:

For many years now, only people of Arab origin have been tried by Israel's military courts, despite the fact that the military court is entitled to try any person who commits an offence under its jurisdiction. For example, when there are demonstrations against the construction of the Separation Wall and people are arrested for committing offences in its vicinity, only detainees of Arab origin are tried by the military courts in the area, whereas Jews or Foreign citizens are brought to trial, if at all, in other, civilian, courts. It is an understatement to say that I am unhappy with this separation. Such conduct on the part of the investigating authorities smacks of racism, the origin of which I do not understand. I believe it is time to reexamine the criteria for bringing people before the military courts, so that all those who commit offences are subject to equal treatment.[21]

The Security Provisions Order (No. 378) of 1970, enacted by the military government, serves as the criminal code and rule of procedure of the West Bank, and it also establishes the jurisdiction of military courts. In fact, military order 378 reflects the general principle of territoriality in criminal law as the courts' jurisdiction is granted over all persons committing crimes in the OPT regardless of their nationality—Israeli, Palestinian, or foreign. Thus, in order to avoid a situation in which Israelis would be bound to military law and tribunals, it was necessary to extend Israeli law over Israelis residing in and travelling through the OPT. For this purpose, the Emergency Regulations Law (West Bank and Gaza—Criminal Jurisdiction and Legal Assistance) 1967 was enacted by the Knesset.[22] According to the High Court of Justice (HCJ), "The aim of these Regulations was to apply the same law to Israelis, wherever they committed the offence, in Israel or in the Region, according to the personal principle—as if Israeli citizens carry Israeli law with them when entering the Region."[23] As a result, a situation of concurrent jurisdiction was created: both Israeli civil and military courts have jurisdiction over offenses committed in the OPT by Israelis. However, although two different legal entities can exercise their authority to judge the same crime, there is no law regulating which system has priority. Thus, a selective policy could be practiced. In early cases, military courts recognized that the parallel jurisdiction of the Israeli courts did not deprive military courts of their authority to adjudicate.[24] That principled ruling was backed by the Israeli HCJ,[25] and indeed, a few cases of Jewish defendants were heard before military courts.[26] However, this practice soon came to an end. Since the violent events committed by Jewish settlers during the evacuation of Yamit settlement in Sinai in 1979, Jewish residents are no longer tried before military courts as a matter of policy.[27] The HCJ ruled later that security offenses committed by Israelis in the OPT should also be tried before Israeli civil courts.[28] Yet, this policy of judging Israelis in Israeli civilian—rather than military—courts, has been practiced through a distinction between Jewish and Palestinian Israeli citizens. While Israeli Jews have been excluded from the military courts' jurisdiction as a matter of policy, Palestinians carrying Israeli IDs (especially those from East Jerusalem[29]), committing an offense within the OPT, have always been tried there. Whenever Israeli Palestinians have argued before military courts that they should be tried in an Israeli civilian court, their claim has been systematically rejected on the formal grounds that the Emergency Regulations Law do not annul the jurisdiction of the military courts.[30] The legal lacuna—that is, the non determination of the rules of priority to regulate the concurrency of jurisdictions—facilitates the practice of racial policy, serving the goal of separating jurisdiction without legislating explicit discriminatory laws, which may not be constitutionally acceptable under Israeli domestic law.

THE EFFECT OF THE LEGAL SEPARATION: TWO EXAMPLES

In order to illustrate the discrimination, I examine below two basic principles of criminal law.

Nullum crimen sine lege

One of the most fundamental principles in criminal law prohibits retroactive legislation.[31] Israeli criminal law indeed requires that for a legislation to be in force it must be published in the official gazette. The Fourth Geneva Convention also sets down this requirement in Art. 65: "The penal provisions enacted by the Occupying Power shall not come into force before they have been published and brought to the knowledge of the inhabitants in their own language."

Yet several authors describe military legislation in the OPT as being partly a secret law.[32] From the first days of the Occupation, more than 2,600 civil and penal orders were promulgated. Despite the obligation set in Art. 65 of the Fourth Geneva Convention, no provision laying down the publication of orders in an official gazette for them to come into force exists in the OPT (unlike the criminal legislation within Israel). The military commander announced that an enactment would be published "in any manner I find appropriate."[33] Any earlier provision which laid down publication in an official gazette (for example, Art. 120 of the Jordanian Constitution) "has to be interpreted as any way of publication which is sufficient to inform the relevant persons, according to the opinion of the Military Commander of the Region."[34] Lacking a general provision, each order contains a specific Article regulating the date of its entry into force. It is usually the date of issue. Thus, from the moment the military commander has signed an order, it is binding, with no legal requirement to publish it. In practice, although some orders are not published at all, such as those regarding administrative provisions and matters concerning settlements,[35] most orders are published in the IDF official gazette in the West Bank, that is, "Proclamation, Orders and Appointments." However, significant time passes until orders are published. During this period, from the date of their issue until their publication, the law is in force without anyone but the army knowing about it. When finally published, these orders are in fact retroactive provisions.

Moreover, the distribution of this publication is very poor and often much delayed. The legislation is not arranged in an organized and updated manner in any book or electronic resource. The orders published in the gazette follow a chronological order and not a thematic one. Therefore, it is very difficult to find an order and to know whether it is the updated one, as they are frequently amended. For example, as of February 2009, the criminal code and rule of procedure of the West Bank—Military Order 378 (1970)—was amended 106 times, of which ten were made in the last year alone. The consolidated version published on the Internet site of the military prosecution office in July 2009 included only a hundred amendments. Military courts decisions, which interpret the law, are also not systematically published. The few selected rulings which are published are available only in Hebrew.[36] It is not surprising, therefore, that the Palestinians and their lawyers only learn of the law when in court. This situation is unimaginable in Israeli regular courts.

Proportionality in punishment

Another basic principle of criminal law is that a punishment should be imposed in proportion to the offense. Although Art. 67 of the

Fourth Geneva Convention reflects this principle, it is not respected by the military courts; moreover, as the two legal systems may practice different levels of punishment for the same offense, a discriminatory policy emerges.

DIFFERENT PUNISHMENTS FOR SIMILAR OFFENSES

Israelis and Palestinians committing similar offences in the OPT do not get the same legal treatment. The following two examples demonstrate this clearly.

Life sentences for murder attempts

The maximal punishment for an attempt to commit murder under Israeli law is 20 years' imprisonment.[37] In the military legal system, it is life imprisonment. Until the second Intifada, military courts rarely used their maximal punishment competence. This jurisprudence was changed by the military court of appeals in June 2003 in the *Nofel* case:

> Until the recent events [that is, the second Intifada] the military system did not have to deal with so many cases in which offenders were charged with attempt to murder. We were familiar with terrorist attacks that took people's life, and with a restricted number of attempts to murder, which fortunately did not succeed … Judges were restricted from imposing life imprisonment on attempts to murder by a barrier based on the fact that in Israel it is impossible to apply this level of punishment, and on the traditional concept that life imprisonment is reserved for murders that were actually committed. Although this barrier is not legally binding, it should be considered. Nevertheless, today it seems that this barrier should be removed … The military legislation enables us to impose life imprisonment on attempts to murder, and the particular reality which exists in the Region justifies this difference between Israel and the Region.[38]

The military court claimed that the difference between those who have accomplished the offense and those who have not is blurred, and the fact that one succeeded whereas the other did not does not in itself justify a lighter punishment for attempts.[39] Thus, two accomplices in an attempt to commit murder charged in two separate legal systems can consequently receive two different punishments: one up to 20 years and the other unlimited years of imprisonment.

Change of heart

In Israeli courts, a person is not criminally responsible for an attempt which was proven to have been stopped by him; therefore the court cannot impose any punishment on him.[40] However, the situation in military courts is radically different: even if there was a change of heart, criminal responsibility remains just the same, and a person who stopped the commission of the offense will nevertheless be charged for attempting it and will be punished. An astonishing example is the case of *Noursi*. On August 2001, he was arrested in Haifa, a city in the north of Israel, having decided to refrain from committing a bombing attack he had intended to carry out because "he had mercy on the women and children who were present in the location [where he was supposed to blow himself up] as they reminded him of his mother and brothers."[41] The court of first instance charged him with attempted murder and sentenced him to 13½ years' imprisonment. The military court of appeals in a majority decision reduced the punishment to "only" seven years in order to encourage this behavior. Noursi could have been tried in a civilian court in Haifa, where he was arrested—there no criminal responsibility or punishment could have been imposed on him. But since the question of concurrent jurisdiction between civilian and military courts is not regulated, the prosecution authorities could bring his case before the military court, where he could be criminally liable.

CONCLUSION

Law can serve an effective tool for exercising arbitrary power. As Sir Adam Roberts stated:

> [T]he law on occupations could be so used as to have the effect of leaving a whole population in legal and political limbo: neither entitled to citizenship of the occupying state, nor able to exercise any other political rights except of the most rudimentary character ... the law on occupations might provide, paradoxically, the basis for a kind of discrimination that might bear comparison with apartheid.[42]

Maintaining the situation as a military occupation over more than 40 years allowed Israel to utilized IHL, when needed, to carry out practices that profoundly violate basic concepts of democracy and human rights. These include practices such as administrative detentions, the exercise of military jurisdiction over civilians and the yielding of all governmental authorities—legislative, judicial and executive—to the military commander, in order to control a population deprived from the rights of self- determination, under legal guise. In fact, the use and misuse of IHL enable the State of Israel to develop a legal framework which opened the door to apply different sets of laws to two populations. The goal of this system was to place the Jewish residents from both sides of the Green Line under the jurisdiction of Israeli law, through its extraterritorial expansion, and to subject Palestinians under the jurisdiction of military courts. Rethinking the legal regime in the OPT is relevant for any process aiming to end the Occupation. As the law of military occupation (IHL) provides detailed rules which *regulate* the Occupation, but is completely unconcerned with bringing it to an end—apartheid and colonialism, not merely the law of military occupation, are the adequate legal frameworks to apply to the analysis of the current situation.

NOTES

1. Many thanks to Dimi Reider, Adv. Nery Ramati and both editors, Dr. Anat Matar and Adv. Abeer Baker, who read earlier drafts of this article and contributed important comments.
2. J. Raz, "The Rule of Law and Its Virtue," *The Law Quarterly Review*, Vol. 93, 1977, p. 195.
3. Ibid.
4. This will only happen if a criminal investigation was opened and handled properly—which is rarely the case in the OPT when the victim is a Palestinian. Since the second Intifada, as a matter of policy, the killings of Palestinian civilians by soldiers are not subject to a criminal investigation, and settlers' violence has a high level of *de facto* immunity. *Law enforcement upon Israeli civilians in the OPT: Yesh Din's monitoring*, Yesh Din data sheet, July 2008; The Report of the UN Fact Finding Mission on the Gaza Conflict, September 2009 (the "Goldstone Report"), p. 496; S. Weill, "The Targeted Killing of Salah Schehadeh: From Gaza to Madrid," *Journal of International Criminal Justice*, Vol. 7, 2009, p. 629. The case of Zeev Brauda, a Jewish settler who shot at unarmed Palestinians, clearly demonstrates the difference in treatment. While the video footage and its media coverage did not leave any choice to the police but to investigate the affair, the Israeli legal system found a way to dismiss the charge: secret evidence, which cannot be revealed because of security reasons, would harm the right of the suspect to have a fair trial.
5. Cases in which the criminal act constitutes a different offense, not involving Israeli victims, will be placed under the jurisdiction of the Palestinian courts in the West Bank, where the applicable law is the Jordanian law and the legislation of the Palestinian Authority. According to the Oslo Agreements, these courts cannot judge Israeli citizens.

6. Legal Consequences of the Construction of a Wall in the OPT, Advisory Opinion of the International Court of Justice, 9 July 2004, (hereinafter: the "ICJ Wall case").

7. The main legal sources of the law of military occupation include the 1907 Hague Regulations, the Fourth Geneva Convention of 1949, the Additional Protocol of 1977, and customary law. In addition, it is generally accepted that international human rights law (HRL) is applicable as well.

8. N. Bhuta, "The Antinomies of Transformative Occupation," *European Journal of International Law*, Vol. 16, No. 4, 2005, pp. 721–40, at p. 725.

9. A. Roberts, "Prolonged military occupations: The Israeli-Occupied Territories Since 1967," *American Journal of International Law*, Vol. 84, No. 1, 1990, p. 47. See, for example, the occupations of Namibia by South Africa and of East Timor by Indonesia, as well as the ongoing occupations of Northern Cyprus by Turkey and of Western Sahara by Morocco.

10. *Jus ad bellum* refers to the legality of use of force. *Jus in bello* refers to the manner in which force is used, which is regulated by IHL.

11. Yesh Din, *Backyard Proceedings: The Implementation of Due Process Rights in the Military Courts in the Occupied Territories*, December 2007; The Report of the United Nations Fact-Finding Mission on the Gaza Conflict, UN Doc A/HRC/12/48, September 25, 2009 (the "Goldstone Report"), para. 1445.

12. S. Weill, "The judicial arm of the occupation: the Israeli military courts in the occupied territories," *International Review of the Red Cross*, No. 866, 2007, pp. 395–419.

13. N. Benisho, "Criminal Law in the West Bank and Gaza," *IDF Law Review*, Vol. 18, 2005, p. 299 (in Hebrew).

14. Article 64(1) of the Fourth Geneva Convention reaffirms that local penal law and tribunals remains in force.

15. Art. 64(2) of the Fourth Geneva Convention provides that: "The Occupying Power may ... subject the population of the occupied territory to provisions which are essential to enable the Occupying Power to fulfill its obligations under the present Convention, to maintain the orderly government of the territory, and to ensure the security of the Occupying Power, of the members and property of the occupying forces or administration, and likewise of the establishments and lines of communication used by them."

16. Art. 66 of the Fourth Geneva Convention.

17. J.M. Henckaerts and L. Doswald-Beck, *Customary International Humanitarian law, Volume I: Rules*, Cambridge: Cambridge University Press, 2005, p. 356; Federico Andreu-Guzmán, Military Jurisdiction, International Commission of Jurists, 2001, p. 10; UN Human Rights Committee, General Comment No. 13 on Art. 14 of the ICCPR, (12 April 1984), UN Doc.HRI/GEN/1/Rev.1: "The Committee notes the existence in many countries of military or special courts which try civilians. This could present serious problems as far as the equitable, independent and impartial administration of justice is concerned"; the UN Special Rapporteur on the independence of judges and lawyers concluded that "international law is developing a consensus as to the need to restrict drastically, or even prohibit, that practice" (UN document E/CN.4/1998/39/Add.1, paragraph 78.)

18. Regarding the impartiality of Israeli judges in military courts see L. Hajjar, *Courting Conflict – The Military Court System in the West Bank and Gaza*, 2005, p. 112. It is worth mentioning that until 2004 the judges did not need to

have any legal background; they were just regular officers, usually very young. See Benisho, "Criminal Law in the West Bank and Gaza," pp. 312–13.

19. Whether it was done through parliamentary legislation, internal policies, HCJ jurisprudence or military orders; see E. Benvenisti, *The International Law of Occupation*, 2nd edn, Princeton, NJ: Princeton University Press, 2004, pp. 129–33.

20. For more details see *Occupation, Colonialism, Apartheid?: A re-assessment of Israel's practices in the occupied Palestinian territories under international law*, The Human Sciences Research Council of South Africa (HSRC), 2009, pp. 115–20.

21. Judge Menachem Liberman, Ofer military court; 4333/08 *Military Prosecutor v. Anbaui Issa*, September 21, 2008. File with author.

22. Art. 2(a) of the Emergency Regulations (legal assistance) states that "Israeli courts have jurisdiction to try according to Israeli law any person who is present in Israel and who committed an act in the Region, and any Israeli who committed an act in the PA, if those acts would have constituted an offence had they occurred in the territory under the jurisdiction of Israeli courts." To prevent the extension of Israeli criminal law to Palestinians, section 2(c) was enacted stating that "this Regulation does not apply on residents of the Region or the PA, who are not Israelis."

23. HCJ 831/80, *Tsoba v. State of Israel*, 36 (2) PD 169, p. 174. The Emergency Regulations (legal assistance) thus constitute a violation of the principle of territoriality, according to which all persons residing in a giving area are subject to the same legal system.

24. See Criminal Appeal 1238/69 *Military Prosecutor v. Abu Ranem* (1969), 1 *Selected Judgment of Military Courts* (hereinafter SJMC), published by the Military Advocate-General Unit of the Israel Defense Forces, p. 130.

25. HCJ *Levy v. General in Chief*, 21 PD 2 (1967); HCJ 507/72 *Arnon v. Attorney General* 27(1) PD 233, 238; English summary: 9, IYHR (1979) p. 334.

26. *Arnon v. Attorney General* 27(1) PD 233, 238.

27. According to the former President of the military court of appeals, Col. Shaoul Gordon, this policy was introduced for substantial and practical reasons. Being tried in Israel, during their investigation, detention and trial, the Israeli accused enjoys the same procedural rights guaranteed by Israeli law, providing a better defense of individual rights. As for the practical reason, it was dangerous to detain Jewish and Palestinian detainees in the same detention units. (Interview with Col. Gordon Shaoul, President of the military court of Appeals, at Ofer military camp on December 4, 2005).

28. HCJ163/82 *David v. State of Israel*, 37 PD 622.

29. As East Jerusalem was annexed by Israel, Israeli law became applicable there, and the status of the Palestinian residents was transformed. See more on this in the interview with Mohammad Abu Tir in this volume.

30. See, for example, HCJ 6743/97, *Zrari v. Israeli Police*, unpublished, 1997; *The Israeli Police v. Nabuls*, 1990, 7 SJMC 189, at p. 198.

31. "No crime can be committed, no punishment can be imposed without having been prescribed by a previous penal law": this principle was incorporated in the European Convention on Human Rights, article 7(1) and in the Rome Statute of the International Criminal Court, articles 22 and 23.

32. A. Rubinstein, "Israel and the Territories: Jurisdiction,", *Iyounei Mishpat*, Vol. 14, No. 3, 1989, p. 415 (in Hebrew); R. Shehadeh, *From Occupation to*

Interim Accords: Israel and the Palestinian Territories, London: Kluweri, 1997, at p. 86.

33. Art. 6 of Military Proclamation No. 2 (1967).
34. *Collection of Proclamations, Orders and Appointments* of the Military Commander in the West Bank Region, Vol. 8, November 5, 1967, p. 330.
35. Benvenisti, *International Law of Occupation*, p. 116.
36. A number of cases appear in *Selected Judgements of Military Courts*, published by the Military Advocate-General Unit of the Israel Defence Forces. Several more recent decisions are published on the Internet site of the HCJ <http://elyon1.court.gov.il/eng/home/index.html>.
37. Art. 305(a) of the Israeli Criminal Code (1977).
38. MCA 120+122/02 *Nofel v. The Military Prosecutor*, pp. 7 and 9.
39. MCA 303/03 *Sorkaj'er v. The Military Prosecutor*, 2004.
40. Art. 35 (a) of the Israeli Criminal Code (1977).
41. MCA 225/02 *Muhamad Tawalba called 'Noursi' v. The Military Prosecutor,* unpublished, 2004, p. 4.
42. Roberts, "Prolonged military occupations," p. 52.

14
Are There Prisoners in This War?

Smadar Ben-Natan

Israel has been holding Palestinians from the Occupied Palestinian Territory (OPT) in detention and arrest ever since the Israeli occupation of the West Bank and the Gaza Strip began in 1967. Most of the Palestinian prisoners are criminally charged and serve their sentences, while some are administratively detained, without charges. Palestinian prisoners and defendants, who are members of armed resistance groups, occasionally argue that they should be treated as prisoners of war. Israel, on its part, frequently refers to the Israeli–Palestinian conflict in terms of "war," to justify its extensive use of force as legitimate self-defense.[1] At the same time, it has never accepted prisoner-of-war (POW) status claims raised by Palestinian defendants. If this is a war, are Palestinian prisoners then Prisoners of War?

The essence of the argument of Palestinians for prisoner-of-war status is the portrayal of their struggle as a legitimate resistance to the Israeli occupation, in line with the right of self-determination, while the opposite position taken by Israel does not recognize this legitimacy.

This chapter aims to address the applicability of prisoner-of-war status under international law to Palestinian prisoners held by Israel, and critically reviews the Israeli positions on this point.

WHO IS A PRISONER OF WAR?

Prisoners of war are combatants of a party to an international armed conflict who fall into the hands of the adverse party. The essence of the claim of prisoner of war is that of being a legitimate combatant in an armed conflict. That is the situation when a national of a state is fighting as a soldier in its armed forces. He is performing a duty, not committing a crime. The Third Geneva Convention of 1949 (GC III) defines the entitlement to POW status.[2] Article 4 reads:

Prisoners of war, in the sense of the present Convention, are persons belonging to one of the following categories, who have fallen into the power of the enemy:

(1) Members of the armed forces of a Party to the conflict, as well as members of militias or volunteer corps forming part of such armed forces.
(2) Members of other militias and member of other volunteer corps, including those of organized resistance movements, belonging to a Party to the conflict and operating in or outside their own territory, even if this territory is occupied, provided that such militias or volunteer corps, including such organized resistance movements, fulfill the following conditions:
　(a) that of being commanded by a person responsible for his subordinates;
　(b) that of having a fixed distinctive sign recognizable at a distance;
　(c) that of carrying arms openly;
　(d) that of conducting their operations in accordance with the laws and customs of war.
(3) Members of regular armed forces who profess allegiance to a government or an authority not recognized by the detaining power.

According to GC III, prisoners of war must be treated humanely, in ways specified by the Convention. The most crucial aspect of POW status is that as combatants they were allowed to take active part in hostilities. Therefore they can not be prosecuted or punished for acts they committed as part of their participation in the conflict, unless they committed war crimes. At the end of the conflict, they must be released and repatriated.

Article 4 distinguishes between regular armed forces of a party to a conflict and any forces who "form part" of such forces, and irregular armed forces. These are also recognized as prisoners of war if they belong to a party to the conflict and meet all the conditions laid by article 4(2) to the convention. Resistance fighters or guerilla fighters who do not belong to a party to the conflict cannot claim the right to be treated as POWs.[3]

The definition given in article 4(2) to GC III can be divided into two parts: the first is belonging to a party to the conflict, while the second is satisfying the requirements in sub-paragraphs (a)-(d), that is, having a responsible command; a fixed distinctive sign; carrying arms openly; conducting their operations in accordance with the laws of war. What distinguishes these two parts of the definition is that the first part is not dependent on the voluntary behavior of the combatants, but on the identity of the parties to the conflict and the relations between the combatants and that party. The second part is dependent on the way the combating force conducts itself.

The Geneva Conventions were adopted right after World War II, and are applicable only to the rights and obligations of states who are party to it. They do not, *prima facie*, apply to rights and duties of non-state actors. However, this perception of international law had changed in the following years in relation to national liberation struggles. The allied support for resistance to the occupation in Axis-occupied countries in World War II, the ending of the European colonial empires and the liberation of African states from colonial regimes, and their inclusion in the UN system strengthened the recognition of the right to self-determination and the status of liberation movements who struggle for that end.[4] The UN Definition of Aggression, of 1974, stated:

> Nothing in this definition ... could in any way prejudice the right to self-determination, freedom and independence, as derived from the Charter, of peoples forcibly deprived of that right ... particularly peoples under colonial and racist regimes or other forms of alien domination; nor the right of these peoples to struggle to that end and to seek to receive support, in accordance with the principles of the Charter ... .[5]

As to POW status, and along the same lines, UN General Assembly Resolution no. 3103 of 1973, titled *Basic principles of the legal status of the combatants struggling against colonial and alien domination and racist regimes*, states that such combatants are entitled to POW status:

> 1. The struggle of peoples under colonial and alien domination and racist régimes for the implementation of their right to self-determination and independence is legitimate and in full accordance with the principles of international law.
> ...
> 4. The combatants struggling against colonial and alien domination and racist régimes captured as prisoners are to be accorded the status of prisoners of war and their treatment should

be in accordance with the provisions of the Geneva Convention relative to the Treatment of Prisoners of War, of 12 August 1949.[6]

Additional Protocol I to the Geneva Conventions (API), adopted in 1977, reflects this view and introduces different definitions on the issue of a POW, than those of GC III.[7] API reflects the legitimacy afforded to armed struggle against foreign colonization and occupation.[8] According to API, the Geneva Conventions are applicable to struggles of self-determination. Article 1(3) and 1(4) provide:

> This protocol, which supplements the Geneva Conventions ... shall apply in situations referred to in article 2 common to those conventions.
>
> The situations referred to in the preceding paragraph include armed conflicts in which people are fighting against colonial domination and alien occupation and against racist regimes in the exercise of their right of self-determination, as enshrined in the Charter of the United Nations ... .

The applicability of API and the Conventions to national liberation struggles means that these struggles are recognized as international armed conflicts.[9] National liberation movements can thus be considered a "party to a conflict," and combatants who belong to them can be recognized as POWs. Article 43 of API stipulates that:

> The armed forces of a Party to the conflict consists of all organized forces, groups and units which are under a command responsible to that Party ... even if that Party is represented by a government or an authority not recognized by an adverse Party.

Article 96 of API further allows for an authority representing people engaged in a national liberation struggle against one of the states party to the convention, to issue a unilateral declaration by which it undertakes to apply the Geneva Convention and the Protocol, and in this way to make the Conventions and the Protocol come into force between that authority and the state it is struggling against. On 4 May 1989 the Executive Committee of the Palestine Liberation Organization decided "to adhere to the Four Geneva Conventions of 12 August 1949 and the two Protocols additional thereto". The decision was reported by the Permanent Observer of Palestine to the United Nations to the Swiss Federal Council, in charge of accession to the GCs.

API introduces further changes in the conditions for entitlement to POW status, which are of less importance in the present context.[10] All the changes introduced by API are allowing irregular forces and armed liberation movements to comply with definitions of POW, which indeed was the intention.[11] The applicability of the protocol to Palestinian armed groups is dependent, therefore, on the classification of the Palestinian struggle as a national liberation struggle for self-determination.

THE PALESTINIAN RIGHT TO SELF-DETERMINATION

The occupation of the West Bank and Gaza in 1967 was the result of an armed conflict between Israel and Jordan, and Israel and Egypt, respectively. All three states were parties at the time to the Geneva Conventions, and therefore the Conventions are applicable to the Israeli occupation of these territories. However, the Palestinian struggle against the Occupation is independent and represents the aspirations of the Palestinian people, not directed by Jordan, Egypt, or under their auspices.

While the existence of a Palestinian people and its claim for self-determination was not self-evident soon after 1967,[12] it has gained general international recognition since then.[13] The West Bank and Gaza are generally referred to as the Occupied Palestinian Territory (OPT).[14] In 1974, the Palestine Liberation Organization (PLO), founded in 1964, was accorded observer status in the UN General Assembly along with several other national liberation movements.[15] The 1978 Camp David peace agreements between Egypt and Israel proposed a Palestinian self-governing authority for the West Bank and Gaza. In 1988, Jordan relinquished any title to the West Bank, dismantling legal and administrative links with it, while accepting "The wish of the PLO, the sole legitimate representative of the Palestinian people, to secede from us in an independent Palestinian state." With the Oslo Accords of 1993, Israel has also recognized the PLO as the legitimate representative of the Palestinian people and agreed to the establishment of the Palestinian Authority. In the International Court of Justice (ICJ) Advisory Opinion on the Construction of the Wall in the West Bank, the Palestinian right to self-determination was explicitly recognized: "the existence of a 'Palestinian people' is no longer in issue," noting that Israel itself has recognized this right.[16]

ARE THE PALESTINIAN PRISONERS AND DETAINEES HELD BY ISRAEL PRISONERS OF WAR?

There is no doubt that GC III applies to the Israeli occupation of the OPT, having been ratified by Israel in 1951. All parties to the 1967 conflict were parties to it, and it resulted in an occupation, meeting the applicability conditions stated in article 2 (common to all four Geneva Conventions):

> In addition to the provisions that shall be implemented in peace time, the present convention shall apply to all cases of declared war or any other armed conflict which may arise between two or more of the high contracting parties, even if the state of war is not recognized by one of them.
>
> The convention shall also apply to all cases of partial or total occupation of territory of a high contracting party, even if the said occupation meets with no armed resistance.[17]

It remains to examine whether the definition of POW applies to Palestinian prisoners, who do not belong to any original party to the conflict that generated the Occupation. The question of being prisoners of war is relevant only for those prisoners who claim to be combatants, not civilians. Many Palestinian prisoners do not view themselves as combatants, but as civilians, who are protected persons under the Fourth Geneva Convention. Only those who are members, or associate themselves, with organized armed resistance groups, are eligible to POW status.

Under GC III, before API, the privilege of being recognized as a prisoner of war was reserved to forces belonging to a party to the conflict, which was understood to be a state. Since Palestinian resistance fighters do not act as part of the armed forces of any such state—namely, not to Jordan or Egypt—they could not be regarded as prisoners of war, even before moving forward to check their compliance with the second part of POW definition. A possible argument for POW status under GC III can only be made on the basis of a claim for statehood of the Palestinian Authority, by members of its security forces.[18]

API changed this situation radically. According to its provisions, Palestinian armed resistance groups' members could, in principle, be entitled to POW status, without having to prove they belong to a state, if they can prove to belong to an organized group fighting alien occupation in the exercise of their right to self-determination.

They would also have to fulfill the second part of the definition: being hierarchically commanded, wearing a distinctive sign and/or carrying arms openly, and having a disciplinary system that enforces obedience to the laws of war.[19]

In fact, this part of the protocol was thought from its conception to be applicable to Israeli-occupied territory, and to Palestinian liberation fighters.[20] It is clear why, then, Israel has never signed the Additional Protocol, and has constantly objected to it.[21]

Since Israel is not a party to API, it would be binding on it only if it was found to reflect customary international law.[22] This is highly doubtful. Although some of the core provisions of API are regarded as customary international law, this doesn't seem to be the case as to the provisions dealing with prisoners of war, which were subject to fierce debate.[23] The United States and Israel along with some other significant states have not ratified the Protocol, due also to its position on the POW status.[24] State practice in national liberation struggles indicates that there is no consistent practice of recognizing liberation movements' prisoners as prisoners of war.[25] This part of the Protocol therefore does not apply, as a matter of law, to Israel, and the possibility of applying it and gaining recognition of POW status to Palestinian liberation fighters is currently theoretical.

All of the above relate to the first part of POW definition, that is, the possibility of members of liberation movements to be recognized as prisoners of war. Candidates for such status would still have to meet the conditions of the second part, dealing with their own conduct. At present, members of the Palestinian Authority's security forces could very likely fulfill these conditions. Fulfillment of these conditions by other Palestinian armed groups is beyond the scope of this article, but it is important to note that they could qualify as POWs, depending on their own conduct and adherence to the laws of war.[26] The possibility of such recognition could serve as an important incentive to conduct the Palestinian struggle according to the laws of war.

The practical implications of POW status in the present context seem to be less significant than the political and symbolic ones. The main features that distinguish prisoners of war from civilians captured by the adverse party in a conflict are that they don't stand for trial for the acts of fighting (their fighting is legitimate), and that they are released and repatriated at the close of hostilities, unconditionally of an agreement between the two states.[27] The convention also specifies conditions of detention and treatment of POWs. The conditions and treatment afforded to prisoners of war are not, in general, any better than the conditions Palestinian prisoners get in

Israeli prisons and detention centers, with possible exceptions in times of active fighting (such as during Operation "Defensive Shield" in the West Bank and the Operation "Cast Lead" war on Gaza). The release at the close of hostilities is probably a disadvantage in the case of Palestinian prisoners. The end of the Israeli occupation, by now well over 40 years old, is at the moment hard to foresee. In any case, according to the Fourth Geneva Convention, all Palestinians that are tried in Israeli military courts should be handed over at the end of the Occupation to the authorities of the liberated territory.[28] This obligation is not dependent on POW status and stems from the liberation of the territory. Although this handover is not formally a release as it is in the case of prisoners of war, it seems that, practically, being handed over to the liberated authority would mean release in the vast majority of cases, if not in all. So the advantage of prisoner-of-war status in these two senses is not of much practical importance.

It is noteworthy that after the Israeli withdrawal from the Gaza Strip and the abolition of the formal military regime and military court that was operating in the Erez crossing, Israel claims to have ended its occupation of the Gaza Strip. However, the hundreds of Gazan prisoners held by Israel haven't been handed over. This is yet another factor that weakens the Israeli argument that the occupation of Gaza has ended.[29]

The most significant difference then is that the status of prisoners of war would entail non-prosecution for acts of fighting. Again, prisoners of war are prisoners, and Israel would be allowed to hold them in captivity for as long as the conflict lasts. In this sense of the punishment as the practical outcome of criminal charges, again the result is the same—a sentenced prisoner and a prisoner of war are both imprisoned. But the POW is not convicted of any offense. He has done nothing wrong but to belong to the forces of the enemy, which is legitimate since he is an enemy national. The sentenced prisoner, on the other hand, is charged and tried as a criminal. This is the aspect that is most acute for Palestinians who regard themselves as freedom fighters: their claim for recognition of the legitimacy of their resistance to the Israeli occupation.

THE RELATION OF ISRAELI COURTS TO POW-STATUS ARGUMENTS

Israeli courts, both military and civil, have repeatedly rejected POW arguments by Palestinian defendants. These arguments have been raised, from time to time,[30] and they continue to rise occasionally in cases where Palestinian members of resistance groups are put on trial.[31] One fairly recent example is that of Marwan Barghouti, a prominent Fatah[32] leader who claimed to be a freedom fighter and not a terrorist. The Israeli judicial system had to relate to arguments regarding POW status of non-regular armed forces also regarding Hezbollah and other armed organizations operating in Lebanon.[33] In all of those cases, the courts rejected POW arguments. However, it is interesting to see that the argument used by Israel has changed over the years, with regard to the Palestinian prisoners.

As early as 1969, the Israeli military court rejected a POW-status claim by Palestinian combatants in the case of *Military prosecutor v. Kassem*.[34] The two defendants, members of the "Popular Front for the Liberation of Palestine" claimed to be prisoners of war. The main argument used by the state was the one of not belonging to a state party to the conflict. The court held that since the Popular Front was not part of the Jordanian Army and was an illegal organization in Jordan, the defendants did not qualify as POWs.[35] The court went on to conclude that they also do not meet the other conditions for POW status.[36] This case is cited internationally as a precedent for the conditions of POW status. The *Kassem* case was decided before API entered into force, and prior to the recognition afforded to the Palestinian liberation struggle, and therefore seems to be consistent with the law at the time. However, seen today in light of later developments, the defendants had a relatively strong claim for POW status, since they were caught wearing uniforms and carrying their arms and a card that associated them with the organization. The court ruled according to an expert opinion by the Israeli Army that the organization targeted civilians and therefore did not conduct itself according to the laws of war. It also concluded that members did not always wear uniforms.

In later cases of Palestinian prisoners, the main argument that was raised by the state was that of not conducting their operations according to the laws of war, and namely, targeting civilians. While there is no doubt that both arguments are valid, it seems that Israel has gradually come to avoid the first argument and rely more heavily on the latter.

The case of Marwan Barghouti demonstrates this line of argument by the state.[37] Barghouti was charged in an Israeli civil court and not in a military court, apparently due to Israel's fear of public scrutiny over the military courts and its wish to make Barghouti's an example case. Barghouti claimed to be a freedom fighter and therefore argued that he was entitled to POW status. He also raised arguments about his trial being a political one, claiming he was a member of the

Palestinian Parliament and that Israel had no jurisdiction over him due to the Oslo Accords and the status of the Palestinian Authority. Barghouti's argument for POW status was argued in the terms of the API, emphasizing that he is fighting an occupation in order to realize the Palestinian people's right to self-determination.[38] The state did not argue that Barghouti did not belong to the forces of a state party to the conflict. Rather, it argued that "He does not meet the accumulating conditions set by the Third Geneva Convention since he systematically breached the laws of war set by international law," that he does not meet any of the conditions of the Convention since he headed terrorist organizations which are not identified by an emblem, do not have a clear hierarchy, don't carry arms openly, and act against civilians. The court accepted the state's positions and ruled that it is sufficient that Barghouti was commanding terrorist organizations which targeted civilians, to conclude that he is not entitled to POW status.

In the Israeli Supreme Court decision regarding the legality of the Detention of Unlawful Combatants Act,[39] the detainees, residents of the Gaza Strip, also argued for prisoner-of-war status. The court stated, "The appellants should not be granted the status of prisoners of war since they do not comply with the conditions of article 4 to the Third Geneva Convention, first and foremost the condition regarding compliance with the laws of war."

The State of Israel and its public prosecution are well aware of the possible argument of not belonging to a state party. That argument has been forcefully raised by the state in the context of members of Hezbollah in the 2006 conflict.[40] Israel argued they were not entitled to POW status, since Hezbollah was not acting on behalf of Lebanon, but independently, or as the long hand of Iran. It therefore seems like a conscious choice not to stress the same argument as to Palestinians.

Thus, in the Palestinian context, the state has notably shifted the emphasis to the second part of POW definition, mainly the argument of obeying the laws of war. This shift could have numerous reasons. While the argument of not belonging to a state might sound formalistic, the argument of keeping the laws of war has its moral appeal while it avoids the issue of occupation and the right to self-determination. This is in line with Israel's line of argument that emphasizes the Palestinians resorting to attacks on civilians while avoiding the question of the legitimacy of occupation, and portraying the conflict in terms of a "war on terror." Due to the adoption of the First Additional Protocol, the demand of belonging to a state is no longer universally accepted, and the state might have wanted to avoid, where possible, the reliance on that principle which would call to question the status of alien occupation, self-determination and legitimate resistance. A line of argument challenging the existence of a Palestinian party to a conflict would also bring into question Israel's compliance with the Oslo Accords that embodied an Israeli recognition of the Palestinian people's right to self-determination and self-governance. The total rejection of POW status for Palestinian resistance fighters was thus weakened significantly over the years.

The legal inapplicability of the standards introduced by API and other GA resolutions, acknowledging the right to self-determination and liberation, is due to Israel's constant opposition to acknowledging those principles and applying them to the Palestinian people. This position remains contrary to the major developments in international law following the liberation struggles and decolonization after 1949. It does not weaken the claim that Israel should acknowledge the Palestinian right to self-determination, as it partially did in the Oslo Accords, but significantly retracted since. Such recognition carries significant implications on the possible status of Palestinian prisoners as prisoners of war.

NOTES

1. For instance, *Legal Consequences of the Construction of a Wall in the Occupied Palestinian Territory* (Advisory Opinion), ICJ Rep 2004, para. 138 (The *Wall* Advisory Opinion).
2. Geneva Convention Relative to the Treatment of Prisoners of War, adopted August 12, 1949, entered into force October 21, 1950, 75 UNTS 135.
3. F. Kalshoven and L. Zegveld, *Constraints on the Waging of War: An introduction to International Humanitarian Law*, International Committee of the Red Cross, 2001, 3rd edn, p. 53.
4. A. Roberts, "Prolonged Military Occupation: The Israeli-Occupied Territories Since 1967," *American Journal of International Law*, Vol. 84, No. 1, 1990, pp. 44, 80. *Commentary on the Additional Protocols of 8 June 1977 to the Geneva Conventions of 12 August 1949*, ed. by Y. Sandoz, C. Swinarski and B. Zimmermann, published by the International Committee of the Red Cross, p. 41.
5. Definition of Aggression, Annex to GA Res. 3314 (XXIX), December 14, 1974, art. 7; a similar definition statement is included in the Declaration on Principles of International Law concerning Friendly Relations and Co-operation among States in Accordance with the Charter of the United Nations, Annex to GA Res. 2625 (XXV), October 24, 1970. Both the Definition of Aggression and the Declaration of Friendly Relations are considered to reflect customary international law.

6. Basic Principles on the Legal Status of the Combatants Struggling Against Colonial and Alien Domination and Racist Regimes, GA Res. 3310 (XXVIII), December 12 1973. See also "Programme of Action for the Full Implementation of the declaration on the Granting of Independence to Colonial Countries and Peoples", GA Resolution 2621 (XXV), October 12 1970.
7. Protocol I Additional to the Geneva Conventions of August 12, 1949, and relating to the Protection of Victims of International Armed Conflicts, adopted June 7, 1977, entered into force December 7, 1978, 1125 UNTS 3. Commentary on the Additional Protocols, p. 506.
8. G. Aldrich, "The Laws of War on Land," *American Journal of International Law*, Vol. 94, 2000, pp. 42, 45–6.
9. As opposed to non-international armed conflicts.
10. Articles 43, 44. See footnote 19 below.
11. Aldrich, "The Laws of War on Land."
12. Palestinian self-determination is not mentioned in Security Council Resolutions 242, 338, which demanded Israeli withdrawal from the territories occupied in 1967.
13. Roberts, "Prolonged Military Occupation," pp. 76–9; O. Ben Naftali, A.M. Gross and K. Michaeli, "Illegal Occupation: Framing the Occupied Palestinian Territory," *Berkeley Journal of International Law*, Vol. 23, No. 3, 2005, p. 551, note 17.
14. Ben Naftali, Gross and Michaeli, "Illegal Occupation," note 2: this term is gradually substituting the terms "the West Bank, Gaza Strip and East Jerusalem" and "Palestinian occupied territories" in the terminology of the United Nations referring to the areas occupied by Israel since 1967, to connote the area where the Palestinians are entitled to exercise their right to self-determination. See, for example, GA Res. ES-10/6, UN GAOR, 52d Sess., Supp. No. 494, UN Doc. A/ES-10/6 (1999).
15. GA Res. 3237 (XXIX) (November 22, 1974).
16. The *Wall* advisory opinion, note 1, para. 118.
17. Israel had claimed that the Forth Geneva conventions are not applicable *de jure* to the OPT; however, that view was repeatedly rejected by the international community. See the *Wall* advisory opinion, paras 86–101; D. Kretzmer, *The Occupation of Justice: The Supreme Court of Israel and the Occupied Territories*, New York: State University of New York Press, 2002. Regarding the Third Geneva Convention, Israeli courts, following the position of the state, relate to it as binding upon Israel. See in the following cases, as well as: C.C. Burris, "Re-examining the Prisoners of War Status of PLO Fedayeen," *NCJ Int'l L. & Com. Reg.* Vol. 22, 1996–97, pp. 943, 976–8.
18. Such an argument is presented by Burris, ibid. This could change if a Palestinian state is declared unilaterally and accepted by the international community, it would then be a state party to the conflict if it signs the Third Geneva Convention or even accepts and applies it, according to article 2 of the GC.
19. This list of conditions incorporates some of the additional changes made by API relative to GCIII: wearing a distinctive sign and carrying arms openly, are, in certain conditions, alternative rather than cumulative; the condition of abiding with the laws of war was replaced by the existence of an organizational disciplinary system which enforces the laws of war.

20. Aldrich, "The Laws of War on Land.", 45–6; Burris, "Re-examining the Prisoners of War Status of PLO Fedayeen," 993.
21. Burris, ibid., 992f. and 1002.
22. According to Israeli and international law, customary international law is binding on the state whether it is a party to the convention or not. The Israeli Supreme Court in Criminal Appeal 6659/06 *Dow v. the State of Israel*, and in other decisions, has acknowledged that some articles in the first additional protocol are customary and therefore apply to Israel, but not the articles relating to prisoners of war.
23. J.M. Henckaerts and L. Doswald-Beck, *Customary International Humanitarian Law – Volume I: Rules*, Cambridge: Cambridge University Press, 2005, p. 387.
24. Henckaerts and Doswald-Beck, ibid., p. 389; Burris, "Re-examining the Prisoners of War Status of PLO Fedayeen," p. 976; Aldrich, "The Laws of War on Land."
25. Burris, ibid., pp. 994–1002. Burris points to releases of prisoners at the end of hostilities in such struggles, but those were taken as a political move and not owing to their POW status or to a legal obligation to do so. A sense of legal obligation is essential for the creation of a binding custom in international law.
26. Based on the condition of conducting operations according to the laws of war, it could be doubtful if Israeli soldiers would be entitled to POW status, more so after the recent wars/operations in Lebanon (2006) and Gaza (2008–09) when international bodies (Human Rights Watch, Amnesty international, and lately the UN "Goldstone Mission") concluded that the Israeli Army was in breach of the laws of war. However, according to the Goldstone Mission, the Israeli captive soldier Gilad Shalit, who was captured in 2006, meets the requirements of prisoner-of-war status: "Report of the UN fact finding mission on the Gaza conflict," p. 285 (Final version).
27. Article 118, GC III.
28. GC IV, article 77.
29. On the legal status of Gaza see K. Mann and S. Bashi, *Disengaged Occupiers: The Legal Status of Gaza*, Gisha, 2007 (NGO Report). The Israeli Supreme Court related to this issue in the case of Criminal Appeal 6659/06 *Dow v. the State of Israel* regarding the Unlawful Combatants Act, where it stated that the detainees there, who were from Gaza, were not released in the end of occupation rightfully, since they still posed a risk to the security of Israel. However, this was stated individually and not generally. To the best of my knowledge, the argument regarding Israel's duty to release the prisoners from Gaza following its withdrawal hasn't been brought up in legal proceedings. In any case, only 10–12 detainees are held under the Unlawful Combatants Law, and there are about 700 detainees in Israeli jails from Gaza.
30. See, for instance, HCJ 403/81 *Jaber v. The military commander of the West Bank*, Israeli Supreme court reports 35(4) 397 (in Hebrew).
31. See, for instance, decisions in the matter of Maslamani (case number not indicated, given April 2, 2003), Naji (case number not indicated, given February 5, 2003). Military Court Beit-El.
32. A branch of the PLO, see Burris, "Re-examining the Prisoners of War Status of PLO Fedayeen," p. 955.

33. See HCJ 102/82 *Tzemel v. The minister of defense*, Israeli Supreme court reports 37(3), 365; HCJ 2967/00 *Arad v. the Knesset*, Israeli Supreme court reports 57(2) 188; Criminal Arrest Appeal 8780/06 *Srur v. the State of Israel*.

34. *Military prosecutor v. Kassem*, 42 ILR, 470.

35. See also Y. Dinstein, *The Conduct of Hostilities Under the Law of International Armed Conflict*, Cambridge: Cambridge University Press, 2004, p. 39.

36. Some of the court's rulings on the other conditions seem more debatable than the one concerning the organization not belonging to a state. The defendants were caught wearing uniforms and carrying their arms and a card that associated them with the organization. The court ruled according to an expert opinion by the Israeli Army that the organization targeted civilians and therefore did not conduct itself according to the laws of war. It also concluded that members did not always wear uniforms.

37. Arrest Request 92134/02, Criminal Case 1158/02 *The State of Israel v. Marwan Barghouti*, Tel-Aviv District court.

38. Description of the arguments of both parties is based on their description in the court's decisions.

39. Criminal appeal 6659/06 *Dow v. the State of Israel*.

40. See *Srur v. the State of Israel*. The writer was one of the defense attorneys on this case.

15
Institutional Schizophrenia: The Release of "Security Prisoners" in Israel

Leslie Sebba *

The possibility of releasing offenders convicted of security offenses[1] in Israel is an issue which may arise in three contexts:

1. routinely, when, like any other offender sentenced to a fixed term of imprisonment, such a prisoner has served two-thirds of the sentence imposed (in the case of offenders sentenced to life imprisonment, only after the sentence has first been commuted to a fixed term);
2. following negotiations for a prisoner exchange, as occurred with the "Jibril transaction" and the release of Elhanan Tenenbaum, and currently since the kidnapping of Gilad Shalit by Hamas;[2]
3. as part of an attempt to improve relations with a current or erstwhile enemy, whether in the framework of peace negotiations such as the Oslo process[3] (and thus an expression of "transitional justice"), or by way of unilateral gesture.[4]

In fact, even for the first category, the term "routine" is distinctly misleading. Prisoner release in Israel is governed by the Conditional Release from Prison Law of 2001 (henceforth "Release Law"), which places the discretionary power to release prisoners who have served two-thirds of their sentence in the hands of Release Boards.[5] Since Israeli laws normally apply only within the official territorial borders, early release provisions did not apply in the Occupied Palestinian Territories (OPT), which were (and are) governed by the law which prevailed prior to the Occupation, subject to later amendments by the military authorities. Moreover, the Military Order issued in the wake of the Six Day War, under which most of the "security offenders" were convicted, granted sole power to modify sentences to the military authorities. A special provision under the Release Law,[6] however, extended the applicability of its discretionary release procedures (with modifications) to all offenders held within the Green Line, where most "security" prisoners are held.

Even in relation to the general prison population, however, penal policies in Israel, like those of other western neoliberal regimes in recent decades,[7] have become increasingly repressive and influenced by political populism and the fears and concerns attributed to a supposedly punitive public. The wording of the Israeli Release Law clearly indicates that the overriding criterion in determining release is the perceived "dangerousness" of the prisoner,[8] and in effect creates a presumption that the prisoner is dangerous unless the contrary can be shown. Moreover, the Release Law allocates a role in the decision-making process to government security agencies.[9] Needless to say, cases in which a release board will grant early release to a "security" offender are rare.

It is true that in a recent case dealing with release policy in "security" cases,[10] a Supreme Court Justice expressed the view that the seriousness of the offense should not necessarily preclude the possibility of an early release—and, indeed, that rehabilitation considerations too should not necessarily be precluded in cases of residents of the OPT, in spite of the difficulty of monitoring such cases—but it seems doubtful whether such rhetoric will be reflected in the practice. Any serious prospect of an early release for these offenders is thus more likely to derive from the "non-routine" channels indicated by options 2) and 3) of my opening paragraph.

For the Palestinian people and their leaders, the release of political activists imprisoned during the course of the Israel–Palestine conflict is a topic of the greatest importance.[11] This is reflected in their official and unofficial discourses and policy positions—and indeed is the main motivation for their attempts to abduct Israeli soldiers. Note may also be taken of the connection between the leadership itself and the prison experience, as illustrated in the "Prisoners' Document"—a statement seen as reflecting the official Palestinian position on peace negotiations which emanated from political leaders held in the Israeli prisons in 2006.[12]

In view of the social, political, legal and military complications and ramifications of this issue, there has been surprisingly little academic interest in the topic. On the one hand, it has not attracted in-depth legal-criminological analysis.[13] More surprisingly, in the light of the burgeoning international literature on Transitional Justice, post-conflict justice issues in the Israel–Palestine context have been neglected, and perhaps for this reason have so far played only a limited role in the formal aspects of the peace process[14]—in spite of their domination of the ongoing political agenda.

*   *   *

This chapter focuses on the legal-structural aspects of this topic. In my view, the current topic may be seen as an example of the approach on the part of the Israeli establishment to legal issues and institutions in the context of the Israel–Palestine conflict. This approach reflects an ambivalence or *duality* in the perspectives and narratives adopted by the professionals, and seemingly shared by the public as a whole, in relation to the so-called "security" offenders in general, and to the legal system applying in the OPT in particular.

In some areas, this duality is reflected in the adoption of distinct narratives by people holding different identities or occupying different roles. Thus, while Palestinian critics and many human rights organizations view the legal system in the territories as a charade,[15] some jurists believe that this system is striving to adhere to due process, albeit in difficult circumstances.[16] This dichotomy may be helpful in understanding an analogous, and indeed directly related, dichotomy which may be identified in the context of the present topic, namely, the prosecution and release of "security" offenders and the perceptions of these offenders. In this case, however, the conflicting perceptions seem to be held not by two ideologically opposed groups, but simultaneously by the same groups.

I refer to the perceptions of these processes on the part of the political establishment (and perhaps also on the part of the public) at the two stages of the process—at the apprehension and trial stage on the one hand, and when their release from prison is mooted on the other. At the point of their apprehension, these detainees are generally portrayed to the public as criminals who deserve to be prosecuted and tried with the full formality of a criminal trial, and sentenced and punished with the full force of the law. When, however, there appears to be a possibility of an exchange in order to secure the release of Israeli captives, or if it is felt that a gesture to the other side would be expedient, these same "criminals" are considered to be merely bargaining chips who can be released at any time at the discretion of the executive.[17]

From a legal perspective, there are four alternative approaches which government authorities can adopt when dealing with persons suspected of involvement in hostile activity: (a) defining them as prisoners of war; (b) issuing administrative detention orders (available under many legal systems in states of emergency)— an approach recently extended to a new category of "unlawful combatants"; (c) prosecution in military courts or tribunals, or (d) prosecution in regular criminal courts. Space does not permit a full discussion here of the various issues arising under international or national law which may be relevant to the choice as among these options.[18] Not all of the four options mentioned will be available in every situation, so their attractiveness as a mode of response in the present context may be hypothetical. It may be noted, however, that options b), c) and d) have all been adopted on different occasions in respect of Palestinians suspected of involvement in terrorist activity, and thus appear to be perceived by the Israeli authorities as legitimate alternatives.

The order in which these options have been presented above is hierarchical, in accordance with the degree of legal formalism by which they are characterized, and the obstacles which have to be overcome to achieve the desired outcome. (A well-known law scholar once described adherence to due process as an "obstacle course".[19]) At the one extreme (option a), the designation of a captive as a prisoner of war involves no formal legal steps. Nor does option b), issuing an administrative detention order, require a judicial process *ab initio*: the authority to issue such an order in the territories is vested in the Military Commander according to his discretion.[20] It is true that since the law was amended such orders have been subject to judicial review (in the same way as administrative detention orders within the Green Line),[21] but if such procedures are invoked, the burden of proof is imposed on the person subject to the order to show that the order was not justified.

By contrast, to bring a prosecution in a military court (option c) requires that sufficient evidence be gathered for the conduct of an adversary proceeding, in which the defendant will generally be represented by an advocate, and that a court be convinced of the defendant's guilt[22] beyond all reasonable doubt. As noted earlier, there are diverse views as to whether trial in the military court and the associated proceedings genuinely accord with due process, but at least in formal terms the similarity with a criminal trial in the regular courts has increased in recent times;[23] and by tradition, at least, the regular criminal trial represents the apogee of formalism.[24]

In statistical terms, it is clear that in most cases the authorities choose to prosecute terror suspects in the military courts.[25] Israel does not recognize terror suspects as prisoners of war, and the use of administrative detention attracts criticism at home and abroad because of the absence of formal charges and a trial proceeding. The state seems to have an interest in showing that those involved in hostile activities are criminals, in order to avoid an acknowledgment of the political-ideological character of these activities which would lend them a veil of legitimacy. For this reason, in prominent cases such as Marwan Barghouti's, who is a Fatah leader sentenced in 2004 to five terms of life imprisonment, preference is given to the proceeding with the maximum formality and the highest public profile—a criminal trial in the courtroom of a district court within the Green Line.[26]

There is, however, a catch here. The greater the formalism of the proceeding adopted for the prosecution of the suspected terrorist, the greater the complications if it is sought to release him before the appointed time. This may be shown in accordance with the hierarchy referred to above. The authority to release prisoners of war falls within the exclusive discretion of the executive branch. As for administrative detention, the military commander has the authority not only to order such detention but also to terminate it at any moment—even if it has been approved by a judge.[27] With regard to a term of imprisonment imposed by a military court, while the sentence itself is no longer (as was the case in the past) conditional on the approval of the military commander, the latter retains the power to "take note at any time of the court's judgment and is empowered to pardon the offender or mitigate his penalty."[28] By contrast, a person sentenced to imprisonment in a regular criminal court may generally be released prior to the end of the term designated by the court only on the authority of the release board following the procedures laid down in the Release Law and its accompanying regulations, and only after serving two-thirds of the term imposed. This, it will be recalled, was the "routine" procedure for release referred to earlier.

If this procedure is unavailable, either because the prisoner has not yet served the required minimum period of the sentence, because other requirements for early release have not been met, or because the release board has rejected the request for early release, the only remaining alternative is the exercise of the presidential power to grant a pardon or commute the sentence.[29]

However, the presidential clemency process is a sensitive procedure from a constitutional perspective, involving a delicate balance between the president on the one hand and the minister whose countersignature will be required to validate the presidential document under the Basic Law on the other.[30] Yet another option where the release of groups or classes of prisoners is contemplated would be a general amnesty incorporated in legislation, a measure adopted following the Six Day War. Such measures, however, are more appropriate in the event of a national transformative event,[31] and are in any case problematic in urgent cases where there is a strict timetable.[32]

The hierarchy according to which the four possible modes of prisoner release have been ordered here is not merely a matter of procedural differences, but also has a substantive dimension. To my mind, the military commander who has authority to release an administrative detainee, may not use this power arbitrarily but only after the exercise of his discretion: his power is of a *quasi-judicial* character. It follows that the military commander should not necessarily comply with the *diktat* of the government, acting through the agency of the Minister of Defense, in spite of his being subjected to the authority of this minister in the administrative structure. This argument is even stronger in the case of a security offender who has been convicted by a military court. The release of such a prisoner in accordance with an arbitrary order from above and without a reasoned application of discretion would make a mockery of the formal procedures which led to the prison sentence, including the prosecution, the trial, the conviction and the imposition of sentence.

Continuing up the hierarchy developed above, based upon the degree of formality of the process, we finally reach the release of the prisoner who has been convicted in a regular criminal court. Again, the matter is more complex not only, as noted above, by virtue of the process itself, but also for substantive reasons. If the Release Board is to be involved, account must be taken of the legislation under which it has been established, which, in addition to specifying its procedures (and that it be headed by a judge), also lays down criteria for the exercise of its discretion. It is by no means clear that the desire of the government to release security prisoners, even if in the last stages of their sentence, can be linked to the statutory criteria for prisoner release which govern the board's decision making, such as the prevention of harm to the public, rehabilitation of the offender and "public trust in the system"—a consideration which has been added in recent years to those guiding the boards in their decisions regarding early release.[33] For all these reasons, the assistance of the pardoning authorities will almost inevitably be necessary.

However, even on the assumption that the ministers involved in the pardoning process support the government's wish to release the prisoners,[34] the expectation—often implicit in government announcements—that the grant of a pardon will necessarily be forthcoming is highly problematical. For in spite of the ministerial involvement in this process, the president has the ultimate discretionary power in making the final decision.[35] Indeed, during the Oslo process, the then president, Ezer Weizmann, refused to agree to the grant of a pardon to a number of Palestinian prisoners with "blood on their hands."[36] Further problems may arise if the consent of the pardon's recipient is required to its conditions or if the pardon is held to be dependent on a petition from its recipient—which may not always be forthcoming.

In an era of judicial activism, the doubts raised here with regard to the advisability of reliance upon the usual procedures for prisoner release in cases where a "deal" is being negotiated is not a problem only for the agencies directly involved. Allegations that governmental initiatives are being undertaken which require the involvement of legal institutions for purposes other than those for which they were established may be grounds for judicial review; indeed, petitions to the High Court of Justice (HCJ) for the purpose of challenging impending releases are regularly brought, primarily by political elements who are opposed to these releases, and by victim organizations—although until now with little success.[37] In relation to objections on the part of victims,[38] it should also be observed that the Victims' Rights Law of 2001 grants the victims of violent (as well as sexual) offenses legal standing in the release proceedings, both in the context of the exercise of the powers of the release boards and in clemency proceedings.[39] Persons with reservations regarding the impending release are thus not exclusively dependent on HCJ proceedings for the expression of their views, the decision makers themselves now being obligated to give appropriate weight to such views.

IN CONCLUSION: A PROPOSAL

The aim of this chapter has been to point out an inconsistency seemingly shared by both the government and the public in their attitude to so-called "security offenders." The latter on their apprehension are regarded as criminals who should be subjected to the formalities of the criminal law in all their severity. Yet once incarcerated, they are perceived as goods which may be bartered at any time or unilaterally released should the political need arise. The outcome of this duality is a legal conundrum: the more the authorities are insistent on observing the niceties of formal legal procedures in securing the detention of the persons concerned, the greater the obstacles encountered if it is desired to release them in the wake of a change in the political situation or in the face of some immediate practical need.

A more satisfactory solution may be sought by way of modifying one or other end of the legal process. Together with a measure of decriminalization in relation to some of the so-called "security offences,"[40] an attempt could be made to minimize the legal measures instigated against those whom it is sought to detain by recognizing them as prisoners of war, or by simply detaining them in prison camps without any status, as did the United States in Guantanamo Bay. However, there is no readiness at present to grant this population prisoner-of-war status, and to hold them without granting them any rights would be in contravention of basic principles of human rights.[41]

The other type of solution would be to seek a solution at the "back end," that is, at the release stage itself. In the long run, it may be hoped that the parties will reach a solution that will provide for a general release of detainees by way of general amnesty, which is traditionally effected by way of legislation. Some jurisdictions and legal traditions, however, are familiar with interim situations where there is recognition that neither comprehensive legislation along the lines of a general amnesty law nor the exercise of individualized discretion may be appropriate. A solution is required which will empower governments to act and to release a particular group or category of prisoners, in apparent derogation of the law enforcement system which has expended great energy in instigating prosecutions, conducting trials and imposing sentences on these groups.[42] It must be acknowledged that solutions which are sufficiently flexible yet consistent with the rule of law, such as those which combine legislative authority with executive discretion, are not numerous even among the plethora of clemency models which have been adopted in different jurisdictions around the world.[43] However, certain uses of Italy's *indulto*[44] may provide guidance here, as well as French hybrid institutions such as collective pardons and *grace amnistielle*.[45]

In this way, it would be possible to become accustomed to a new duality which would be recognized by the law, obviating the need for government officials to bend the law to meet their expediency needs.

The working assumption here is that persons suspected of hostile acts will continue to be designated "criminals" under the laws of the state and attract severe punishments. However, since it will be recognized that their activities are related to a national struggle, an institution will have been established—openly and sanctioned by the law—which will provide for their early release in accordance with geopolitical and military expediency.

NOTES

*   I am grateful for the comments and suggestions made by Rachela Erel, Smadar Ben-Natan and the editors of this volume.
1.   This article regards the terms "security offenses," "security prisoners," and so on, as social and legal constructs. These terms have been adopted by the Israeli authorities (and the public in general) to describe various persons or activities perceived or presented as a security threat. (Specific, but arbitrary, definitions have been adopted for this purpose in the IPS Orders to guide the prisons administration: cf. n. 40 below.) The conduct of the authorities in this context is the subject of this article, which consequently adopts the official terminology.
2.   During the first period after the kidnapping, parallel negotiations took place for the return of Uri Regev and Ehud Goldwasser, Israeli soldiers captured by Hezbollah. The exchange indeed took place—but the soldiers were no longer alive.
3.   See C. Bell, *Peace Agreements and Human Rights*, Oxford: Oxford University Press, 2003, pp. 280ff.
4.   The differentiation between categories (b) and (c) may, however, not be clear-cut. The release of some 250 Fatah prisoners by the Israeli authorities in July 2007 appears to have been a unilateral gesture on the lines of category (c); but it seems to have been accompanied by the hope that this gesture would hasten a deal on the release of Gilad Shalit. For a comprehensive survey of prisoner releases since the beginning of the Oslo process, see Addameer, *Reaching the 'No-Peace' Agreement: The Role of Palestinian Prisoner Releases in Permanent Status Negotiations*, Jerusalem, 2009 < http://addameer.info/?cat=24&paged=3>.
5.   As with parole in Britain or the United States, the release here is, as indicated by the title of the law, subject to conditions. Unlike parole, however, there is routinely no supervision.
6.   S. 42.
7.   D. Garland, *The Culture of Control*, Oxford: Oxford University Press, 2001; C. Cavadino and J. Dignan, *The Penal System: A Comparative Approach*, London: Sage, 2006.
8.   Sec. 2 of the Law refers to two main criteria when deciding whether to grant an early release: dangerousness to the public, and whether the release of the prisoner would be appropriate. The latter criterion is elaborated in sec. 9 of the Law where, again, dangerousness plays a part. Moreover under sec. 42 (see previous note) the concept of dangerousness is specifically extended to include danger to the security of the OPT. For a critique of the concept of dangerousness in the context of social control, see J. Pratt, *Governing the Dangerous*, Annandale, New South Wales: Federation Press, 1997.

9. See sec. 9 of the Law.

10. Application to Appeal 10844/08 *Anonymous v. The State of Israel*, delivered February 1, 2009.

11. See, for example, L. Hajjar, *Courting Conflict*. Berkeley: University of California Press, 2005, p. 207, and Addameer, *Reaching the 'No-Peace' Agreement*.

12. The document is also known as the National Conciliation Document, as it was compiled by members of the different Palestinian organizations. The full text (including the revised version) is available on the *mideastweb* website <www.mideastweb.org>. On the Israeli side, the issue of prisoner release has been repeatedly raised by Ilan Paz, former Head of the Civil Administration in the West Bank.

13. See, however, the many articles authored by Kevin McEvoy in relation to Northern Ireland, some adopting a comparative approach.

14. In the original Oslo Agreement, there were no references to these topics. There were, however, "understandings" not included in the formal agreements, and the Cairo and "Oslo B" agreements included undertakings for the gradual release of prisoners (Bell, *Peace Agreements and Human Rights*; K. McEvoy, "Prisoner Release and Conflict Resolution: International Lessons for Northern Ireland," *International Criminal Justice Review*, Vol. 8, 1998, pp. 38ff.). For other occasions in which the issue arose in the course of negotiations, see Addameer, *Reaching the 'No-Peace' Agreement*.

15. Hajjar, *Courting Conflict*; Yesh Din, *Backyard Proceedings: The Implementation of Due Process Rights in the Military Courts in the Occupied Territories*, Tel Aviv, 2007.

16. A. Strasnov, *Justice under Fire: The Legal System during the Intifada*, Tel-Aviv: Yediyot Aharonot, 1994; N. Ben-isho, "On the Legal System in the Areas of Judah, Samaria and the Gaza Strip: Perspective and Trends," *Law and Army*, Vol. 18, 2005, p. 293.

17. On the tension between legalism and *realpolitik* in this area, see also McEvoy, "Prisoner Release and Conflict Resolution," p. 35.

18. For a relevant discussion, see Smadar Ben-Natan's chapter in this volume.

19. See H. Packer, "Two Models of the Criminal Process," *University of Pennsylvania Law Review*, Vol. 113, 1964, p. 1.

20. Sec. 87(a) of the Order for Security Provisions states as follows: "If the Area Commander has reasonable grounds for believing that ... security ... requires that a certain person be held in detention he may, by his signature, order that the person be detained for the period specified in the order which will not exceed six months." See, generally: E. Noon, "Administrative detention in Israel," *Plilim—Israel Journal of Criminal Law*, Vol. 3, 1993, pp. 168–98 (in Hebrew). The provisions operating in the OPT under the Order were amended in 1980, 1983 and 2005.

21. Administrative detention inside the Green Line is generally carried out pursuant to the Emergency Powers (Detention) Law, 1979. The authority to issue such an order is vested in the Defense Minister. The authority to detain "unlawful combatants" under the Incarceration of Unlawful Combatants Law, 2002, is vested in the Chief of General Staff.

22. Since the majority of prisoners, military judges and military commanders are male, the masculine form is used throughout this article.

23. See above and Ben-isho, "On the Legal System in the Areas of Judah, Samaria and the Gaza Strip."

24. There is in fact a considerable literature doubting the extent to which there is due process in the regular criminal trial. Nevertheless, military courts or tribunals are generally assumed to be inferior in this respect, as was evident in the debates surrounding the tribunals established by the US government to try the detainees of Guantanamo Bay. Sharon Weill discusses this in her chapter in this volume.

25. According to an NGO analysis, in January 2009, there were 7,720 Palestinians in Israeli prisons who were classified as security offenders, of whom 570 were administrative detainees: see Adalah, *Newsletter*, Vol. 59, April 2009 <http://www.adalah.org/newsletter/eng/apr09/apr09.html>. The number of security offenders prosecuted in the regular criminal courts is small.

26. On the Barghouti trial, see the report by Simon Foremen to the Inter-Parliamentary Union. Mr. Barghouti has recently been reelected to the Fatah Council. In keeping with the duality referred to above, he is also seen by some Israeli politicians as a future negotiating partner, and his release has been advocated by at least one government minister.

27. Sec. 87I of the Order for Security Provisions. See also sec. 4 of the Incarceration of Unlawful Combatants Law, 2002.

28. Sec. 44 of the Order for Security Provisions.

29. The law also provides for the release of prisoners in extreme cases of illness: see section 7 of the Release Law.

30. In most clemency cases, the Minister of Justice, but where the military courts are involved, the Minister of Defense.

31. Cf. L. Mallinder, *Amnesty, Human Rights and Political Transition: Bridging the Peace and Justice Divide*, Oxford: Hart. 2008.

32. The release of prisoners which took place within the framework of the Cairo Agreements, however, was sanctioned by legislation: see The Law for the Implementation of the Agreement on the Gaza Strip and the Jericho Area (Jurisdiction and Other Provisions) (Legislative Amendments), 1994.

33. See sec. 10 of the Release Law. Cf., in the context of the release of political prisoners, McEvoy, "Prisoner Release and Conflict Resolution," pp. 43–4.

34. As in the other situations discussed here, the question arises whether the minister charged with preparing the pardoning file and ultimately adding the ministerial counter-signature should be implementing the government's policy in these cases or exercising his or her own discretion.

35. A recent Further Hearing procedure in the High Court determined that the President cannot exercise this power on his own – but it certainly cannot be exercised without him.

36. C. Burris, "Re-examining the Prisoner of War Status of PLO Fedayeen," *North Carolina Journal of International Law and Commercial Regulation*, Vol. 22, 1996–97, p. 943. President Weizmann appeared to have fewer inhibitions when dealing with petitions for clemency on the part of Jews convicted of violence against Palestinians. On the other hand, he was consistent in refusing to act as a rubber-stamp in non-security cases, when asked to commute the life sentences of murderers. This was the reason for the establishment of a Special Release Board to deal with this category of prisoners—although even here the president's role was not totally excluded.

37. The HCJ generally defers to the authorities, both on the issue of procedural correctness and on the substantive issues: see, for example, HCJ 1539/05 and the precedents cited therein. However, in a minority opinion in HCJ 6316/07,

Rubinstein, J., favored the issuing of an injunction to prevent (or delay) the release of 250 prisoners and detainees.

38. Inevitably, victims and victim-sympathizers are found on both sides of the divide in these cases, depending upon whether they identify with the families of victims of terrorist acts committed by perpetrators who are candidates for release, or with the families of hostages whose release the negotiations are intended to secure.

39. See secs. 19 and 20 of the Victims' Rights Law, 2001.

40. See, for example, Addameer, *Reaching the 'No-Peace' Agreement*, p. 19, n. 71. Other criminal offenses become "security offenses" by virtue of Prison Service Order 04.05.00.

41. It is interesting to note that the United States government encountered less problems with their judicial system before they began to instigate prosecutions against the detainees; but the status and the circumstances of the apprehension of these detainees was different from the Israeli case, and it is doubtful that this solution could stand the test of the Basic Law: Dignity and Freedom of the Person.

42. To some extent there is an analogy here in sec. 68c of the Prisons Ordinance (sec. 68C), whereby certain categories of prisoners are released when the number of prisoners exceeds a maximum; but in this case no discretion is exercised, and the candidates for release are identified, by their proximity to the end of their sentences.

43. L. Sebba, "The Pardoning Power—A World Survey," *Journal of Criminal Law and Criminology*, Vol. 68, 1977, p. 83; Mallinder, *Amnesty, Human Rights and Political Transition*. In Mallinder's survey of the processes of amnesty (ibid., 30ff.), "Exercises of Executive Discretion" were the most frequent model to have been adopted, but her illustrations indicate that the survey is mainly concerned with post-conflict amnesties.

44. Sebba, ibid., p. 119.

45. Cf. R. Levy, "Pardons and Amnesties as Policy Instruments in Contemporary France,", in M. Tonry (ed.), *Crime, Punishment and Politics in Comparative Perspective* (*Crime and Justice Series*, Vol. 36), Chicago, IL: University of Chicago Press, 2007, pp. 551–90.

16
Prisoner Exchange Deals:
Between Figures and Emotions

Mounir Mansour

The record of prisoner exchanges between the Arabs and Israel is one of the most sensitive and publicly debated issues, for it concerns the lives and future of thousands of sons and daughters who await release. Release under a prisoner exchange deal holds a special place amongst prisoners, who desire this form of liberation in particular. It is different to any other type of release, such as completing the prison sentence, or release on humanitarian grounds. To be freed through an exchange reinforces a sense of belonging and brings a great sense of pride and strength, leaving those freed with an extraordinary feeling that surpasses all others. This is what I felt when I was released in an exchange in 1985.

The Arab and specifically Palestinian prisoners' movement has known numerous exchanges. Arab prisoner exchange deals through Egyptian mediation began in February 1949; while Palestinian prisoner exchange deals mediated by the PLO began in July 1968, Fatah and the Popular Front for the Liberation of Palestine (PFLP) General Command followed. There have been 36 such exchanges. I cannot list every exchange deal, but I can tell you about the deal that secured my release after I had been sentenced to life imprisonment.

The exchange that saw my release is considered the biggest exchange witnessed during the Arab–Israeli conflict, and the most momentous given that it took place in accordance with Palestinian conditions. On May 20, 1985, Israel concluded an exchange deal with the PFLP General Command, which was named Operation Gull (Nawras).[1] For its part, Israel released 1155 prisoners who were being held in various prisons; among them 883 prisoners held in the prisons situated within the Occupied Palestinian Territories (OPT), 118 prisoners who had been snatched from Ansar Prison in South Lebanon during an exchange with Fatah on 1983, and 154 detainees who had been transferred from Ansar Prison to

175

Atlit Prison during the Israeli withdrawal from South Lebanon in exchange for three Israeli soldiers captured by the PFLP: Sgt. Hezi Shai who was imprisoned during the battle of Sultan Yacoub on June 11, 1982 after he was captured by the PFLP General Command, and Yosef Grof and Nissim Salem who were imprisoned at Bahmadun in Lebanon in 1982.

There is much talk of prisoner exchange deals in terms of figures, but little is said of the tensions caused by these deals within the prisons; some of these tensions are mixed with joy and others with disappointment. Drawing from personal experience, I will attempt in the following to shed a little light on what happens inside the prisons during these deals.

The most difficult stage in a prisoner exchange is between the announcement of the possibility of a deal along with the commencement of negotiations, and the moment when it actually goes ahead. As prisoners, we are accustomed to naming this time "the period of expectation and mortifying anticipation." Perhaps the only thing that lightened its severity for us at the time was that the prisoners only learnt about it a few days before it took place. After the names of the prisoners to be released were announced, we entered a more difficult stage of dealing with the tragedy of those prisoners we would leave behind. We made every effort to cushion the blow for the prisoners who had not been chosen for release. I recall cases of refusal where prisoners set to be freed insisted that another prisoner with a longer sentence take their place.

Perhaps the most difficult situation we faced during our release was that of the prisoner Kareem Younes, sentenced to life imprisonment. It had been decided that Kareem would be released with us in 1985. All the relevant procedures were carried out for his release, just as with us; yet at the last minute, and as the deal began to take place, he was returned to his cell and his name was taken off the list. He languishes in prison until this very day. When I met him once in prison in 1993, I found him strong and forbearing, but he was very hurt by what had happened to him. Something I will never forget was what happened to Rafiq Omar al-Qasem in the desert prison of Nafha. The prison administration chose Qasem to read out the names of the prisoners to be released. When he finished reading out the list, he realized his name was not included and he would not be released. His utter shock and bewilderment echoed outside the prison. To this day and after his death, we all feel weak and powerless whenever we remember him. We almost feel responsible for what happened.

Our feelings were not simply those of disappointment; to varying extents it traumatized us all. If we were united by a desire for release from prison as soon as possible, then the time factor was very important for those of us sentenced to life, for none had a set release date. So if our release did not take place in an exchange deal, then that meant we would remain in prison for life. This is how we spent our nights and days: dreaming of a deal that would lead to what we used to term as a "laundering" for the prisons, though we understood all too well the difficulty of its actual implementation.

The atmosphere of prisoner exchange deals is filled with joy for oneself on the one hand, and on the other, with sadness for the brothers left behind in prison. On a personal note, it was difficult for me to leave behind in prison to face an unknown fate friends like Kareem Younes, whom I mentioned above, and Maher Yousef, who is also still imprisoned. Emotions were running high in those difficult days. We tried through discussion and negotiation to keep the prisoners calm and convince them that this deal was not the last and that we would never forget them. And indeed, I have since then determined to never let go of the prisoners' problem and up to this very day I have been trying to keep our promise as much as I could.

I remember, when news first got out at the beginning of the deal on Radio Monte Carlo, joy and excitement raced in all our hearts merely because the deal would finally go ahead, even though we did not yet know the specific details. After we had taken in the news a difficult debate began, along with questions and speculation. Who would be released? Would they return to their homes or be released outside the borders of the homeland, and if they did go home would the people know them and would they know the people? How would they be treated, would they be able to live outside prison? Many other questions along these lines occupied our thoughts. We could not sleep. As for the prison administration, it treated us with the usual suspicion as though nothing had or was going to happen. The first time they entered into the issue was on the day of the exchange when we were summoned to hear the names of those to be freed.

In the prison, I worked as a member of the committee that oversaw the verification of the names of the prisoners to be released. This was to check the names, so that no room would be left for the prison service to play with the official list by replacing some names with others. The original list was kept in my possession after the Red Cross representative had given it to me. The day of my release my friends Fowzi Nimer and Mohammad Abu Tir were with me.

After the names had been confirmed we were gathered together in a section of the Ramla prison, then we were moved by night to Ashkelon (Asqalan) Prison, and on the next day we were released. That was on May 20, 1985 at 9 p.m. Two military cars and one from the Red Cross accompanied us as we headed home.

In actual fact, the prisoners have a lot of say on the general conditions of the exchange deals and how those to be included on the list are chosen. The Palestinian negotiator takes into account the opinion of the prisoners, which he then works to implement. Through our understanding of the complexity of the situation, it was clear to us that it would be impossible to release all the prisoners in one go, because we did not have the bargaining power for such a deal. Most often we chose the criteria that had been adopted by all national action factions, according to the following:

1. Very long sentences/life imprisonment.
2. The length of time already spent in prison.
3. Women and girls.
4. Sick prisoners.
5. Young prisoners/minors.

As for myself, I was released after having spent 13 years in prison since my arrest on November 15, 1972 during armed clashes with the Israeli Army close to Nahariya. I was chosen to be included in the exchange for reasons to do with the Palestinian leadership outside and perhaps because at the time I was a representative of the National Prisoners' Movement and of the inmates in Ramla Prison. The issue of my Israeli citizenship did not make my chances of release any better. Things have worsened since then. In recent years, Israel has absolutely refused to include the names of Palestinians who carry Israeli citizenship in prisoner exchanges. Israel describes its refusal as being based on political considerations: it considers the demand to release its Palestinian citizens in exchange deals as Palestinian interference in an internal Israeli matter, that is, the relationship between Israel and its own citizens.

Yet despite my release, I have suffered and continue to suffer many curtailments on my freedom of movement and my work and activities in solidarity with the prisoners. When I was released in 1985, I was prohibited from leaving my village for three months and my passport was confiscated for three years. Other sanctions were also imposed, for example, sanctions that limited my employment opportunities; moreover, provocative searches of my home were conducted, and sometimes resulted in the confiscation of every material that was relevant to the prisoners and my work for their cause. Two associations for which I worked to defend the rights of Palestinian prisoners were closed by order of the Israeli Minster of Defense. All this was done under the pretext of national security.

NOTES

1. For Galilee. The exchange is better known as "Jibril's exchange" on the name of Ahmad Jibril, the founder and leader of the PFLP General Command.

Part III
Inside Prison

17
Female Prisoners and the Struggle: A Personal Testimony

Ittaf Alian (Hodaly)

For a Palestinian woman to become involved in any political or military activities is not coincidental. The Occupation has left her harmed; it has molested her land, children, husband and family and changed the course of her life. The collective suffering influences her directly and makes it impossible for her to detach herself from her surroundings.

Ever since I was young, I believed that women should be entitled to greater roles than the ones allowed within Arab and Palestinian realities. Comparing the role of women in Islamic history books and our present reality reveals a large gap between the two eras on intellectual, theoretical and practical levels. The Quran addresses women and men alike, as cited: "I do not waste the effort of any of you whether a male or a female for you are both equal." Women enjoyed a powerful presence and obtained important positions during Prophet Mohammad's time. On the other hand, in our days, women's roles are being dominated by backward mentalities which challenge their involvement in the society and limit their roles to traditional functions. I was determined to change this prominent negative role of women into a positive and constructive one.

I was honored to experience the Jihad (national struggle) with much confidence and competence, proving to myself and others that women's involvement in the struggle is not to be questioned, except maybe for those who intend to marginalize the Palestinian struggle. If colonizers succeed in keeping women away from lining up at battle side by side with men, they achieve victory even before battle had started.

USE OF AGGRESSION AGAINST WOMEN DURING DETENTION AND INTERROGATIONS

At first when I joined the resistance act, my function was limited to offering logistical services and intercommunications among resistance groups. Later on, my responsibility was modified to direct resistance actions involving a full membership in a military cell. Thus, I was the first woman to take the mission of executing Jihad actions for an Islamic resistance movement. In 1985, I was assigned to carry out a martyrdom operation with a car bomb in the Government Buildings in Sheikh Jarrah neighborhood. Planning the operation took two years, and just before the intended execution of the operation, in 1987, I was arrested.

I was detained for more than 40 forty days during which I underwent the worst of all kinds of torture. Male interrogators used, intentionally, particular investigation methods to interrogate female detainees, mainly through enforcing their superiority as men and as investigators. During detention, my most basic needs were not met. For instance, I was not provided with hygienic pads to use during menstrual periods so that I had to tear the dirty bedcover and use it as a pad; I was not allowed to bathe or change my clothes for the ones given by the Red Cross. The interrogators abused the fact that I was religious to desecrate me, call me names and to violate me. I remember that one of them had forcefully removed my veil and torn my traditional *jilbab* and threatened to molest me sexually. Moreover, I was exposed to excessive beatings that led to breaking my nose and one of my fingers.

Psychological torture methods were deployed similar to the ones used with male detainees, such as imprisoning a family member to put pressure on the detained so he/she will confess. However, I can recall a few things I was told mainly because I was a woman which had negative influence on me. The interrogators worked hard to create in me a feeling of isolation and loneliness. They held me in isolation cells and kept repeating common Arabic proverbs about abandonment and exploitation, such as "You fall inside the fence while others eat the chickens," and "One hundred eyes cry but your mother's eyes do not cry for you." It was clear they wanted me to think that as an Arab woman I was exploited and taken advantage of to promote the interests of the "masculine and patriarchal Arab Islamic society."

Detained mothers get special treatment in interrogations as well as during detention. In 2003, I was taken from home when my daughter Aishah was less than 18 months of age. The hardest thing was to be deprived from seeing and holding her. I had to endure a hunger strike for 16 days in order to put pressure on the prison's administration to bring my child to prison. I was then 44 years old and the hunger strike was exceedingly difficult for me; nevertheless, my yearning to be with my daughter pushed me to fight for this to happen. Aishah stayed in prison with me until she turned 2 and then she was taken away from me and I only got to hug her again when I was acquitted and released.

Assaulting and humiliating Palestinian women was not limited to female suspects and detainees; other women were also harassed in order to put pressure on their brothers, husbands and loved ones during interrogations. Women are brought to the interrogation room, they are humiliated and are forcefully undressed, in order to weaken the men and break their willpower. Another manner of using women is when the interrogators tell detainees bad news about their wives' manners or behavior, with the intention of harming their relationship and damaging their marriages.

PORTRAYING WOMEN AS VICTIMS AND OBLITERATING THEIR ROLE IN RESISTANCE

The interrogators repeatedly offered to release me or reduce my penalty if I only admitted that all I had done was against my will, that I had been submissive and fearful of men. I have rejected the offer unhesitatingly. My act of resistance wasn't motivated by anything like fear, subordination, or an attempt to "remove a cone of shame," or any personal problem of this kind. Unfortunately, many people assume that women's involvement in national struggles must have a reason behind it, such as a failed love story, illegitimate relationships with men, or subjection to violence, rather than strong political vision or belief.

Rejecting this approach is for me not merely subjective; I have proved it scientifically as well. In 2000, during my Bachelor degree studies in the Social Sciences Program, I conducted a study which indicated that society's perception of women who are freedom fighters is distorted. Although women might have personal tragedies or societal challenges, this doesn't necessarily mean that they are discharged of political or national objectives. As part of this study, I met 15 Palestinian women who had experienced detention. The main result of the study was that over two-thirds of these women were influenced by the Occupation and the atrocities they witnessed on the television, and they had decided on revenge.

NEGATIVE AND POSITIVE ASPECTS OF WOMEN'S DETENTION

Undoubtedly, the detention experience has some positive influence on women. On being detained, women are taken away from their homes, families and surrounding environment; although they are then forced to resist their occupier and jailer, they are liberated from the internal social struggle and gain their independence. The detention experience makes the father's role one of support of and solidarity with the detained daughter, granting her more confidence and strength.

In prison, women are influenced by each other; they are challenged to develop their skills. I have witnessed women developing leadership skills and becoming active, in contrast to what they were before detention. The organizational structure, including working committees and political movements inside prison, provide women with more personal and leadership development opportunities than in the outside world, enabling them to become leaders within their communities. As for myself, I can say that although I had a certain amount of autonomy before I was arrested, my detention experiences offered me the highest levels of independency and mobility.

It is very important to emphasize that the experiences of Palestinian women in their national struggle have proven no less successful than those of men. I, for example, set a record in the number and duration of hunger strikes initiated in protest against the harassment and sufferings I went through for 4½ years. I have set the longest record in the history of the Palestinian prisoners' movement with my 40-day hunger strike in objection to my administrative detention.

As women, our achievements inside prison were at times greater than those of our male fellow prisoners. For instance, when the occupation forces tried to classify the prisoners and divide them in preparation for a prisoners' exchange deal, all women took a firm decision to reject this deal, while the male prisoners adopted the position of "accept and demand." Remarkably, those who accepted the deal back then were not released and some of them are in prison up to this very day.

When women are released, they have high expectations and aspirations for making significant changes in their personal lives. Many of them initiate unique developmental programs for women and children. I myself have established a kindergarten and an elementary school that I run myself. Ibtisam Issawi, a woman who spent 15 years in detention, had established—along with several ex-detainee women and prisoner's wives—a charity organization upon her release. They started by carrying out educational and cultural activities; later, they established a kindergarten, a school, a surgery clinic and a health centre. Aishah Odeh, who was deported following her release in 1979, became a member in the National Palestinian Council in 1981.

Unfortunately, there are also negative aspects of women's detention. These are manifest in the various attempts and efforts for excluding and alienating ex-detainee women after their release. Even given the compassion of the Palestinian nation towards prisoners, the reality proves otherwise. For example, marrying an ex-prisoner raises various controversies and is usually accompanied by fear, doubt and the wish to keep a distance; as the saying goes, "Praise the evil from afar." There are only few exceptions, mainly those who experienced detention themselves and therefore pay more respect for detained women. Among them is my husband and companion Walid Al Hodali. Many people advised him not to marry me because of my detention, claiming that I might be detained over and over again, that I have a strong personality and that I would bring him trouble.

Some families impose limitations on women after their release, such as banning them from pursuing their education, or having any social involvement. Families of political prisoners in general—and prisoners' wives in particular—need strong moral support. They may get financial support, but what they actually need much more has to do with their value as a human being.

To sum up, I would like to state that the freedom of a nation is intertwined with the freedom of its women and vise versa; therefore, I believe that as Palestinians we will not be able to end the Occupation unless we unleash our women from their social restraints and empower them to take a genuine and active role in both political and social struggles. Having had the experience of national political struggle, I say with confidence that women's struggle is not limited to the national resistance; rather, it includes also the long wait for the return of a detained husband, being a provider for the family during his absence, guaranteeing her children a good future and above all, fighting to improve her society while living under a vicious Occupation and oppressive political conditions.

18
Devil's Island: The Transfer of Palestinian Detainees into Prisons within Israel

Michael Sfard

THE PROBLEM: THE PRISON ACROSS THE BORDER

Hamed[1] hasn't seen his mother for four years. He hasn't seen his brothers and sisters ever since his arrest, 24 years ago. He has brothers who were born after his arrest, whom he has never met. But most troubling for Hamed, so he told me when last I met him, is his concern that he will never again see his 75-year-old mother who is ill.

With all the checkpoints, the fences, the monstrous bureaucracy requiring three permits—a permit from the military to enter Israel, a permit from the Civil Administration to pass through the Seam Zone,[2] a permit from the Israeli Prison Service (IPS) to hold the specific visit, and the involvement of the General Security Service (GSS) and the Israeli Police in the process of clarifying entitlement to all these permits—the chance of Hamed's mother ever being able to visit him again, in her medical state, is very slim. No more than 80 kilometers separate Ramallah and Ashkelon, the Israeli city where the prison in which Hamed is held is located, and yet Ashkelon, for the residents of Ramallah, is like Devil's Island for the residents of Paris. A penal colony somewhere across mountains and oceans: mountains of movement prohibitions and preventions and an ocean of walls, checkpoints and a bureaucracy of segregation.

Hamed, resident of a Ramallah suburb, was arrested in 1985 and convicted for involvement in the murder of a Palestinian suspected of cooperating with the Israeli Defense Force (IDF). He was sentenced by the military court in Ramallah to serve a life sentence. At an early stage of his incarceration, he was transferred from a holding facility in the West Bank to a prison in Israel. Disconnection from his family is a direct result of his being held in Israel. Had he served his sentence in the West Bank, his parents would not have needed entry permits to Israel in order to visit him. The prohibition imposed by Israel preventing young Palestinians from entering its boundaries, a prohibition resulting in Hamed not seeing his brothers and sisters for so many years, would have been irrelevant, had he been incarcerated in the West Bank.

The holding of detainees and prisoners of an occupied territory within the territory of the occupying state creates an assortment of problems, of which Hamed's case represents only one aspect. Transferring the detainees to incarceration facilities outside of the occupied territory severs, in one fell swoop, their contacts with their community, their lawyers and their families, and uproots them from their organic environment. Such forced transfer makes fundamental rights of prisoners and detainees impractical or turns them into privileges subject to the whim of the hosting state.

When a forced transfer of an individual prisoner from the occupied territory to the territory of the occupying state takes place, his individual fundamental rights are being violated. However, when thousands and tens of thousands of prisoners and detainees, residents of the occupied territory, are forcibly held outside it, this has a collective significance. An entire sector of the society from which the prisoners come is removed from its homeland. It is therefore not only the systemic violation of individual fundamental rights at a scale of thousands and tens of thousands, but also a severe injury to the community, from whose land thousands of sons and daughters are being forcefully removed. Whether we see this as a violation of collective rights of the Palestinian community, or as a violation of the individual rights of each and every prisoner, deriving from their membership in the collective group, this constitutes an additional violation, on top of the violation of each and every prisoner's fundamental right to have contact with their family. The forced mass transfer of prisoners outside the West Bank constitutes a violation of their right to live in their homeland and amongst their people, even as prisoners.

These are the reasons why international humanitarian law, in its branch dealing with occupation, completely forbids the transfer of prisoners and detainees, individually or in mass, outside of the occupied territory. This is why occupation laws positively determine that detainees shall be arrested and brought to trial in the occupied territory and that prisoners shall serve their sentence within it.

The State of Israel is flagrantly violating these norms of international law. This violation has harsh implications in the three aspects mentioned earlier: the practice of prisoners' rights to have contact with the outside world, especially their families and relatives; the ability of detainees held suspect for offenses to make use of the right of due process and properly participate in their own defense in criminal trial; the ability of convicted prisoners to be represented by attorneys of their own people in all matters pertaining to the conditions of their imprisonment and other matters; and the ability of the Palestinian community to have community life with the participation of a significant part of the community—its prisoners.

THE HOLDING OF DETAINEES AND PRISONERS IN ISRAEL: FIGURES AND RAMIFICATIONS

In March 2009, 8,171 Palestinians were being held in detention or incarceration for security reasons by Israeli authorities. These are divided into categories according to the following segmentation:[3] of the 8,171 security prisoners, 1,052 were being held, as of March 2009, in the Ofer base, a military base located in the West Bank, south of Ramallah. This means that *in March 2009, 7,119 Palestinian prisoners, detainees and administrative detainees were being held in prison and detention facilities within the territory of the State of Israel.*

The transfer of these thousands of prisoners outside of the Occupied Palestinian Territories (OPT) in effect stripped them of many significant rights to which they are entitled according to basic legal standards. This stems from the closure policy imposed on the Palestinian residents of the West Bank by Israel since the early 1990s. The gist of this policy is the abolition of the general permit issued to the Palestinians of the West Bank and the Gaza Strip, in the early days of occupation, by Defense Minister Moshe Dayan, to freely enter and move within the territory of Israel. The new policy criminalized the act of entry without an individual permit. In fact, entry without permit of a Palestinian resident of the West Bank into Israel constitutes a criminal offense according to both Israeli law and the military law applying in the West Bank.[4] During the first decade of the twenty-first century, the closure policy was accompanied by a massive-scale project of constructing a physical barrier, separating the State of Israel and parts of the West Bank from the vast majority of the Palestinian populace. The separation fence redivided the area between the Jordan River and the Mediterranean Sea in a manner to create an unhindered continuity of land from the sea to the fence, including approximately 9 percent of the West Bank (between the fence and the Green Line), this being the "Seam Zone." In order for the wall to be effective in preventing (only) Palestinians from coming through from the eastern ("Palestinian") side to the western ("Israeli") side, the separation wall system includes not only fences, patrol roads, concrete walls and other physical features, but also a monstrous legal permit regime, allowing for the filtration of those seeking passage through gates installed in the fence. The permit regime is a legal mechanism, which includes a declaration of the Seam Zone—that is, the entire area between the fence and the Green Line—as a closed military zone, a zone into which entry is prohibited and which compels those within it to exit, and a bureaucratic system of permit issuing to farmers, tradesmen and permanent residents in the Seam Zone.[5]

Thus, since the early 1990s, and more rigorously in the first decade of the twenty-first century, the implication of a Palestinian detainee being held in Israel has been the severing of his ties to his community and family. The permit system—to enter Israel, to pass through the Seam Zone, to meet with the prisoner—created a reality of disconnection for hundreds and thousands of prisoners. According to activity reports for 2000–06 of HaMoked, family visits were prevented in this manner; on some occasions, no visits of any kind took place for many months, and in some cases years.[6]

This disconnection is especially grave with regard to detainees not yet tried. These individuals have difficulties in meeting with their attorneys, and are therefore denied the possibility of properly preparing their defense. A research report prepared by Israel human rights organization Yesh Din, regarding the implementation of due process rights in military courts in the West Bank, based on over a thousand observation visits made by its volunteers, reveals a very harsh picture.[7] The state of affairs described in the report can be viewed by anyone visiting the military courts: attorneys meet their clients for the very first time in the court compound, where the latter are brought from their detention facilities in Israel. At best, the guards allow the attorneys to meet their clients for a few minutes in the overcrowded holding cells where detainees await the hearing on their matter. At other times, the first encounter takes place in a military courtroom, and one may occasionally observe a client and attorney getting acquainted for the first time, whispering in the courtroom, while another case is being discussed.[8]

The fact that lawyers cannot meet their clients in reasonable conditions and have free access to them violates the right of defendants to consult with their attorneys and prepare an effective defense. The possibility of having attorney-client meetings under appropriate conditions, and an unhindered access of lawyers to their clients, constitute fundamental preconditions to the realization of due process. The current state of affairs does not allow this to happen, and, alongside other reasons mentioned in detail in Yesh Din's report, brings pressure to bear on defendants to accept plea bargains with the military prosecution. In the absence of the appropriate ability to meet with an attorney and prepare a legal defense, the belief (inasmuch as it existed) in the possibility of facing the criminal procedure and in its fairness evaporates completely.

In actual fact, of all Palestinian defendants held in Israel, only those retaining the services of Israeli lawyers or lawyers who are Israeli residents (for example, lawyers from East Jerusalem) are able to conduct a full evidence trial. It is therefore no wonder that the number of cases in the military courts in which a full evidence trial was conducted is miniscule: according to the Yesh Din research, only 1.42 percent of the cases concluded in 2006 had full evidence trials, while the rest took the path of plea bargains.[9]

And there's more. Another violation of due process rights— *which derives from the holding of detainees in Israel in a reality of closure*—is the *de facto* violation of the right to a public hearing. This is a result of the fact that Israel not only holds Palestinian detainees and prisoners in its territory, but also conducts some of the detention hearings in "branches" of the military courts which were also transferred into its territory.

The significance of the public hearing principle derives from the idea that without publicity, public scrutiny of legal proceedings cannot take place, and as this is absent, concerns for the miscarriage of justice grow. This is one of the most important principles in the due process group of rights.

However, some of the hearings regarding remands and arrest extensions of Palestinian suspects take place in branches of the military courts within the territory of Israel: at the Petah-Tikva police station, at Ktzi'ot (Ansar) Prison in the Negev, at the Kishon detention facility, at the Russian Compound in West Jerusalem. The branches of the military courts in Israel were established for the purposes of the ease of interrogation: as detention and interrogation facilities are located in Israel, transporting detainees to the courts in the West Bank for remand hearings would "waste" interrogation time and place a logistic burden on the authorities. Thus, in order to conduct remand proceedings close to the interrogation facilities, branches of the military courts in the West Bank were established inside Israel. As part of the policy of closure over the OPT, Israel does not allow the families and defense attorneys of the detainees to attend these hearings. Hence, the location of remand hearing courtrooms inside the territory of Israel completely prevents the relatives of the Palestinian detainees from observing these hearings and thwarts the principle of public hearing.

Thus, the ramification of the changed reality—the hermetic sealing of Israel against Palestinians residing in the West Bank, as described above—is that the holding of Palestinian administrative detainees, criminal detainees and prisoners from the West Bank, in Israeli territory, violates a group of fundamental rights which, absent the said change, might have not been violated so severely. Among these rights can be listed *the right to legal counsel*, in the sense that such legal counseling and representation will not only exist formally but be real and effective, *the right to mount a proper legal defense, the right to public hearing*. All these are basic due process guarantees, without which the danger of miscarriage of justice is imminent and of course in addition, *the right to lead a family life* and especially to have contact with family members is also severely violated.

Until now, we have mainly discussed the violation of due process rights of detainees not yet tried. However, one must remember that prisoners already tried, who are serving their sentence and being held in Israel, also require legal representation—for the purpose of appeal, applications for a new trial, matters regarding the conditions of their imprisonment and also matters unrelated to their incarceration. The procedural rights of these prisoners are violated in a manner similar to that of those not yet tried.

THE LEGAL OBLIGATION TO HOLD DETAINEES AND PRISONERS— RESIDENTS OF AN OCCUPIED TERRITORY—*IN* THE OCCUPIED TERRITORY

As is commonly known, the West Bank is an occupied territory. It was belligerently occupied during an armed conflict, in a war between Israel and several Arab states including Jordan, in 1967. The international laws of war (also referred to as international humanitarian law) legally regulate the Do's and Don'ts in a case an armed conflict between states leads to a situation where the military forces of one state effectively controls a territory outside the sovereign borders of that state. This branch of international law—called the "international law of belligerent occupation"—is regulated by general principles of international law, by treaties, resolutions and declarations of states and of international organs. The two main treaties codifying the laws of occupation are the Fourth Hague Convention respecting the Laws and Customs of War on Land, 1907 and the Fourth Geneva Convention relative to the Protection of Civilian Persons in Time of War, 1949. Both Conventions contain a chapter pertaining to a situation of belligerent occupation, which include provisions determining the authority of the occupying power (the state conquering the territory), its duties, its powers and the rights of the conquered civilians (defined as "protected persons" in the Fourth Geneva Convention).

Three provisions of the Geneva Convention also deal with the issue of holding prisoners and detainees of an occupied territory. These provisions are clear and unequivocal, and categorically prohibit the removal of prisoners and detainees to detention facilities outside the occupied territory. To cite the provisions (all emphasis are mine):

Article 76 of the Convention:
Protected persons accused of offences shall be detained in the occupied country, and if convicted they shall serve their sentences therein … .

Article 66 of the Convention:
In case of a breach of the penal provisions promulgated by it [the occupying power] by virtue of the second paragraph of Article 64, the Occupying Power may hand over the accused to its properly constituted, non-political military courts, *on condition that the said courts sit in the occupied country.* Courts of appeal shall preferably sit in the occupied country.

And Article 49 of the Convention:
Individual or mass forcible transfers, as well as deportations of protected persons from occupied territory to the territory of the Occupying Power or to that of any other country, occupied or not, *are prohibited, regardless of their motive … .*

While Article 49 sets forth the principle rule and prohibits any type of forced transfer of citizens of the occupied territory outside that territory, whether they are suspect of committing offenses, convicted persons, or just innocent civilians, Article 76 speaks specifically of defendants and convicted prisoners, and clearly determines that they "shall be detained in the occupied country," and if convicted "shall serve their sentences therein."

It is commonly believed that these provisions were included in the Convention in order to prevent the practice that brought about long years of disconnection between prisoners and their families, as the Convention drafters had in their mind's eye the massive forced transfers of populations performed by the Nazis during World War II. Accordingly, the purpose of these prohibitions is twofold: to prevent demographic changes in the occupied territory by means of deportations and forced transfers, but also to protect the rights of the individual not to be disconnected from family, community, people and country.

It would be difficult to dispute the fact that the Israeli policy—to hold thousands of the prisoners of the occupied territory in Israel—constitutes, at least in a textual sense, an obvious and blatant violation of the provisions of the Geneva Convention, by which it is obviously bound as an occupying power. In the past, the State of Israel may have been able to argue that this is only a "technical" violation, since the potential harm to the prisoners and detainees that these provisions aim to prevent did not in actuality take place, as there used to be free movement between the West Bank and Israel and therefore the transferee did not suffer disconnection from his family and community. However, nowadays, in an era of closures, segregation and prohibition to enter Israel, one can hardly dispute the fact that the violation is substantive, that the danger which the Geneva Convention sought to prevent is actually taking place.

FROM THE SAJADIA JUDGMENT TO THE YESH DIN JUDGMENT: THE SUPERIORITY OF ISRAELI LAW AND THE PATERNALISM OF THE CONQUEROR

The legality of the policy of holding Palestinian prisoners and detainees, residents of the West Bank, in Israel, was challenged twice in the Israeli High Court of Justice (HCJ): once at the close of the 1980s, just before the closure policy came into being, while the state could still argue that inasmuch as a violation occurs, it is merely "technical"; and again, 20 years later, after the area was bound in the web of segregation and the permit regime, in 2010.

The first attempt to prevent the transfer of prisoners and detainees to Israel took place in 1988.[10] A group of administrative detainees, incarcerated at the Ktzi'ot (Ansar) base in the Negev, filed a petition with the HCJ, arguing that according to Article 49 of the Geneva Convention, and by analogy to Article 76 (which does not apply to administrative detainees but only to pre-trial detainees and convicted prisoners), their transfer outside of the occupied territory is prohibited. At the time the petition was filed, only a small proportion of Palestinian prisoners were held in Israel, in two detention facilities: Ktzi'ot, and Megiddo prisons. The majority of Palestinian prisoners were held in prisons located in the large towns of the West Bank. Visits from families and attorneys were not a problem at the time, as the closure barring Israel to the residents of the West Bank was not yet declared. The Court denied the petition, mainly on grounds of the three following determinations: (a) Article 49 does not apply to the transfer of prisoners but to the forcible relocation of entire populations (there was dissent in this matter, and this was the ruling of the majority, Chief Justice Meir Shamgar and Justice Menachem Elon; Justice Gabriel Bach disputed this interpretation of Article 49 and opined that Israel is violating this provision). (b) Even if Israel is violating Article 49, a contradicting local law (Israeli law), allowing Israeli authorities to hold Palestinian prisoners and detainees in Israel, supersedes. In this matter, the judges relied on a doctrine accepted in most countries in the world, whereby in a frontal conflict between local law and a norm of international law and inability to resolve the two norms, the local court must apply the municipal law.[11] (c) Article 76 does not apply to administrative detainees, as it speaks of those "accused" and of those "convicted," while these administrative detainees were never accused and in any case never convicted.[12] The judges were not required to discuss the question of family or attorney visits, as at the time the issue was not yet a problem. In fact, the Court was only required to address the "technical" violation of international law.

Twenty years later, following the publication of the Yesh Din report, *Backyard Proceedings*, three Israeli human rights organizations involved in promoting rights of Palestinian prisoners and detainees—Yesh Din, the Association for Civil Rights in Israel and HaMoked—joined forces to file a new petition in the matter, to once again challenge the policy, this time through bringing to the forefront the "substantive" violation, which is no longer a vague danger but an actual wrong. The petition was filed in 2009, and requested the HCJ to rule that the policy of holding in Israel those Palestinian detainees, prisoners and administrative detainees who are residents of the West Bank, and conducting remand proceedings in branches of the military courts in Israel—is illegal.[13]

A major change occurred in the period between the first judgment (the "Sajadia judgment") and the filing of the second petition (the "Yesh Din petition"), not only with regard to the freedom of movement for Palestinians between Israel and the West Bank, but also in the scale of prisoners and detainees held in Israel. After the Oslo Accords and the ending of permanent IDF presence at the centers of Palestinian cities, all Israeli prisons in the West Bank were closed, and with the exception of one facility, Palestinian prisoners were distributed between prisons across Israel. Thus the exception became the rule.

In the Yesh Din petition, the human rights organizations argued that the Sajadia judgment applies only to administrative detainees, and therefore the holding of criminal prisoners must be reviewed in accordance with the prohibition in Article 76. It was further argued that in light of the violation becoming "substantive" and in light of the actual violation of fundamental rights of the prisoners and detainees, the Israeli law allowing the holding of Palestinian prisoners from the West Bank in Israel must be narrowly interpreted. The petitioners proposed an interpretation whereby the discretion of the authorities in transferring a prisoner to Israel must be such as will prevent as much as possible the violation of international law, by determining, for example, that only in cases where a Palestinian prisoner cannot be held in the West Bank (because he faces mortal danger there, or because he requires medical treatment unavailable in the West Bank, and so forth)—only then shall the prisoner's detention in Israel be allowed. Another argument was that in any event, a policy of holding all or the majority of prisoners in Israel and completely refraining from attempting to find incarceration solutions in the West Bank cannot be allowed.

The HCJ denied this petition as well. This time, contrary to the reasoning of the Sajadia judgment, the judges made no attempt to argue that the policy conforms to international law. Even the interpretational virtuosity of Chief Justice Shamgar in the Sajadia case was to no avail in the face of such a clear provision as the prohibition set forth in Article 76 of the Geneva Convention ("shall be detained in the occupied country ... [and] serve their sentences therein"). Instead, the HCJ judges adhered to the principle of the superiority of local law over international law.[14] It is interesting that in addition to this determination, which brought an end to the petitioners' arguments, the judges also expressed their opinion whereby the holding of the prisoners in Israel is *beneficiary both to the prisoners and to their people*:

> ... the facilities of the Israel Prison Service, as well as the incarceration facility in Ofer base in the Seam Zone, have seen

great improvements in the holding conditions of the detainees, and the possibility of reviewing the conditions, making grievances regarding them, or adding and improving them, is much greater than it had been in the incarceration facilities under military control and those located in the area ... .

Under the current circumstances one must consider the practical ramifications of constructing new incarceration facilities in the area at the scale required after IDF forces have left the cities in which facilities were located in the past, a construction project that may harm both the detainees and the conditions of their detention, and the local residents on whose lands the facilities would be constructed.[15]

On reading the judgment, one is asked to believe that it is not for its own political, logistical and financial convenience that Israel holds the prisoners and detainees of Palestine in its territory. *It is for the Palestinians' own sake* that we do so. So that we would not have to misappropriate even more lands to build prisons on, so that incarceration conditions would be properly sanitary, so that prisoners may file petitions and enjoy modern judicial review procedures regarding the conditions of their incarceration. This judgment is a part of a central genre in Israeli case law regarding the OPT, wherein Israel's injurious actions which constitute a violation of international law find their reasoning in the well-being of the injured occupied subject. The logic path of reasoning of this genre intensifies the exclusion processes of the injured people by denying them the slight advantage they supposedly always have over their oppressor: their moral status as victims. The paternalism underlying the determination whereby although the injured party or their representatives seek to abolish a certain policy or practice, the strong, ruling party knows what is best for the injured party, takes away from the victim the acknowledgment of the price it is paying for the interests of the strong party. In the Yesh Din judgment, this reasoning is made through referring to the alternative (the establishment of detention and incarceration facilities in the West Bank) as if, in case it takes place, it would be executed by a completely different authority, over which the State of Israel has no control. For, what are the HCJ judges telling us? They are saying that while in Israel it is possible to ensure appropriate conditions of incarceration and detention and proper judicial review, over there—in a far, uncharted land—the West Bank, only God knows what would happen. As if this is an extradition to another country, to a government over which we have no power. As if it is not the same power that rules, for over four decades, over both sides of the Green Line.

NOTES

1. The name is fictitious, the account is true.
2. The Seam Zone is the area enclosed between the separation fence erected by Israel inside the West Bank territory and the Green Line demarcating it (the armistice line of the 1949 Rhodes Armistice Agreements). Since 2002, the Seam Zone has been gradually declared a "closed military zone," that is, an area in which Palestinians may not stay and which they may not enter without permit from the Military Commander. Tourists and Israelis have a general permit and they do not require an individual permit. The Seam Zone comprises an area of approximately 9 percent of the West Bank.
3. Data from human rights organization HaMoked—Center for the Defense of the Individual (hereafter HaMoked), based on data received from the IPS.
4. Sec. 12 of the Entry to Israel Law, 5712-1952. In military legislation, the West Bank was declared a closed military zone, the exit of which requires a permit from the Military Commander. Violation of this declaration bears a penalty of five years' imprisonment (Sections 90, 92 of the Decree regarding Security Provisions (Judea and Samaria) (no. 378).
5. Declaration regarding the Closure of an Area no. C/2/03 (the Seam Zone), dated October 2, 2003, declared the area between the Green Line and the separation fence a closed military zone. Provision regarding Permit for Permanent Residents in the Seam Zone (Judea and Samaria), 5764-2003 and Provisions regarding Entry Permits to the Seam Zone and Staying Within (Judea and Samaria), 5764-2003 (both signed on October 7, 2003); these instituted the bureaucratic mechanism for the granting of entry permits to the Zone for Palestinian residents of the Seam Zone and the owners of farmlands and businesses. Various amendments have since been introduced both to the Declaration and the Provisions, but the principle remained the same. For further reading regarding the separation fence see the book I co-authored with LTC (res.) Shaul Arieli, *The Wall of Folly* (published in Hebrew as "Fence and Failure: the Separation Fence—Security or Greed?" by Aliyat HaGag Publishing, 2008), hereafter: "Fence and Failure." A petition challenging the legality of the "permit regime" was filed by HaMoked, and is still pending (HCJ 9961/03 *HaMoked v. Government of Israel*. I represent the petitioner in this case). Another petition filed regarding the legality of the permit regime is the petition of the Association for Civil Rights in Israel (HCJ 639/04).
6. See Anat Barsella and Sigi Ben-Ari's chapter in the present volume.
7. See *Backyard Proceedings: The Implementation of Due Process Rights in the Military Courts in the Occupied Territories*, Yesh Din, December 2007, p. 108.
8. Palestinian Attorney Fares Abu-Hassan describes the problem of Palestinian attorneys representing detainees in the Military Courts in ibid., p. 109.
9. Full evidence trials took place in 130 of the 9,123 cases concluded that year: ibid., p. 136.
10. HCJ 253/88 *Ibrahim Hameed Sajadia v. Minister of Defense*, judgment dated November 8, 1988, IsrLR 42(3), 801.

11. Regarding the superiority of local law over norms of international law see CivA 25/55 *Trustee of Absentees' Assets v. Samara*, IsrLR 10, 1829-1831, and also in HCJ 253/88 *Sajadia v. Minister of Defense* IsrLR 42(3), 801, paragraph 6 of the opinion of Chief Justice Shamgar; these judgments determine the superiority of a local law over a norm set forth in a treaty (international treaties law). A similar principle was determined also regarding norms originating in international *customary* law, that is, what is practiced by most nations and therefore regarded as binding even nations not signing it—in CriA 336/61 *Eichmann v. Attorney General*, IsrLR 16, 2033, at p. 2040. These principles were adopted into Israeli law from the English common law.

12. It is of interest to note the absurdity of adopting an anti-textual interpretational approach toward Article 49, whereby it applies only to the deportation and forced relocation of entire populations (contrary to its language, which specifically says: "Individual or mass forcible transfers ... of protected persons ... are prohibited"), while adopting a narrowly textual approach to Article 76, whereby it does not apply to administrative detainees, as they were not "accused" or "convicted."

13. HCJ 2690/09 *Yesh Din: Volunteer Organization for Human Rights et al. v. Commander of IDF Forces in the West Bank*, judgment of March 28, 2010, not yet published; I represented the petitioners in this petition.

14. See *supra* note 11.

15. Paragraphs 8, 14 of the Yesh Din judgment.

19
Family Visits to Palestinian Prisoners Held Inside Israel

Sigi Ben-Ari and Anat Barsella

The importance of family visits in prison cannot be overstated, particularly in the case of prisoners labeled "security prisoners," who are subject to an occupying regime, often sentenced for many years, held far from their homes and denied any other contact with their loved ones. Unlike any other prisoners inside the prison, contacts between Palestinian prisoners and their families are at the mercy of an occupying army, changes in the security situation and shifting political interests. These and other factors have often prevented, sometimes for years, contacts between the prisoners and their closest relatives—spouses, children and parents.

We begin with the importance of the right to family life and its enshrinement in international and Israeli law, followed by a review of the arrangements for family visits in prisons and the many restrictions imposed on them. We conclude with a description of the hardships the relatives face on the day of the visit itself.

THE RIGHT TO FAMILY VISITS AND FAMILY LIFE

The right to family visits in prison facilities is a fundamental right of both the prisoners and their families. It is a basic right which stems from the perception of humans as social creatures living in families and communities.

Preventing family visits with incarcerated loved ones severely infringes upon the fundamental right of the relatives and the prisoners to family life. Society has always treated the right to family life as a supreme value throughout time and across cultures. The rights of families are recognized and protected in public international law. Article 46 of the Hague Regulations stipulates: "Family honour and rights, the lives of persons, and private property, as well as religious convictions and practice, must be respected."[1]

The right to family visits is enshrined in a number of international legal sources. Among these, one may note the Fourth Geneva Convention, which stipulates in Article 116: "Every internee shall be allowed to receive visitors, especially near relatives, at regular intervals and as frequently as possible," and the UN Standard Minimum Rules for the Treatment of Prisoners, 1955 which stipulates in Article 37 that "Prisoners shall be allowed under necessary supervision to communicate with their family and reputable friends at regular intervals, both by correspondence and by receiving visits." Article 92 addresses untried detainees and stipulates that "An untried prisoner ... shall be given all reasonable facilities for communicating with his family and friends, and for receiving visits from them, subject only to restrictions and supervision as are necessary in the interests of the administration of justice and of the security and good order of the institution." It should be noted that the right to visit relatives who have been tried and imprisoned is not enshrined in Israeli legislation. The Prison Ordinance specifies only that "visits from friends may be permitted"[2] and accordingly, the Israeli Prison Service (IPS) treats family visits as a privilege that can be withheld.[3]

The right to family visits in prison facilities also stems from the concept, which governs both international and Israeli law, that the mere fact of incarceration does not deny the prisoner's fundamental rights. The walls of the prison may restrict the prisoner's freedom of movement, with all that this entails, but they do not invalidate his other fundamental rights. It follows that incarceration is not to invalidate the prisoner's right, as a human, to family life and continued contacts with his family and friends.[4]

Article 10(1) of the International Covenant on Civil and Political Rights stipulates that "All persons deprived of their liberty shall be treated with humanity and with respect for the inherent dignity of the human person." This article received a very broad interpretation by the Human Rights Committee, the organ charged with implementing the Covenant, in CCPR General Comment No. 21, dated April 10, 1992: "... respect for the dignity of such persons must be guaranteed under the same conditions as for that of free persons. *Persons deprived of their liberty enjoy all the rights set forth in the Covenant, subject to the restrictions that are unavoidable in a closed environment.*"

Articles 1 and 5 of the Basic Principles for the Treatment of Prisoners which were adopted by the UN General Assembly (in Resolution 45/111 on December 14, 1990) also set forth the principle that prisoners are entitled to all human rights with the exception of those denied as a result of the incarceration itself. Article 1 stipulates that "All prisoners shall be treated with the respect due to their inherent dignity and value as human beings." According to Article 5:

> Except for those limitations that are demonstrably necessitated by the fact of incarceration, *all prisoners shall retain the human rights and fundamental freedoms set out in the Universal Declaration of Human Rights*, and, where the State concerned is a party, the International Covenant on Economic, Social and Cultural Rights, and the International Covenant on Civil and Political Rights and the Optional Protocol thereto, as well as such other rights as are set out in other United Nations covenants.

THE ARRANGEMENTS FOR AND RESTRICTIONS ON PALESTINIANS' VISITS TO PRISONS IN ISRAEL

The right to family visits and family life is severely impinged in the framework of the arrangements for and restrictions on family visits by Palestinians from the Occupied Palestinian Territories (OPT) to their loved ones in prisons inside Israel.

The foundation for this severe impingement is the fact that Palestinian prisoners are held inside Israel in contravention of international law.[5] Article 49 of the Geneva Convention prohibits the forcible transfer of protected civilians outside the occupied territory: "Individual or mass forcible transfers, as well as deportations of protected persons from occupied territory to the territory of the Occupying Power or to that of any other country, occupied or not, are prohibited, regardless of their motive." The convention also explicitly stipulates, in Article 76, that "Protected persons accused of offences shall be detained in the occupied country, and if convicted they shall serve their sentences therein." If Palestinian prisoners were held in the OPT, at least some of the difficulties and restrictions currently imposed on family visits would have been prevented—primarily, the need for permits to enter Israel and the hardships the visitors face on the day of the visit.

Between late 2000 (the beginning of the second Intifada) and March 2003, no family visits by residents of the OPT to their loved ones in prisons were made possible. Following petitions to the High Court of Justice (HCJ) filed by HaMoked: Center for the Defense of the Individual (hereafter: HaMoked),[6] the military gradually began to allow family visits from the West Bank to imprisoned relatives. Initially, visits were allowed only from the districts of Ramallah, Jericho and Qalqiliya. During the second phase, the arrangement was extended to the districts of Bethlehem, Tulkarm and Salfit and today it includes all districts. The military established narrow criteria, defining who is entitled to visit: spouses, parents, grandparents, as well as siblings and children, all of whom must be under the age of 16 or over the age of 46. In July 2005, the military removed the age restriction on daughters and sisters eligible for visits. The military later stipulated that males between the ages of 16 and 35 could visit an incarcerated father twice a year and an incarcerated brother once a year only.

The military does not allow residents of the West Bank to arrive at the prison for the visits independently and does not itself see to any visitation arrangements, despite being obligated to do so under international law, due to its control over the OPT. The visits are organized and executed exclusively through the International Committee of the Red Cross (ICRC). Applications for visits are submitted by residents of the OPT to ICRC offices in the various districts; the ICRC submits these to the military which examines the applications and transmits its response to the ICRC, which, in turn, notifies the applicants of the answer. The ICRC also provides and pays for the transportation to the visits, in coordination with security forces and the IPS, including strict security procedures.

According to routine procedure, when an application for a prison visit is approved, the military grants the applicant a permit which is valid for three months. The military has recently begun issuing permits for six months and also a year. The permit is valid only for the ICRC prison visit shuttles and in the period of validity, one can visit the prison once every two weeks, or once a month, depending on the restrictions imposed by the IPS.

When the visits were renewed in March 2003, it soon became clear that in many cases, the military refuses to allow relatives to visit prisoners on "security grounds." This applied to a large segment of the population which was designated by the Israel Security Agency (usually referred to as GSS) as "precluded from entering Israel." Such persons were automatically denied prison visits in Israel as well.

In late 2003, following petitions filed by HaMoked against this sweeping restriction,[7] the military changed its policy and determined that in principle, individuals classified as "precluded from entering Israel" would be able to take part in ICRC-organized prison visits on condition that a GSS examination determines there is no impediment to their entering Israel solely for the purpose of prison visits. Following this policy, a new arrangement was put in place by which prison visit applications by residents of the OPT who are precluded from entering Israel are submitted to the military via the ICRC and transferred to the GSS for individual examination and screening. If there is no impediment to allow the applicant to visit his loved one in prison via the ICRC shuttles, the applicant is issued a single-use entry permit to Israel for the purpose of a prison visit, valid for 45 days. This permit, which is transferred via the ICRC allows a single prison visit and can be used on a date when there is an ICRC shuttle from the applicant's district to the prison in which his relative is held. At the end of this visit, the permit is revoked and the applicant may submit a new application via the ICRC which would then be transferred to the GSS for reexamination. So long as the security diagnosis remains unchanged, the applicant would receive a new permit of the same kind and the cycle will repeat itself.

This process which involves many agencies and necessitates individual examination by the GSS before each and every visit is cumbersome and takes several months. At best, those who are "precluded from entering Israel" are able to visit their loved ones three times a year. They are often issued a permit to enter Israel once a year only. Every year, HaMoked files dozens of petitions regarding prolonged delays in responding to prison visit applications by persons precluded from entering Israel. Of the applications by such individuals which were processed by HaMoked in 2009, some 80 percent received a response only three to eight months after the prison visit application was submitted.

Another obstacle which stands in the way of relatives from the OPT wishing to visit prisons is a regulation which stipulates that a person who was previously incarcerated for a criminal offense may not visit a prisoner in prison unless approved by the IPS commissioner (Article 30(a) of the Prison Regulations 5738-1978). This regulation has been preventing hundreds of Palestinians formerly incarcerated in IPS facilities from crossing the gates of prisons in Israel. It applies also in cases where the applicant was a prisoner 20 years ago, a detainee who was tried and acquitted, or a person who was detained but released without charges. It is possible to contact the IPS and request the preclusion be lifted, and it often is indeed lifted, yet many Palestinians are not aware of the preclusion and/or have no access to IPS officials. After waiting for many months to receive a permit to enter Israel and the excruciating journey on the ICRC bus, these individuals are unable to actually visit due to the former-prisoner preclusion imposed on them. HaMoked and the Association for Civil Rights in Israel petitioned against this arbitrary and sweeping regulation which infringes on the rights of the prisoners and their families.[8] Following the petition, some changes, mostly procedural, were made to the Prison Commission Ordinance which stipulates how the regulation is implemented. Yet, the regulation enshrining the preclusion remained intact.

PREVENTION OF FAMILY VISITS FROM GAZA

Family visits from Gaza to prisons in Israel were held, in principle, under arrangements similar to those practiced in the West Bank. On June 6, 2007, family visits from the Gaza Strip to prisons in Israel were halted. The fundamental right of some 900 prisoners from the Gaza Strip who were incarcerated in Israel at the time and that of their relatives was denied. The explanation for the revocation of prison visits was that in view of the Hamas military takeover of the Gaza Strip, there was no Palestinian agency with which to conduct security coordination of movement through the crossings which were now under the control of terrorist entities. This, despite the fact that the visits had always been coordinated through the ICRC and that it is willing to continue to coordinate the visits and calling for their reinstatement.

In June 2006, after two years during which no family prison visits were held, HaMoked and other human rights organizations[9] petitioned against the revocation of the visits, arguing that the fundamental rights of thousands of Palestinians (prisoners and their relatives) are being denied and that the state is practicing collective punishment which is prohibited under international law. In response, the state argued that the major component of the policy denying the visits is political, that the state is entitled to determine who may enter it and that residents of the Gaza Strip have no legal right to enter Israel. As for captive soldier Gilad Shalit—the state argued it was obliged to consider his matter and his return when reviewing the policy regarding entry from Gaza.

The High Court held a hearing on the petition in October 2008 and delivered its ruling a year later, in December 2009. The court found that there was no cause to intervene in the decision of the competent officials and that family visits in prisons do not amount to a basic humanitarian necessity which is incumbent on the state to provide. Thus, to this day, for almost four years, more than 700

Gazan prisoners and their relatives have been cut off from one another. Since the vast majority of them are defined "security" prisoners, they are not permitted to make telephone calls and rarely get letters from their families via the ICRC.

HARDSHIPS ON THE DAY OF THE VISIT

The trials and tribulations facing relatives of prisoners do not end once they receive the permit to enter Israel. Relatives who obtained such permits go through many hardships on the day of the visit itself. Visitors arrive at a predetermined central meeting place in one of the major cities in the West Bank. From there, they travel on buses organized by the ICRC to a checkpoint located at an entry point into Israel. For many, particularly those residing in villages around the large cities, the day begins in the early morning hours and ends well into the night as a result of the many restrictions on movement and roadblocks on the way to the meeting place.

At the checkpoint leading into Israel, following meticulous examinations of all persons and luggage, the visitors board Israeli buses, also rented by the ICRC. From the moment they leave the checkpoint until they reach the prison, the buses are accompanied by Israeli police cars. Due to the limited number of police cars allocated for accompanying the buses transporting Palestinians to the prisons, the visitors are forced to wait at the checkpoint until everyone is security screened and the buses can continue to travel together. The delay sometimes takes a few hours. The buses are prohibited from stopping and passengers cannot get off until they arrive at the prison.

The passengers arrive at the prison facility in the late morning and spend the rest of the day waiting for their turn to visit or for other visitors to finish.

The number of visitors varies on different visit days and at different facilities, but in most cases there are at least four or five buses, and sometimes as many as ten, arriving on a given day to a single facility. This is a result of the restrictions the IPS imposes on the number of visit days. The immediate effect of the large number of visitors is long waiting periods for the visit. The conditions in which visitors wait vary from one facility to another. In some facilities, the visitors wait in halls or rooms with benches, beverage vending machines and toilets. In others, visitors wait outside in both summer and winter. Sometimes, the waiting room is not large enough and has a limited number of seats and toilets which does not match the number of visitors. After waiting for many hours, the visit with the imprisoned relative lasts no longer than 45 minutes.

The many prohibitions, the long hours necessitated by each visit, the hardships on the way and the dire conditions during the wait often prevent adult relatives from visiting, particularly men who are breadwinners, as well as elderly and infirm parents. As a result of this and of the security preclusions often imposed on adult family members, in some families, only the children or minor siblings of a prisoner are able to visit. On every visit day, dozens of children aged three to 16 leave their homes in the early hours of the morning and travel alone, sometimes with another young sister or brother or a neighbor, for a visit which can take an entire day.[10]

In some facilities, the IPS holds separate visit days for criminal and "security" prisoners. IPS regulations stipulate that, with the exception of extraordinary cases, visits with criminal prisoners should be open, without barriers between prisoner and visitor, both children and adult. Visits with prisoners labeled "security" prisoners are held in complete separation. Physical contact between the prisoners and their relatives is impossible as they are separated by thick glass. Conversations are held via a telephone receiver or small holes in the plastic sheets separating between the prisoner and the visitors. The visits are held in large long halls. Prison guards walk amongst the families and dozens of relatives sitting in front of their loved ones try to listen and be heard and overcome the bustle around them.

Since the ICRC provides its visitation program without any help or support from Israel, it is unable to provide separate shuttles for families of Palestinian prisoners classified as "security" prisoners and those classified as ordinary criminal prisoners, unless the IPS issues a specific demand to do so. The separation is done only in the prison, with an IPS representative organizing the groups entering for the visit according to classification. According to a representative of the legal advisor for the IPS, the visit itself is carried out in the same visitation room, which means that in many cases, Palestinian criminal prisoners receive visits in conditions harsher than those of criminal prisoners who are citizens of Israel.

As noted, the visits are particularly significant for "security" prisoners, as this is their only contact with their families other than letters which are limited and often do not reach their destination or arrive late. Physical contact during the visit is of particular importance to the children of the prisoners, but such contact is denied to the children of "security" prisoners. In the past, the IPS allowed children and siblings of "security" prisoners who are under 10 years old to go into the prisoners' section for the final 15 minutes of the visit. However, since the visits were reinstated, the IPS has prohibited children of "security" prisoners to make any physical contact with their incarcerated relatives. Approval of such contact is granted as an exception.

In response to a petition on this matter filed by Adalah on behalf of children of prisoners,[11] the IPS notified that it would permit children under the age of six to have physical contact with their incarcerated relatives, but refused to guarantee such contact would be allowed in every visit. The IPS also subjected physical contact to the behavior of the prisoner in the prison and the absence of a security preclusion.

According to the state, the denial of physical contact during visits stems from concern that contact with relatives and children would be used for the purpose of transmitting messages and prohibited objects to and from the prisoners. This claim cannot justify such a sweeping infringement. The arbitrary and sweeping nature of the restriction on contact and the fact that this prohibition has been in place for years do not meet the test of minimal infringement on human rights. It is doubtful that the harm done to the children is proportionate to the number of cases in which children's visits were abused. The prohibition constitutes prohibited collective punishment of all children of "security" prisoners in response to a few and specific cases in which visitation regulations were breached. Rather than making the restriction of a right the exception which is based on an examination of each case as per concrete information justifying the same, the IPS opts to make its job easier and deny this right to all children in a sweeping manner.

The judgment in the petition which was handed down in March 2010 instructs that the "open visit" arrangement shall apply to all children under the age of eight, at least once every two months and subject to individual circumstances which may justify denying an open visit to a prisoner. The arrangement will come into effect on August 1, 2010.

CONCLUSION

As they stand today, the arrangements for prison visits by Palestinian families with their relatives incarcerated in prisons inside Israel severely impinge on the right to family visits and family life of both the prisoners and their relatives. The source of the impingement is primarily the breach of international law which prohibits holding prisoners from the occupied territory in the occupying power's territory. Additionally, the state shirks its responsibilities toward the prisoners and their relatives using all manner of security and political excuses, and often changes the policy regarding visits in view of changing circumstances. The state also makes use of the right to family visits as leverage in the context of the overall conflict. As such, recently, a number of bills seeking to worsen the holding conditions of "security" prisoners, including denial of family visits, have been tabled.

At the same time, there are severe restrictions on physical contact between those labeled "security" prisoners and their relatives. Additionally, the various preclusions the IPS is empowered to impose on all prisoners have a particularly far-reaching effect on Palestinian prisoners and their relatives. These restrictions include preventing former prisoners from visiting the prison (a large number of the OPT's residents, certainly the men, are "former prisoners") and denying visits to prisoners as a punishment or as a result of a classified security preclusion which, for the most part, does not pass judicial review. Relatives who wish to visit their incarcerated loved ones and preserve a modicum of family life must overcome many hurdles imposed by the state, the military and the IPS, in order to get a mere taste of family contact which does nothing to alleviate their hunger.

NOTES

1. See also: Arts. 17 and 23 of the International Covenant on Civil and Political Rights, 1966; Arts. 12 and 16(3) of the Universal Declaration of Human Rights, 1948; Art. 12 of the European Convention on Human Rights; Art. 27 of the Fourth Geneva Convention; Art. 10(1) to the International Covenant on Economic Social and Cultural Rights of 1966; Preamble to the Convention on the Rights of the Child of 1988.
2. Prison Ordinance [new version] 5732-1971, Sec. 47(b).
3. See for example: Prison Commission Order 04.42.00 Arrangements for Visits with Prisoners and Prison Commission Order April 17, 2000 Granting and Withholding Privileges.
4. HCJ 337/84 *Hokma v. Minister of the Interior*, Piskei Din 38(2) 826, 832; Prisoner's Petition Appeal 4463/94 *Golan v. Israel Prison Services*, Piskei Din 50(4), 136, 152–3; Prisoner's Petition Appeal 4/82 *State of Israel v. Tamir*, Piskei Din 37(3) 201, 207; HCJ 114/86 *Weil v. State of Israel*, Piskei Din 41(3) 477, 490.
5. The Supreme Court of Israel ruled that transferring prisoners to the territory of the state is legal in two judgments handed down at different times. See: HCJ 253/88 *Sajdiya v. Minister of Defense*, Piskei Din 42(3) 301 (1988), HCJ

2690/09 *Yesh Din v. IDF Commander in the West Bank,* not yet published, handed down on March 28, 2010. For more on this issue, see the chapter by Atty. Michael Sfard in this volume.

6. HCJ 11198/02 *Diriya v. Commander of the Ofer Military Prison Facility,* unpublished, decision dated October 1, 2003.

7. HCJ 8851/03 *Nahleh v. Commander of IDF Forces in the West Bank* (unpublished), HCJ 11193/03 *Nazal v. IDF Commander in the West Bank* (unpublished).

8. HCJ 5154/06 *HaMoked v. Minister of Public Security,* unpublished, decision dated March 12, 2009.

9. HCJ 5268/08 *Anbar v. GOC Southern Command,* unpublished, decision dated December 9, 2009.

10. For further information, see *Barred from Contact: Violation of the right to visit Palestinians held by Israel,* B'Tselem, September 2006.

11. HCJ 7585/04 *Kana'aneh v. Israel Prison Service,* not yet published, decision dated March 25, 2010.

20
Isolation and Solitary Confinement of Palestinian Prisoners and Detainees in Israeli Facilities

Sahar Francis and Kathleen Gibson

INTRODUCTION

Since the Israeli occupation of Palestinian territory in 1967,[1] an estimated 700,000 Palestinians have been detained under Israeli military orders in the Occupied Palestinian Territories (OPT),[2] which constitutes approximately 20 percent of the total Palestinian population in the OPT, and as much as 40 percent of the total male Palestinian population. There are currently at least 6,584 Palestinians in Israeli prisons and detention centers, of whom 35 are women and 300 are children under the age of 18.[3]

Every year, dozens of Palestinian prisoners and detainees[4] are held in solitary confinement, as a disciplinary measure, or in isolation, for reasons of state, prison, or prisoner's security. An unknown number of detainees who pass through interrogation facilities are held at any given time in isolation. With regards to persons in prison custody, at least 20 prisoners are currently held in isolation for mental health conditions, and approximately 15 are held in isolation for reasons of state or prison security.[5] An unknown number of prisoners are held at present in solitary confinement. Although rules exist under Israeli and international law to closely govern the use of solitary confinement and isolation, both measures are often used impermissibly and at great cost to Palestinian prisoners and detainees.

DIFFERENCES BETWEEN "SOLITARY CONFINEMENT" AND "ISOLATION"

1. Solitary confinement

Solitary confinement and isolation are both measures imposed during a prisoner's detention or prison sentence. On the face of it, solitary confinement is used by Israel as a disciplinary measure and is also common practice during interrogation, typically employed immediately following arrest. Solitary confinement combined with a monetary fine is the most common punishment meted out to Palestinians held in Israeli prisons.

Detainees and prisoners held in solitary confinement are completely cut off from the world. They are held in an empty cell containing only a mattress and a blanket. Other than their clothes, they are not allowed to take anything with them into solitary confinement, including reading materials or a television set. The detainee or prisoner is held in their solitary confinement cell, which does not contain a toilet, 24 hours a day. When the detainee or prisoner wishes to use the toilet, he or she must call out for a guard and wait until one agrees to take the prisoner out.

Article 56 of the Israeli Prisons Ordinance (New Version), 1971 (Ordinance), lists 41 disciplinary offenses for which solitary confinement may be imposed on prisoners and detainees, and establishes who among the prison officials may order such measures. According to the Ordinance, the commissioner, the prison director, and prison officers of the rank of captain or higher who have been so authorized by the commissioner each have the power to take disciplinary action against a prisoner by imposing a punishment of up to seven days in solitary confinement. The prison director is authorized to sentence a prisoner to a maximum of 14 days in solitary confinement; each successive confinement period may not exceed 7 days.

Article 56 also includes a number of broadly defined offenses that may engender solitary confinement, such as "made noise unnecessarily," or "any action, behavior, disorder or neglect that disrupts good order or discipline, even if not detailed in the preceding clauses." These open provisions establish no restrictions on what may be considered "disruption of order," and therefore leave the imposition of solitary confinement vulnerable to abuse.

2. Isolation

By comparison, the Israeli Prison Service (IPS) uses, or claims to use, isolation as a preventive measure. The Ordinance provides five general categories that warrant the isolation of a prisoner: state security; prison security; protecting the well-being and health of the prisoner or other prisoners; preventing significant harm to discipline and the proper prison routine, and finally, preventing violent offenses, offenses included in the Law to Combat Organized Crime, or drug transaction offenses. As with solitary confinement, broad definitions of "harm" to state security, prison security, discipline, or proper prison routine leave considerable liberty for authorities to claim that there are grounds for isolation.

Prisoners held in isolation are held in a cell alone or with one other prisoner[6] for 23 hours a day. They are allowed to leave their cell for a daily one-hour solitary walk; on the way to the recreation area, the prisoners' hands and feet are typically shackled. Handcuffs may sometimes be removed during the recreation period, but prisoners have reported to Addameer[7] that, in many cases, they remained handcuffed and sometimes even leg-shackled during the walk. During every transfer from the isolation cell, including for attorney visits, the prisoner's hands and feet are shackled, and he or she is accompanied by a prison officer.

Isolation cells in the various Israeli prisons are similar in size—typically from 1.5m by 2m to 3m by 3.5m. Each cell usually has one window measuring about 50cm by 100cm, which in most cases does not allow in sufficient light or air from the outside. One prisoner held in isolation reported that there was no natural light or fresh air in his cell and that for two months his cell was lit by artificial light, day and night. Isolation cells also include a toilet and shower; prisoners typically hang a curtain to separate the toilet and shower area from the rest of the cell. The cell usually has an iron door, which includes an opening at its lower part, through which guards insert food trays. Prisoners held in these cells are thus prevented from having any eye contact with other prisoners in the isolation wing, or even with guards.[8]

Isolated prisoners are generally allowed to keep a television set, radio, electric hotplate and electric kettle in their cells. These appliances may be bought at the prisoners' own expense in the canteen and are sometimes taken away as a punitive measure. Isolated Palestinian prisoners may receive books from the ICRC and occasionally obtain permission for their family to send a book through the mail, but the prisons impose many restrictions as to the kinds and number of books prisoners are allowed to receive. Prisoners also receive newspapers in Arabic free of charge, such as the Jerusalem Arabic daily *Al-Quds*, but other newspapers in Hebrew or English are distributed only to those holding a subscription. The newspapers are always distributed after a delay and are typically not current. Although Palestinian prisoners in Israeli prisons are allowed to study via correspondence at the Open University of Israel, prisoners who are held in isolation are not allowed to do so.[9]

Prisoners and detainees are typically reliant on canteens for food, clothing, personal hygiene items and most cleaning products, as the IPS does not provide many essential items. Sometimes, an isolated prisoner's canteen account is closed, as has occurred to dozens of prisoners, especially those who have been identified with Hamas.[10] When this occurs, prisoners whose canteen accounts have been closed receive essential personal hygiene products and cleaning products for their cells but may be forced to go without other basic items.

Isolation can be ordered by the courts, and by security authorities such as the General Security Service (GSS), but is most frequently levied by prison officials. The length of time in isolation that prison officials may order depends entirely on their rank, and can extend from 12 hours to longer periods of up to six to 12 months, with approval of the court. The courts may order that a prisoner be isolated for up to 12-month renewable periods, and the GSS may order isolation for similar long periods as well when citing security concerns.

Under Article 19D of the Ordinance, prisoners subjected to isolation have the right to a court hearing if the duration of isolation exceeds 96 hours.[11] The hearing must be conducted in the presence of the prisoner and his or her attorney, though broad provisions disable any protections engendered for the prisoner by enabling the courts to use confidential material not disclosed to the prisoner or his or her counsel.[12] The court's decision at this hearing may be challenged on appeal to the Israeli High Court of Justice (HCJ).

SOLITARY CONFINEMENT AND ISOLATION UNDER INTERNATIONAL LAW

Treaties and international agreements that address prisoners' rights prohibit the use of solitary confinement as a punitive measure or attempt to limit its use significantly. For example, Article 10 of the International Covenant on Civil and Political Rights (ICCPR) provides that all persons deprived of their liberty shall be treated with humanity and with respect for the inherent dignity of the human person.[13] The Standard Minimum Rules for the Treatment of Prisoners[14] clearly express that solitary confinement, as a form of punishment, should be used infrequently and exceptionally. It also stipulates in Article 31 that corporal punishment or punishment by holding a prisoner in a dark cell and any other cruel, inhuman or degrading punishment are prohibited as a disciplinary measure.[15]

The Basic Principles for the Treatment of Prisoners (1990), a UN General Assembly resolution, encourages the severe restriction or abolition of solitary confinement as a punishment.

In addition, in certain cases and in specific circumstances, solitary confinement and isolation can rise to the level of torture and ill-treatment and are therefore prohibited by international law.[16] The European Committee for the Prevention of Torture has stated that "Solitary confinement can, in certain circumstances, amount to inhuman and degrading treatment; in any event, all forms of solitary confinement should be as short as possible."[17] Similarly, in its general comment on article 7 of the ICCPR, the Human Rights Committee stated that "Even such a measure as solitary confinement may, according to circumstances, and especially when the person is kept incommunicado, be contrary to this article."[18] It therefore becomes a question of fact whether a particular form or incident of solitary confinement or isolation amounts to torture or ill-treatment in violation of article 7 of the ICCPR. Factors to be considered in this assessment may include: the duration of the solitary or isolated confinement; whether the use of solitary confinement or isolation is more extreme than necessary to achieve reasonable disciplinary objectives or the protection of the prisoner from other inmates, and whether the decision to institute solitary confinement or isolation was made following a controlled decision-making process or whether it was the result of arbitrary or vindictive behavior by the prison administration.

ISSUES ARISING FOR PALESTINIAN PRISONERS AND DETAINEES

Any use of solitary confinement or isolation exacerbates underlying structural isolation

The use of solitary confinement and isolation against Palestinian prisoners and detainees further exacerbates the underlying structural isolation imposed on all Palestinian prisoners resulting from their illegal imprisonment inside Israel. In 1995, Israel transferred all Palestinian prisoners from the OPT to facilities inside Israel, directly violating international humanitarian law[19] and effectively isolating them from their families, community and the outside world. The International Committee of the Red Cross (ICRC) runs a Family Visit Programme in the OPT to help family members visit their detained relatives inside Israel. However, access criteria and visit frequency are limited by Israeli authorities. For prisoners from Gaza, also held inside Israel, this underlying isolation has been even more devastating: following the capture of an Israeli soldier by armed groups on June 25, 2006 at the Kerem Shalom crossing on the Gaza Strip border, family members resident in Gaza have been prohibited from visiting their detained relatives.[20]

Documented restrictions imposed by the IPS and other security authorities exacerbating the isolating conditions for the general population of Palestinian prisoners and detainees include: restrictions on or the prohibition of family visits; the prohibition of telephone communication between prisoners and their families and friends; restrictions on the receipt of letters, newspapers and books; the requirement to coordinate attorney visits, which is in contrast with the ability of prisoners of all other categories to meet their attorneys without delay during designated hours and without prior coordination; and education and work restrictions. These restrictions all serve as indicators of an intentional policy to disconnect the population of Palestinian prisoners from one another, from their families and from their community.

Degenerating Israeli laws regarding the imposition of isolation

The Israeli HCJ has established through their rulings that a prisoner's right to "sunlight, air, and ventilation" should be anchored in legislation.[21] In 2000, the Knesset passed an amendment to the Ordinance, which established internal and external mechanisms for review of isolation. The amendment stipulated that isolation be employed as a last resort only, that a judge's ruling be required in order to extend individual isolation beyond six months and joint isolation beyond twelve months, and that prisoners had a right to a hearing during isolation proceedings. This amendment resulted in a significant decline in the number of prisoners held in isolation.

In 2006, however, the law was amended again, producing many of the provisions detailed above. The criteria for isolating a prisoner were expanded, as were the powers of those authorized to order isolation, and additional controlling mechanisms were canceled. The amendment also broadens the ability of the detaining authorities to use confidential material in justifying isolation, critically limiting the prisoner's ability to challenge their detention conditions and nullifying the effectiveness of court proceedings.[22]

Solitary confinement and isolation during interrogation

Following the September 1999 Israeli HCJ decision in *The Public Committee Against Torture v. The Government of Israel*,[23] in which the court ruled that some of the interrogation methods used by the GSS against Palestinian detainees were illegal and unacceptable, alternative, non-physical methods of interrogation—not necessarily in accordance with the court's decision—began to be used more frequently. These include solitary confinement, separation from legal counsel, insults and curses, threats of harm against the detainee or a family member, threats of being imprisoned for an indefinite period of time, allegations that family members have been arrested or imprisoned, threats that the detainee's work or study permits would be revoked, and threats that the detainee would be sexually abused, attacked by a dog, or that their family home would be demolished.[24]

In most cases during interrogation, Palestinian detainees are held for varying periods in total isolation. According to Israeli military law, security authorities may hold a detainee for interrogation without charge for up to 188 days without charge,[25] and may prohibit a detainee from meeting with a lawyer for up to 90 days. Delayed access may also apply to meetings with ICRC representatives, who are authorized by international agreements to visit Palestinian detainees who are under interrogation. The detainee is thus completely disconnected from the outside world for a prolonged duration.

The use of collaborators and isolation in combination

Frequently, detainees held for interrogation allege that after an often lengthy period in isolation, they are transferred to what appears to be a normal prison section, but is actually a mock-up unit created by Israeli interrogators. Inside the unit, referred to as "the birds" by detainees, they are held with persons who they perceive to be fellow Palestinian detainees, but who are actually collaborators working for the interrogators. After a certain period, during which the collaborators persuade the detainee to reveal information, incriminating or not, the detainee is transferred back to the main interrogation unit where the interrogation resumes. The period in which the detainee is held in isolation clearly is designed not merely for the safety of the detainee or the detained population, or to preserve the integrity of any information the detainee may have, but is instead utilized to exert pressure, to "break" the detainee, and is, in extreme uses, one element of the methods of ill-treatment applied against Palestinian detainees.

Isolation during detention and imprisonment

As mentioned above, isolation in prison is typically used for one of three reasons: as a punishment with the sentence or for offense in the prison (referred to as "security isolation" by the IPS); for health issues, typically in cases of mental illness, and, occasionally, at the detainee or prisoner's request. However, isolation is also used to silence prominent Palestinian political figures, as a form of punishment, as a method to push prisoners to collaborate and as a means of vindictive long-term treatment.

Isolation of political leaders

Isolation is a frequent measure used against prominent political detainees and prisoners, in an effort to keep them from contributing to internal facility and external community political discourse. The case of Ahmad Sa'adat, the former Secretary-General of the Popular Front for the Liberation of Palestine (PFLP), and an elected Palestinian Legislative Council member, directly illustrates this trend. Now serving a 30-year prison sentence following his conviction in December 2008 for offenses arising from his leadership of the PFLP, Sa'adat has been held in continuous isolation or solitary confinement since his abduction by Israeli authorities from Jericho jail on March 14, 2006. The IPS has also moved him repeatedly since his conviction, shuttling him from Hadarim Prison north of Tel Aviv to Nafha Prison between Beersheba and Eilat in the Negev Desert and back, to Ashkelon and Rimonim prisons, to Damon Prison near Haifa, Eshel Prison in Beersheba, then Ohalei Keidar Prison, also in Beersheba, then back to Damon, where he remains at present. Sa'adat's isolation extends further than his confinement to a particular cell: he suffers from cervical neck pain, high blood pressure and asthma, and has reportedly not been examined by a medical doctor. For the first seven months of his detention, he received no family visits. When Sa'adat went on a nine-day hunger strike in June 2009 in protest of his ongoing isolation, the Ashkelon prison administration imposed further restrictions on him, including denial of family visits, a ban on visits to the prison canteen and smoking, a fine of 200 shekels and an order to serve an additional week in isolation. It is clear that Sa'adat serves as a particular target both because he is a Palestinian political leader and because he has become a leader among the prisoners as well. The IPS is often quick to use isolation to remove those whose presence within the prison strengthens the prisoners' unity and steadfastness.

Isolation as a punishment

Isolation is also used in some cases not as a security measure as allowed under the Ordinance, but as a punishment. Akram Moussa

Khalaf Jebreen was held in isolation for nearly two months as punishment for the offense of another. Detained by Israel on January 22, 2009, Jebreen was charged with a number of offenses relating to membership in Hamas, communication with Hamas and Syria and plans to commit violent acts and engage in illegal arms trading. Jebreen confessed to these charges, and was sent to Ofer Prison, where he was visited by his family, including his father, Musa, his 10-year-old brother Mohammed, and two sisters, 12-year-old Israa and 16-year-old Maimoona. When prison officials searching his family discovered a knife on Maimoona, Jebreen was taken to his cell and held in there for 12 days with no recreation period and bathroom visits limited to just 10 minutes a day. Jebreen was then moved to Ashkelon Prison, where he was held in further isolation for a month and a half. He was allowed no visits for a month, and was denied receipt of any mail. After one month held alone in isolation, he was placed with another isolated prisoner who suffered from mental illness and talked to himself constantly.

Noura Mohamed Shokry El Hashlamon was held in isolation for nearly a month as punishment for her decision to go on a hunger strike protesting her ongoing detention without trial. Hashlamon was detained on September 17, 2006 and held under administrative detention orders. Following a HCJ ruling on December 12, 2007 that offered her the options of moving to Jordan or continuing as an administrative detainee, Hashlamon refused these options and embarked on a hunger strike. As a result, she was moved into isolation for the entirety of her 27-day strike. During her time in isolation, Hashlamon was held in a 2m-square cell, with sewage leaking from the plumbing, glass fragments on the floor and a 1m by .5m barred window without any glass to protect the cell from the cold weather. Prison officers repeatedly came to her cell, insulting and taunting her. She was allowed a recreation period of one hour after two weeks in isolation, and went a full two weeks without any electricity. She ended her hunger strike after the prison manager promised that her administrative detention order would not be renewed and she would be released, and that he would bring her young daughter and would allow Hashlamon to visit her husband, also held in administrative detention, and her parents. None of these promises were ever carried out and Hashlamon remained in administrative detention until August 2008.

Long-term isolation

Of significant concern is the use of permanent, long-term isolation for a limited number of Palestinian prisoners. Such extreme isolation measures may be ordered in specific cases, such as by the GSS on the premise of state security or by the courts, citing the mental health of the prisoner. However, as with shorter-term isolation, little or no proof is required in practice to make such an order, and prison authorities often have no say in its imposition. Long-term isolation takes an enormous mental toll on the prisoners and detainees involved, who have little effective recourse under the law to challenge their detention conditions.

Mahmoud Ahmed 'Abd Allah El Helbi has been imprisoned in isolation since October 23, 1989. Convicted along with his brother Mohammad of the murder of seven Jewish Israelis, he was sentenced to serve seven life sentences. Every six months, Helbi's isolation is renewed on the premise that he poses a danger to the other detainees. Transferred from prison to prison over the years—from Ramleh to Ashkelon and Eshel, again to Ashkelon, and then to Ohal Keidar, Shatta and finally Gilboa—Helbi has suffered greatly from his years under permanent isolation, without family visits, or meaningful social interaction. He stated during an interview in January 2009 that he feels as though the prison management intends to push him into a state of depression where his only option is to commit suicide or do something to himself, and wants only to be moved from isolation.

Resulting mental health toll on those subjected to isolation

Addameer contends that, as the above case indicates, isolation causes mental and physical damage, both among mentally healthy prisoners and prisoners with a history of mental illness. This becomes a complicated problem, as mental health services in Israeli prisons are wholly inadequate. Services are typically limited to medication only and do not include accompanying supportive therapy sessions; in most cases, prison psychiatrists do not speak Arabic but rather must interact with patients through a prison staff translator. Prison mental health personnel are generally unfamiliar with the culture and social codes of the Palestinian population, which creates additional barriers to the provision of optimal mental health treatment.[26]

Like Mahmoud El Helbi, Fares Baroud has been held in isolation for a period of many years, and wishes only to be moved back into the regular units. Baroud hasn't had any visit from family since 2001, and says that despite a number of requests, he hasn't been allowed to phone his family either. Baroud suffers from migraines, fits, tightening around the chest and says his ongoing isolated detention causes "horrible thoughts that get into his head." According to Baroud, though it is of utmost importance that he sees a doctor, he dreads dealing with the prison administration, as they levy emotional stress on him after any request he makes and well before they act on it, if ever.

Difficulties inherent in legal challenges to isolation orders

Both the Prisons Ordinance (New Version), 1971, and the Commissions Ordinance provide isolated prisoners with the right to a hearing.[27] Most Palestinian prisoners do not receive legal representation during court proceedings on isolation. The proceedings are conducted in Hebrew with poor or ineffective translation. Isolation orders on state security grounds are typically based on undisclosed information to which neither the prisoner nor his attorney is privy. Thus, prisoners and detainees subjected to isolation have no effective recourse to challenge the conditions of their detention under the law.

CONCLUSION

The excessive use by the Israeli authorities of solitary confinement and isolation against Palestinian detainees held in prison custody as well as under interrogation are matters of serious concern. The use of isolation under interrogation is particularly worrisome as it is applied in combination with other methods in order to exert pressure which may amount to ill-treatment or torture. In addition, the severe, sometimes irreversible mental reactions to isolation, resulting from the minimal environmental stimulation and social interaction, undermine the very definition of isolation as a preventive measure.

NOTES

1. Addameer operates under the legal assumption that the West Bank, East Jerusalem and the Gaza Strip comprise the OPT, which Israel has held in belligerent occupation since 1967.
2. UN Human Rights Council, *Human Rights Situation in Palestine and Other Occupied Arab Territories: Report of the Special Rapporteur on the Situation of Human Rights in the Palestinian territories occupied since 1967*, John Dugard, A/HRC/7/17, 21 January 2008.
3. IPS statistics, as of 31 May 2010.
4. For the purposes of this article, "prisoners" refers to persons who have been held in prison custody—remandees or convicts. "Detainees" refers to persons held prior to indictment or under administrative detention orders.
5. Addameer statistics, as of May 31, 2010 See <www.addameer.org>.

6. A prisoner held in isolation may be held with additional prisoners also requiring isolation. However, this remains a rarely used provision.

7. Addameer Prisoner Support and Human Rights Association is a Palestinian non-governmental, civil institution that focuses on human rights issues in the OPT. Established in 1992, Addameer offers support to Palestinian prisoners and detainees, advocates for the rights of political prisoners, and works to end torture through monitoring, legal procedures and solidarity campaigns.

8. In a few prisons, the doors of isolation cells are made of iron grid, allowing eye contact to be maintained.

9. Palestinian prisoners in Israeli prisons are allowed to study *only* at the Open University of Israel, and may not continue their studies at any other institution, even if they were enrolled there prior to their incarceration, or if the university so approves. The IPS claims that prisoners are barred from participating in study programs in conjunction with Arab universities for security reasons.

10. Palestinians resident in Gaza have been prohibited from visiting their relatives detained inside Israel since the Israeli government suspended the International Committee of the Red Cross Family Visits Programme in June 2007. These Gazan family members are also often unable to transfer money to their incarcerated relative's canteen accounts due to their inability to enter Israel, as prison authorities have in some cases insisted such money transfers can only be done from inside Israel.

11. Commission Ordinance 04.03.00, Article 6, states that extending individual or joint isolation beyond the initial 96 hours requires holding an oral hearing before the person who made the decision. Article 7 of the Commission Ordinance indicates that the hearing is to take place only prior to the first extension; subsequently the prisoner may make his or her arguments in writing against the decision to extend isolation. Article 7E stipulates that the IPS has the authority to order isolation even after the court has denied the IPS' request to isolate, if grounds for isolation continue to exist after the decision.

12. Articles 19B and H authorize the court to review confidential material that is not disclosed to the prisoner or his attorney on the grounds of state security, prison security, or prevention of real harm to discipline, or to the prison's proper routine, on the condition that doing so is crucial for the making of justice.

13. International Covenant on Civil and Political Rights, 999 UNTS 171, 6 ILM 368. (March 23, 1976).

14. Passed by the UN in a 1995 convention ratified by the Economic and Social Council in Decisions 663C (D-24) on 31 July 1957 and 2076 (D-62) on May 13, 1977.

15. The Standard Minimum Rules for the Treatment of Prisoners, adopted August 30, 1955 by the First United Nations Congress on the Prevention of Crime and the Treatment of Offenders, UN Doc. A/CONF/611, annex I, ESC res. 663C, 24 UN ESCOR Supp. (No. 1) at 11, UN Doc. E/3048 (1957), amended ESC res. 2076, 62 UN ESCOR Supp. (No. 1) at 35, UN Doc. E/5988 (1977). Articles 9–14 of the Standard Minimum Rules for the Treatment of Prisoners also stipulate the conditions of prison cells: each prisoner must have appropriate living space, sufficient daylight, and proper ventilation. Article 39 of the Standard Minimum Rules stipulates that the prisoner must be kept informed regularly of the more important events in the world outside prison via newspapers, periodicals, radio, or lectures. Article 40 stipulates that each prison must have a library that meets prisoners' needs and from which prisoners can receive the maximal benefit.

Article 77 stipulates that prisoners should be allowed to continue their studies and that illiterate minors must be taught to read and write. It is important to note that the Standard Minimum Rules emphasize that the prison sentence must be utilized to rehabilitate prisoners, support them, and help them be integrated into society upon their release, partly in order to prevent recidivism, and that prisoners may not be punished or oppressed.

16. M. Howells, "A Study of the Effects and Uses of Solitary Confinement in a Human Rights Perspective," 10th World Congress on Medical Law, Jerusalem, August 30, 1994, p. 4.

17. See N.S. Rodley, *The Treatment of Prisoners under International Law* (2nd edn), Oxford: Oxford University Press, 1999, pp. 295–6.

18. Report of the Human Rights Committee, General Comment No. 07: Torture or cruel, inhuman or degrading treatment or punishment (Art. 7), 30/05/82, Sixteenth session (1982), para. 2.

19. All but one of the more than 17 prisons where Israel detains Palestinian prisoners are located inside Israel. The one prison located inside the 1967 borders of the West Bank, Ofer Prison, near Ramallah, is still located inside an Israeli military base, on the Israeli side of the Annexation Wall, and is therefore similarly inaccessible to Palestinians from the West Bank who need a permit to visit relatives detained there. This practice is a direct violation of Article 76 of the Fourth Geneva Convention, which states that an Occupying Power must detain residents of occupied territory in prisons inside the occupied territory. See Michael Sfard's chapter in this volume.

20. The ICRC Family Visits Program in the Gaza Strip was suspended by Israel on June 6, 2007.

21. HCJ 4624/04 *Physicians for Human Rights-Israel and the Association for Civil Rights in Israel v. the Minister of Public Security and the IPS Commissioner*, Piskei Din.

22. As for evidence, the new amendment allows the court to hear evidence in the presence of one party, not only on security grounds, but also for the reasons listed in Article 19B, that is, prison security or prevention of real harm to discipline or to the prison's proper routine, on the condition that doing so is crucial for the making of justice.

23. HCJ 5100/94 *Public Committee Against Torture in Israel v. Israel*, [1999] IsrSC 53(4) 817.

24. See Bana Shoughry-Badarne's chapter in the present volume.

25. Palestinian detainees may be held for up to eight days before being brought before a judge in the Israeli military courts; the judge can authorize up to 90 days of detention for interrogation, which can be extended by another 90 days by a judge in the Military Court of Appeals.

26. See Ruchama Marton's chapter in this volume.

27. See *supra* footnote 11.

21
The Impact of Isolation on Mental Health

Ruchama Marton

In his book *The Carrot and The Stick*, Israel's first coordinator of government activities in the Occupied Palestinian Territories (OPT) (1967–74), Shlomo Gazit, states that since the earliest days of the Occupation, solitary confinement has served as the most important strategy for breaking the spirit of Palestinians and coercing them to collaborate. Gazit writes:

> The great advantage of defense regulations and administrative measures was the creation of circumstances in which the detainee was "broken", confessed his guilt and cooperated with his interrogators. Here the most important means for "breaking" interrogated persons (at a time when there existed strict instructions to avoid exerting physical pressure during the interrogation) was the absolute isolation of the interrogated person (from his family, his attorney, Red Cross personnel and even other detainees) during the initial phase of detention and interrogation.[1]

The Occupation is the broader context in which solitary confinement of security/political prisoners, as well as its reasons and effects, should be viewed. Social, national and individual aspects are all relevant. For the purposes of this discussion, we are referring to the Occupation which began in 1967 and that includes the Gaza Strip, East Jerusalem, the West Bank and the Golan Heights. The detention of most political/security prisoners begins with periods of solitary confinement of varying lengths. Psychologists employed in the service of security agencies and the accumulated experience of detention in isolation in Israel and worldwide have all served as the scientific and particularly the practical foundation for the use of this type of detention. An examination of the psychological impacts of solitary confinement can fill Gazit's statement with concrete content, and explain why isolation has served as such a central strategy in "breaking" Palestinians since the earliest days of the Occupation.[2]

Human beings seek to achieve equilibrium among the needs and demands of their external and internal worlds. This process continues throughout one's lifespan and is guided by one's ego, which uses perceptions for this purpose. It is through perceptions that one develops and forms one's lifestyle, behavior and occupation. Therefore, perceptions represent the tools for building cognition and judgment of reality. Some people require more stimulation, while others require less. Stimulation can be positive or negative, but in any case is an absolute human need. In a state of sensory deprivation, disequilibrium occurs between the internal and external worlds, producing extreme anxiety and loss of control over one's ego, judgment of reality, activity level, and regularity of behavior and thought. We need to receive information through our senses in order to maintain our sanity.

It is precisely the damage that solitary confinement causes to the prisoner's psyche and personality that is often viewed by the detaining authorities as its most useful aspect. According to Haney[3] and Rhodes,[4] one of the destructive effects of solitary confinement is the transformation of the detainee into an asocial, shattered being. In this chapter, I will demonstrate how the psychological, physical and social damage of solitary confinement is employed in the service of the Occupation, owing to its horrific effects, while it earns the official backing of "security grounds."

Many studies have been conducted on the psychopathological effects of solitary confinement[5] and their findings are unequivocal. Solitary confinement produces:

- Deep psychotic reactions such as visual and auditory hallucinations, paranoid states, disorientation in time and space, states of acute confusion and thought disturbances.
- Emotional instability and extreme emotional disturbances, the experience of depersonalization and derealization, rage and anger, negative attitude and affect,[6] compulsiveness, memory loss, attention and concentration difficulties, fear, panic, fear of death, depression, hopelessness, apathy, loss of *joie de vivre*.
- Disturbances of body image, self-mutilation, experience of suffocation, excessive masturbation, startle reaction.
- Physiological states created by the anxiety that results from solitary confinement: prisoners develop symptoms of the

gastroenterological, vascular and sexual/urinary systems. Sleep disturbances and extreme fatigue. Tremor, recurrences of heart palpitations, recurrences of excessive perspiration.

- Long-term effects: Solitary confinement frequently produces permanent mental disturbances and a feeling of insecurity.[7] In fact, each of the pathologies described above may become chronic both in prison and outside.

- Social pathologies: The total social isolation sometimes causes prisoners to withdraw and fear relationships with other people. It may be said that the prisoner's social personality is obliterated or distorted to such an extent that prisoners have lost the ability to handle themselves and live their lives in the company of others.[8] This may be manifested in prisoners' preference to remain isolated even when they are given the option to leave solitary confinement. Prisoners may also suffer attacks of irrational violence and rage.

PSYCHOTIC REACTIONS

There are several types of psychotic reactions to solitary confinement: visual and auditory hallucinations, disturbances of thought and concentration, and memory loss.

A large percentage of prisoners in solitary confinement suffer from hallucinations: one study reports 38.4 percent[9] while another indicates 50 percent.[10] In a study of 31 persons, Siegel[11] indicated that such hallucinations were liable to occur despite a conscious effort to avoid them, and they are typically considered to be a conscious reaction to stressful and traumatic situations. Often the initial images, which may occur after only 15 minutes in solitary confinement, are flashes of white light, followed by the appearance of geometrical forms. More complex visual hallucinations of insects, small animals, people, or places, may occur several hours or days into isolation. Hallucinations of tunnels and the experience of floating through them have also been reported, particularly in cases in which isolation has been accompanied by the threat of death.

Several explanations have been offered as to the cause of these hallucinations. Williams[12] suggests that the brain may require a certain quantity of stimuli in order to function, in the absence of which it creates its own stimuli.

Most people who were placed in solitary confinement described an experience of thought disturbances, as well as the inability to control their thought processes. One described tasteless, odorless, confused thoughts. The appearance of thought disturbances creates fear and panic. One person said he thought this meant he was going mad.[13]

Following a few days in solitary confinement, states of acute confusion have been reported. In research carried out at the Massachusetts Correctional Institute at Walpole, one prisoner cut and injured his elbow while completely disoriented, and was unable to recall what had happened during the few days when the event had occurred. Nor could he remember the thoughts or feelings he had experienced at the time. Another prisoner described difficulty concentrating and memory loss: "I can't concentrate, can't read ... Your mind's narcotized ... sometimes I can't grasp words in my mind that I know. I get stuck; have to think of another word. Memory is going. You feel you are losing something you might not get back." They attempted to retain their cognitive capabilities by using self-discipline techniques. One said, "Got to try to concentrate. Remember list of presidents, memorize the states, capitals, five oceans, seven continents, nine planets ... ."[14]

The importance of an environment with varied stimuli on the development of intellectual abilities such as thought, concentration and memory has been demonstrated in a great many studies and experiments on human and animal behavior.[15] It is understandable how a person held in solitary confinement where the level of stimuli is significantly lower may suffer from various forms of thought disturbance and loss of control over thought processes.

EMOTIONAL DISTURBANCES

Extreme, deep anxiety is the most common feeling among prisoners in solitary confinement. Gradually, fear and despair take over and break down the prisoner's mental and physical soundness. The feeling of deep anxiety and total abandonment along with thought disturbances and hallucinations produce an ongoing state of doubt and insecurity. All of these cause the loss of self-confidence and self-worth and bring about the loss of identity. An example may be that of the Palestinian prisoner "A," who had been held in individual isolation in an Israeli prison for about six months, as she did not get along with other prisoners. She was held in individual isolation during her previous three-year sentence as well. When the prison authorities wished to remove her from isolation, she refused: "I no longer believe in anything or anyone ... I feel alone and am trying to survive the rest of my sentence," she said. The

Israeli Prison Authority's psychiatrist wrote about her need to talk, just in order to shatter her loneliness, adding that she clearly uses her visits to him as an opportunity for conversation: "The prisoner agreed to have a conversation. She does not want to be examined [and] is interested only in conversation." Yet he was unresponsive: "During the examination she speaks in a stressful manner about many things, many topics ... It is impossible to speak with her ... She talks about how she is being harmed and not treated ... goes into long, irrelevant explanations, asks for help."

It is important to add that in many cases isolation produces violence and rage, so that while it is intended to "restrain" the prisoner, the result of confinement may be the reverse.

PHYSIOLOGICAL SYMPTOMS

The extreme anxiety caused by solitary confinement may produce acute physiological disturbances. Victims of solitary confinement suffer from symptoms affecting their digestive, vascular, urinary and sexual systems, as well as tremors, migraines, headaches, sleep disturbances and extreme fatigue. According to Hocking,[16] these symptoms may persist long after confinement and even become permanent. Symptoms such as recurring heart palpitations, excessive perspiration and shortness of breath have been described.

LONG-TERM EFFECTS OF SOLITARY CONFINEMENT

According to Williams,[17] solitary confinement "is designed to induce disorientation and confusion ... [and thus] ... isolate the individual from his or her sense of self in such a way that it will prove very difficult for the victim ever to recover and function normally again ... ." Persons who were placed in solitary confinement have reported that symptoms continued after their release. They often suffer from dependency, limited concentration, attention and memory, and confusion. Research has shown that these long-term symptoms do not disappear over time, but rather become worse if left untreated.[18]

SOCIAL PATHOLOGIES

Solitary confinement requires the prisoner's maximum adaptation in order to survive under the difficult, abnormal conditions. Sometimes adaptation is total, transforming the prisoner's mental structure into a replacement of their previous one. Thoughts, the manner of organizing life's activities and the emotional system all undergo complete transformation to enable survival in solitary confinement. The prisoner suffers from flattened emotion, shallow thought, inability to withstand minor external stimuli, irrational rage, inability to plan and initiate normal activity, dependence on external systems to organize one's life, loss of ability to control one's behavior, and anxiety triggered by the presence of another human being. For some prisoners, these symptoms become permanent and do not enable them to readapt to life within a social system. Most importantly, in some cases, it is impossible to heal these social pathologies. One of the presumed objectives of imprisonment is the prisoner's rehabilitation and return to society as a better citizen. Solitary confinement stands in stark contrast to this possibility.

In fact, prison not only denies basic human rights during confinement, but may even prevent prisoners from conducting new lives outside of prison. It eradicates and reshapes their personality, rendering it inappropriate for "normal" life.

MENTALLY ILL PRISONERS IN SOLITARY CONFINEMENT

Some prisoners have suffered from emotional problems prior to their detention, for example, from mental illness such as schizophrenia. For these prisoners, adapting to life in prison is especially difficult. They become the "unsolvable problem" of prison authorities and other prisoners, due to the behavioral disturbances they manifest as a result of their mental illness. Subsequently, they are placed in solitary confinement. The prison thus punishes prisoners for their mental illness. Prison authorities do not know what to do with them, there are no budgets for psychotherapy, and solitary confinement is a practical "solution" for these prisoners. Certainly, solitary confinement is not a substitute for the psychotherapy that mentally ill patients so desperately need. Solitary confinement irreparably shatters whatever is left of these prisoners' personality.

Over the years of PHR-Israel's activity, we have found that schizophrenic prisoners are often systematically given a wrong diagnosis. Although they are typically on anti-psychotic drugs, the commonplace diagnosis is "manipulative," "malingerer," "hysterical"; the most common diagnosis is "impostor," or some other odd diagnosis that does not exist in the diagnostic manuals, such as "anxiety of imprisonment." All these misdiagnoses fail to define Palestinian prisoners as mentally ill, placing them outside the realm of mental illness. Subsequently, they are perceived as responsible for their actions, and specifically, fit to stand trial and carry out prison sentences.

I recall a clear-cut example elucidating this method: Prisoner "M." from Gaza was accused of attempting to run over an IDF soldier. During his trial, the military judge was impressed by M.'s mental state and ordered a psychiatric exam for him. M. was examined at a psychiatric hospital, where the psychiatrist who examined him found him to be mentally ill, chronically schizophrenic. The judge then determined that M. was unfit to stand trial. At this point, Major-General Matan Vilnai, Commander of the Southern Command,[19] intervened. He sentenced M. to three years in prison, by power of Vilnai's authority as commander, under Article 36B of Security Provisions Order (No. 378) of 1970.

In other words, the army disregarded and canceled out the psychiatric opinion as well as the military judge's ruling, so that a Palestinian prisoner would not escape a prison sentence.

In prison, the authorities could not find a solution to M.'s difficult behavior, and he was soon placed in solitary confinement. When I examined him some time later, M. was devoid of humanity. He spread feces on his cell walls, was unable to identify his family members and could not utter a single coherent sentence.

SOLITARY CONFINEMENT AND THE OCCUPATION

In his book, *Imagined Communities*, Benedict Anderson argues that a nation is an "imagined political community." It is imagined because for the most part, its members do not know and have never met each other. According to Anderson, the important point for our purpose is that despite the differences among the different individuals who make up the community, it is founded on a deep affinity among its members: "The nation ... is always conceived as a deep, horizontal comradeship. Ultimately it is this fraternity that makes it possible, over the past two centuries, for so many millions of people, not so much to kill, as willingly to die for such limited imaginings."[20]

In Israel, solitary confinement should be viewed as one of the practices of the Occupation, whose objective is to shape submissive, compliant subjects who will fail to develop a national consciousness, develop into a community, as defined by Anderson.

Another reason for holding Palestinian prisoners in solitary confinement is that the GSS or IPS have determined that the prisoner would put Israeli security at risk if allowed to be in contact with other prisoners. The case of Marwan Barghouti[21] who has been held intermittently in solitary confinement, is just one example of how security grounds are sometimes used merely as an excuse to exert pressure on the confined individual or others to act in a manner desirable to Israeli agencies. The grounds for placing someone in solitary confinement notwithstanding, its impacts on one's mental and physical condition may be severe and permanent, as I have described.

Among the most basic stimuli that we need and which are indeed essential to our very existence is the feeling of solidarity—that we are accepted by others—and the need to hear, speak with and touch another human being. These essential needs are denied to prisoners in solitary confinement. As a result, development of a powerful sense of the loss of ability to feel is unavoidable. An individual who suffers from a feeling of emptiness and hollowness feels nothing. To lose the ability to feel means risking the death of the psyche.

Charles Dickens wrote of confinement: "I hold this slow and daily tampering with the mysteries of the brain to be immeasurably worse than any torture of the body." I believe that solitary confinement is equal only to lobotomy—except that the process of solitary confinement is longer and more cruel. Solitary confinement is nothing but a specific form of torture. People do not die from solitary confinement; they only lose their minds.

NOTES

1. S. Gazit, *The Carrot and the Stick*, Tel Aviv: Zmora-Bitan, 1985, p. 297 (in Hebrew).
2. It is important to note that the Israeli law does not prohibit such a practice. On the contrary, it even allows for holding detainees in severe conditions during the interrogation period. Article 22 of the detention regulations permits the imposition of harsher conditions of confinement on persons classified as security detainees simply because they are alleged to have committed offenses defined as security offenses under section 35(b) of the Criminal Procedure Law (Enforcement-Detention) 1996.
3. C. Haney, "Mental Health Issues in long-term solitary and 'supermax' confinement," *Crime & Delinquency*, Vol. 49, 2003, pp. 124–56.
4. L.A. Rhodes, *Total Confinement*, Berkeley: University of California Press, 2004.
5. *Voices for Vanunu*, Papers from the International Conference, Tel Aviv, October 1997, p. 35.
6. Haney "Mental Health Issues in long-term solitary and 'supermax' confinement."
7. 40 CHR (Agenda Items) at 8, United Nations Human Rights Committee, Doc. E/CN. 4/Sub/ 2/1988/28 (1988).

8. Haney "Mental Health Issues in long-term solitary and 'supermax' confinement," p. 141.

9. R.K. Siegel, PhD, "Hostage Hallucinations – Visual Imagery Induced by Isolation and Life-Threatening Stress," in *Journal of Mental and Nervous Disease*, Vol. 17, No. 5, 1984, pp. 264–72.

10. S. Grassian, "Psychopathological Effect of Solitary Confinement," *American Journal of Psychiatry*, Vol. 140, No. 11, 1983, pp. 1450–54.

11. Siegel, "Hostage Hallucinations," p. 266.

12. L. Williams, "Psychological Aspects of Torture," Newham College, University of Cambridge, August 1990, p. 13.

13. S. Smith and W. Lewty, "Perceptual Isolation in a Silent Room," *The Lancet*, September 12, 1959, pp. 342–45.

14. Grassian, "Psychopathological Effect of Solitary Confinement," p. 1453.

15. P. Suedfeld, "Introduction and Historical Background," in *Sensory Deprivation: Fifteen Years of Research*, John P. Zubeck (ed.), Appleton-Century-Crofts, Educational Division, Meredith Corporation, 1969, pp. 4–5.

16. F. Hocking, "Extreme environmental stress and its significance for psychopathology," *American Journal of Psychotherapy*, Vol. 24, 1970, pp. 4–26.

17. Williams, "Psychological Aspects of Torture," p. 7; re F.E. Somnier and I.K. Genefke, "Psychotherapy for victims of torture," *British Journal of Psychiatry*, Vol. 149, 1986, pp. 323–9.

18. R.I. Daly, "Compensation and Rehabilitation of Victims of Torture," *Danish Medical Bulletin*, Vol. 27, No. 5, 1980, pp. 245–8.

19. Currently Deputy Minister of Defense.

20. B. Anderson (1983), *Imagined Communities*, London: Verso, New Left Books, 1983; revised edn 1991, pp. 6, 7.

21. One of Fatah's most prominent political leaders, captured by the Israeli Army in 2002 and sentenced to five life sentences.

22
Consciousness Molded or the Re-identification of Torture

Walid Daka

INTRODUCTION

The Palestinian prisoner in the prisons of Israel's occupation is experiencing a state of impotence which is a result of the difficulty in describing the state of oppression he has been in since the beginning of the second Intifada. In adapting to current human rights discourse, oppression and torture have become modern and complex. This discourse, employed by human rights organizations, concentrates its special efforts in order to prove specific violations considered by the Israeli judiciary and media as the exception to the rule, which is respect for human and prisoners' rights. The result is that contrary to the pretense of exposing and being transparent, in reality this discourse hides facts and obscures the truth.

Modern oppression is hidden. It is a shapeless oppression, indefinable by a single picture. It is composed of hundreds of small isolated actions and thousands of details, none of which appears as a tool of torture, unless the whole picture and the logic underlying the system are understood. It is comparable to exploitation in free market economies under globalization, which is always presented as necessary to raise the rate of economic growth. Your exploiter is devoid of face, homeland, or address. Its monopolist arms reach into every corner of the world, into every detail of your life, while you, oppressed as a worker or a consumer, may concomitantly become a shareholder in the same cartel which exploits you. When the borders between exploiter and exploited are thus erased, understanding exploitation becomes almost impossible.

Oppression and torture in Israeli prisons are not similar to the cases of oppression and torture known from prison literature. There is no serious denial of food or medicine; no one is buried underground, denied sunlight. Prisoners are not chained in irons. In our postmodern era, the prisoner's body is no longer the direct target; the spirit and the mind are. Our conditions are neither what Fučik faced under fascism, described in his *Notes from the Gallows*, nor those in Tazmamart Prison depicted in Taher Ben Jelloun's *This Blinding Absence of Light*. You shall not find here anything like Malika Oufkir's description of Moroccan prisons. We are not in Abu Zaabal, not even in Abu Ghraib, or Guantanamo. In those prisons, one knows one's torturer, the form of torture and the tools used; one has the certainty acquired in experiencing physical torture. But in Israeli prisons, you face a harder torture, because it is civilized; it turns your own senses and mind into tools of daily torture, quietly creeping without any club, without making any noise. It is part of your life, together with the cell, the time, the sunny courtyard and the relative material abundance.

Prison as an example is the subject of this study: the state of losing the ability to interpret reality, the feeling of impotence and the loss of initiative are not only the fate of prisoners; this description applies to *all* Palestinians. The similarity of the conditions of Palestinian citizens to those of prisoners is not restricted to the form of oppression, in which the citizens are closed off in separate geographic enclaves, just as prisoners are isolated from one another in wings and in sectors, totally dependent upon the will of the jailer. The essential similarity relates to the purpose of the jailer: to remold them according to an Israeli vision, by means of molding their consciousness, and especially by molding the consciousness of that fighting elite locked in prison. Therefore, in order to understand the general picture of Palestinian reality, it is worthwhile to study the life of the Palestinian prisoner, as a parable of the lives of civilians in the Occupied Palestinian Territories (OPT).

Palestinian prisoners in Israeli prisons complain of a condition that does not exist. And they are incapable of describing what does exist. They face torture whose form and source they are incapable of defining. The following pages do not pretend to be a scientific study; they were written in prison where there are no available research sources. They are based mostly on my memory, at least in that part of my discussion that deals with the reality in the enclaves created by Israel, since I have been detained and isolated from the world outside prison for almost a quarter of a century. My principal purpose is to explain that what happens in the smaller prisons is not just detention and isolation of people considered to be a security risk for Israel, but is part of a general, scientifically planned and calculated scheme to remold the Palestinian consciousness. The success or failure of this scheme depends on our ability to uncover and understand it and its details, without falling into self-delusion and self-deceit. What we need are clarity and honest scientific research rather than enthusiastic speeches glorifying the prisoners, their struggles and their sacrifices.

POLITICIDE: DEGRADATION WITHOUT ANNIHILATION

The South African delegation that visited Palestine[1] was astonished by the extent and nature of the measures imposed by Israel on the Palestinians and described them as having far surpassed the measures taken by the governments of South Africa during the Apartheid period. In the worst times of racial segregation in South Africa, there were never segregated roads for blacks and whites like the existing segregation in the OPT between roads for Jews and for Arabs. The segregation was never as total and absolute as it is here now; there always remained certain zones where whites and blacks met. The one thing which astonished the South African delegation and rendered the term "racial segregation" insufficient for describing and defining the Palestinians under the Occupation, was the system of roadblocks separating not only Palestinians and Israelis, but also Palestinians from each other. Israel, as we know, divided the OPT and cut them into small enclaves, which has made life unbearable for the inhabitants.

There is a difference between the final goal of the Israeli governments since the second year of the Intifada and the goals of the South African governments in their Apartheid policies. This difference is the reason for the totality and depth of the Israeli measures and for Israel's absolute control over Palestinian lives. In this latter case, racism is basically the means of achieving the remolding of Palestinian consciousness, in accordance with the plan of the Jewish state. Racism in this context is not a popular, spontaneous and illogical phenomenon, but an organized racism, initiated by the entire Israeli establishment, with its logic, legal and moral justification. The Israeli idea is that the real problem does not lie with the official Palestinian leadership; it is the Palestinian community which rejects the Israeli maximalist solution and expresses its readiness to oppose it, supplying an endless flow of fighters to the resistance organizations and rendering every possibility of agreement with the Palestinian negotiators impossible to implement. The former Israeli chief of staff, Moshe (Bogey) Ya'alon, declared several times, clearly and openly, that the Palestinian consciousness must be remolded,[2] and that this goal dictated his army's military plans. The division of the OPT into enclaves must be understood in this context, that is, as part of the Israeli plan of molding Palestinian consciousness.

Initially, the Israeli Army targeted its actions against the material infrastructure of the resistance, seeking to reach the point of "consciousness molding" by making the very idea of resistance too costly for individuals and society as a whole. But eventually, those actions strengthened the moral infrastructure of the resistance, leading to the opposite result: the production of large numbers of resistance fighters. When this became clear to the Israeli leaders and the army command, they reevaluated the ways and means used for "consciousness molding." The new targets were the elements of the moral infrastructure of the resistance, that is, the system of collective values that embodies the concept of one unified people, with a purpose shared by the majority of its members. I tend to think that, since 2004, Israel has created a strict system, based on the most updated theories of human engineering and social psychology, in order to mold Palestinian consciousness by shattering its collective values. Thus, this Israeli system in its totality constitutes a case of what Baruch Kimmerling defined as "politicide."[3] The reason is that it consists of plans, schemes and positions which appear to the observer as chaotic, confused and contradictory components of the Israeli policy; however, in reality, this "chaos" aims at the following purposes:

1. Breaking up Palestinian economic, cultural and civil society structures and organizations. These should reach a level below full organization, but not devolving into total chaos.
2. Adhering to ongoing political negotiations, thus creating an illusion that a solution is within reach, right around the corner. At the same time, creating facts on the ground, so that the situation always remains unsolved but not a stalemate.
3. Breaking up the self-image of a people by destroying Palestinian collective values. An emphasis is on destroying central forces and groups representing these values, such as the prisoners, the front line of the struggle. Thus the Palestinian people are reduced to something less than a nation, but safe from material annihilation.

Israeli prisons are the laboratory where policies targeting the Palestinian moral and social situations are tested. It is in this sense that what happens in prison represents the policy implemented by the Israeli Army in the enclaves of the OPT. The similarity might be helpful in solving the conceptual problem of describing the Palestinian reality, sometimes depicted as apartheid and sometimes as a ghetto. But these interpretations describe only parts of the Palestinian situation. For example, the segregation between the Palestinians themselves cannot be described as apartheid; the Palestinian enclaves are not provisional ghettoes. They consist of the final solution, whose target is not the body, not collective extermination, but rather the soul—the extermination of the Palestinian culture and civilization.[4]

THE HUNGER STRIKE AS A SECOND SHOCK: MOLDING PRISONERS' CONSCIOUSNESS

When Israel repeatedly invaded and bombed Palestinian cities and populated areas with F-16 airplanes and Apache helicopter gunships, when it attacked populated neighborhoods with its tanks, entering each and every lane and alley in Nablus, Jenin and Ramallah, when it destroyed houses along with their inhabitants with its huge D-9 Caterpillar bulldozers—its purpose was not to pursue and annihilate those little fighter bands, armed at best with AK-47 rifles, who lacked any military training or experience worth mention.

As its leaders incessantly declared, Israel sought to extract "a high price tag," that is, to bring the Palestinians to a state of deep shock, which could be used to mold their consciousness after the moral infrastructure of the resistance was destroyed. The basic objective of the shock situation Israel tried to induce in the minds and souls of Palestinian citizens was to replace national values with pre-national ones and to render Palestinian society and elites incapable of rational and balanced thinking. This explains the dismemberment of the OPT into enclaves, so that ordinary Palestinians would be incapable of grasping the national scene and immerse themselves in the concerns and details of the part of the homeland in which they lived. The next stage was that of the implantation of new values. This is the role of the Dayton Plan, whose danger lies in the values taught to hundreds of young people enrolled in the security apparatuses. Just as the "Palestinian Revolution" was replaced by the "Palestinian Authority," the mobilization of these young people signals the replacement of "struggle" with the "rule of law" and "resistance" with the "prevention of armed chaos." The slogan "Fighting corruption" became the focus of political discourse, instead of "Liberty and independence." These new slogans do not belong to a discourse of a liberation movement; they were invoked in order to make the movement disappear.

I cannot elaborate here on the implementation of the shock doctrine in the OPT. I do wish to describe that aspect of the shock doctrine that has to do with the Palestinian prisoners, during and after the second Intifada. Waves of prisoners arrived daily, and the IPS officers regarded them as a dangerous mass which needed to be absorbed quickly and brought under tight control. There were two options:

1. To deny the new prisoners the possibility of pulling themselves together, by creating a state of instability through their constant transfers between the prisons. This option prevents their transformation from individuals into a body or a group obeying certain rules, yet such a transformation would make it easier to predict their future steps and control them.
2. To enable the prisoners' movement to absorb this mass of new prisoners into its existing framework. They would thus continue relations with the jailers, as before. Now on one hand, the IPS thus immunizes itself to unexpected behavior by the prisoners, but on the other, it encounters an organized body, a struggling moral force not only within prison but also for the Palestinian people and its political leadership.

From the end of 2003 to mid-2004, the IPS handled the prisoners according to the second option; but during this period it paved the road for implementing the first one. Outside the prisons, Israeli public opinion pushed to create an alternative Palestinian leadership, a "Palestinian partner" who could sign the right agreement. Inside the prisons, the idea of building an alternative leadership for the prisoners was implemented by separating the symbolic leaders of the various organizations and isolating them from the other prisoners. Except for a few cases, this wasn't achieved by solitary confinement, and hence wasn't limited in time. Rather than a punitive measure, it was a step towards creating a vacuum in the leadership. After the prisoners' hunger strike of 2004, a similar logic to that of breaking the OPT into enclaves operated within the prisons. By the time Yaakov Ganot, the new head of the IPS, took office, our prisoners' national movement—as we used to call it—was no longer what it used to be.

The current situation is described by older prisoners as "materially high," but "morally low." This is not the familiar nostalgia of older people, a mere longing for the past. Indeed, prisoners are not exceptional in this regard. Yet it is true, as one prisoner once described it, that "in the past we were one with each other, now we are one against each other." The contrast between the relatively good material conditions and the prisoners' feeling of moral deterioration is hard to grasp: since oppression does not appear in its rude, explicit and familiar physical form, prisoners cannot diagnose it and develop ways of coping with it.

Prime Minister Sharon's government sought to mold prisoners' consciousness in coordination with the general plan to mold Palestinian consciousness. For this purpose, the following steps were taken:

1. In mid-2003, the blatant racist Yaakov Ganot was appointed as head of the IPS, enjoying personal support from Prime Minister Sharon. This personal connection removed all the bureaucratic obstacles which could have hindered the restructuring of the IPS to fit its new functions. Sharon gave Ganot the freedom to act as he wished; his budget was increased, enabling him to equip old prisons with modern control technology and to build new prisons for the thousands of new prisoners arrested daily by the Israeli Army.

2. Ganot imposed a unified policy in running the prison, applicable from the lowest warden to the highest official. It was made clear that there is only one master, one decision maker. No room was left for spontaneity, improvisation, or different interpretations of the rules.

3. From his first minutes in office, Ganot sought conflict with the prisoners in several prisons. The first clash was in Ashkelon [Asqalan] Prison; its prisoners were harshly suppressed, with tear gas and batons, which resulted in many injuries. These clashes were followed by further steps which were premeditated, I now believe, with benefit of hindsight. These steps were designed to push the prisoners into the corner of an open-ended hunger strike. Ganot prepared everything required to turn the hunger strike into a turning point in the prisoners' lives. He wanted the strike to turn into a second, stronger shock (after the shock of the mass invasions and arrests), which would be followed by consciousness molding and brainwashing.

4. The IPS started to put into practice frequent strip searches upon prisoners' bodies, using physical and mental violence.

The IPS also used dogs to search prisoners and their possessions, and while transporting them between prisons, in order to humiliate them and hurt their religious feelings. In Islamic culture, dogs represent pollution, which requires purification. This policy left very grave moral and mental scars upon the prisoners, and was one of the main reasons that they adopted the tactic of the open-ended hunger strike.[5]

5. Isolating plate glass was fitted in the visiting rooms. Prisoners weren't capable of touching their families, including their children; contact with them was limited to hearing. This measure was implemented right before the strike: Ganot knew that the introduction of the plate glass barriers would make the prisoners respond by canceling their visits. This led to the prisoners' isolation from their most important and supportive social circle: family visits, which help the prisoners recover their mental balance and self-esteem and help them survive.

Never before, in the history of Israeli prisons, had the IPS provoked the prisoners to start an open-ended hunger strike. Because of the large number of inexperienced prisoners, the leadership of the National Prisoner Movement tried to cooperate with the new policy in return for easing the harsh measures which targeted human dignity and religious feelings. The prisoners delivered several messages in this vein, but they were all rejected. A hunger strike seemed like the only option available.

Throughout the preceding year, Ganot had prepared the means for breaking the strikers, as if he was facing a great army, rather than incarcerated prisoners whose only weapon was their empty stomachs. He relied on modern theories in social psychology, psychological warfare and demagoguery, and mobilized for that purpose professionals and experts from outside the system. Together, they processed the plan to the finest details, down to the daily actions of the lowliest warden, leaving nothing to chance or individual interpretation. It was clear that we were facing an aggregation of oppressive measures, frightening in their rationality, implemented together in every prison, from Gilboa [Jalbu'a] Prison in the north to al-Nafha in the south. These measures received total support from the highest ranks in the Israeli government. Internal Security Minister Tzahi Hanegbi declared in the Israeli media: "As far as I'm concerned, they can strike for a day, a month, until death," since he had no intention of relaxing the new rules.[6]

These rules, which taken separately do not amount to an unusual and unbearable level of torture, together created mental stress, since they were used against weak and exhausted prisoners. Let me cite just several among them:

1. Lights were left on in the rooms, day and night.
2. Anything that could function as a means of physical comfort was expropriated: from pillows to plastic containers and cups that could be filled with water and put beside the prisoners' beds. This prevented the simple means of manifesting mutual solidarity by giving water to the most exhausted prisoners.
3. Table salt was confiscated: prisoners used to take in salt during hunger strikes, in order to prevent permanent health damage. The IPS won an appeal submitted by prisoners to the High Court of Justice (HCJ) regarding this matter. Cigarettes were also confiscated; this indeed was the first means of pressure against the striking prisoners.
4. Prisoners were often taken out of their rooms in order to "search for forbidden items," although the rooms had already been emptied of all their contents and left with only a bed for each prisoner. Prisoners were transferred between the prison's rooms and wards constantly, sometimes twice a day. In addition to the physical exhaustion caused by all this to the hunger-striking prisoners, the aim was to break up their circles of acquaintance and friendships which were formed during years of detention, and thus to weaken their moral and mental support.
5. Loudspeakers sounded incessant calls and fliers were distributed, in order to weaken prisoners' confidence in the strike and the leadership. Rumors were spread that the strike was initiated by Hamas in order to serve its own political agenda, or that a certain leader of Fatah had broken the strike and eaten, and so on.
6. Daily barbecue parties were held for the wardens. In every ward, a room was allocated for regular criminal prisoners, whose role was to cook, eat, and play loud music, day and night.
7. When prisoners were transferred from one prison to another, to the prison's clinic, or to a hospital, violence and electric cattle prods were used to make them move faster. Metal detectors (manometers) were used to search for sharp objects hidden on the prisoners' naked bodies.

8. Lawyers were prevented from visiting prisoners and making contact with them in any way, throughout the strike. Thus prisoners were totally isolated from the outside world, deprived of any information on the solidarity campaigns and mass demonstrations supporting them.

The IPS adjusted its actions during the strike to the developments in each prison and each ward individually, yet these adjustments were calculated, rather than mere bursts of anger towards the prisoners. The IPS based its actions—both the means used to crush the strike and the overall goals—on international experience, for example, that of US Intelligence and its clients in Latin America during the 1970s. Prisoners arrested and tortured by the military junta in Argentina testified later that the objective of their torture wasn't primarily to extort information from them, but to force them to betray a basic principle—the principle of solidarity and empathy for their comrades. In prisons like Guantanamo and Abu Ghraib, prisoners were broken and their personality and mental makeup crushed through the use of Islam and religious convictions against Muslim prisoners. Two forms of torture recur in their testimonies: being stripped naked, and harassment regarding their religious beliefs.[7]

Stripping the Palestinian prisoners naked was customary before and during the hunger strike, and was actually one of the main reasons for the strike. But most of the measures taken in order to crush the prisoners targeted their feelings of solidarity and the values of collective national action. Solidarity had the ability of turning the prisoners from a group of individuals and diverse factions, with various beliefs and ideologies, into one force. Destroying this solidarity, which had developed throughout decades of Palestinian prisoners' struggle, was crucial not just in order to end the hunger strike, but to end the idea of collective action in any strike in the future.[8]

It was impossible to implement the new policy desired by the IPS without the shock of the strike and its results. Only thus could the prisoners be molded according to the role prepared for them. Before the strike, Palestinian prisoners used to appeal to such concepts as the National Prisoner Movement, the Dialogue Committees, a general strike, and so on. These terms represented the values of the collective national prisoner struggle. A shock was necessary in order to crush the framework of nationalist committees, to undermine these collective ideas.

The prisoners failed to achieve their goals through the hunger strike; however, the crucial failure, whose consequences will persist for years to come, was the success of the IPS in breaking up the striking body. The strike didn't end in the way that it had been first declared—that is, in a unified manner, through the decision of one collective leadership—but instead in an individual and chaotic fashion, without any plan or agreement. As a former military officer, Ganot knew that it is not enough to conquer the enemy's strongholds and make it retreat; withdrawal and defeat must be chaotic. In practice, the end of the strike resembled chaos more than orderly retreat. The disorderly manner in which the hunger strike was ended ensured the total collapse of the leadership structure in prison, as well as the set of shared values which turned soldiers from individuals into fighting units. The Palestinian prisoners were now ready for consciousness molding.

STEPS TAKEN AFTER THE STRIKE: MATERIAL ABUNDANCE AS A TOOL OF TORTURE

Just as Israel dismantled the Palestinian national struggle through the divisive measures taken in the OPT, the prisoners were also individualized. Thus, for instance, there's a parallel in demands by the groups of the prisoners from, say, the Nablus area, regarding an increase in the number of visitors and visiting time, and the demands of the inhabitants of Nablus fighting to improve their particular living conditions, like opening roadblocks, or similar issues. Palestinian suffering, just as the Palestinian prisoners' suffering, was broken apart into local scenes, each focused on particular sections divided according to geographic region. The individual is not allowed to see or be concerned with the larger scene; his visual field is blocked, either by the wall and the checkpoints, or through control over his time, so he will collapse under the yoke of daily trouble and constant oppression.

To achieve the surveillance and control of the prisoners after the hunger strike, the IPS sought to exploit the ensuing post-hunger strike depression and the disappointment with the leadership. The most important steps taken then were:

1. Segregating the different divisions among prisons and within the same prison according to geographic considerations. Thus, Gilboa [Jalbu'a] prison now holds prisoners from the northern West Bank, from Nablus to Jenin, and two

divisions where prisoners holding Israeli identity cards are detained: one mostly for people from Jerusalem and the other for Palestinians of '48.[9] This division is usually presented as a benefit to the prisoners, complying with the demands of human rights committees to detain prisoners close to their homes. However, this cannot account for the inner divisions among the wards, according to smaller geographic units. For example, there is a special ward for the inhabitants of the town of Jenin, and another for prisoners from Jenin's refugee camp; there is a ward for prisoners from Qabatiyya and the surrounding villages, one for Tulkarm, and another for Qalqiliya and its villages. These separations coincide with the closed enclaves that Israel created in the OPT. Thus, geographical divisions yield geographical affiliations, replacing the national one.

2. The IPS stopped working with the Dialogue Committees. Before the strike, each prison had an elected committee representing all the political factions, whose role was to present to the authorities the common problems and demands of all prisoners in that prison. This mechanism has now been replaced by a spokesman from each ward, who in practice represents a geographic region. This representative is chosen by the prison administration, out of two or three names suggested by the prisoners. Meetings are held with each representative separately. He is only allowed to discuss problems regarding his division/region alone, usually personal ones; he also carries the warnings and regulations of the prison's administration back to the prisoners. Thus, the IPS emptied the representational function of its national content.

3. Heavy punishments, personal or collective, are given in response to any sign of struggle, even one as small and symbolic as refusing a meal.

4. Any collective gesture, such as consolation in the case of death, reception of a new prisoner, or a farewell party to a released prisoner, is strictly forbidden. Although Friday prayers are still allowed, they may not transcend religious matters. Discussion of the Palestinian situation, or even the mention of Palestine, is counted as expressing an opinion, and freedom of expression is denied.

5. Prisoners keeping photographs of Palestinian leaders or of *shaheed*s are heavily punished; for example, by solitary confinement, prohibition of visits and monetary fines. Such

photographs, not exhibited in public, are usually taken from a Hebrew newspaper, and the *shaheed* could even be the prisoner's next of kin. The significance of this prohibition is that freedom of thought is denied, especially when it involves feelings of affiliation with the struggle or belonging to a nation.

6. During decades of detention, the National Prisoner Movement shaped organizational traditions for solving internal conflicts. Those traditions were based on the principle of fair representation of the political factions and sought to strengthen the democratic spirit. There were codes of conduct regarding rotation in leadership and its renewal, submissions of periodical reports to assure transparency, and so on. To counter this reality and hinder the democratic process, the IPS started to transfer activists on a national and organizational level.

7. The IPS favored personal contact with the prisoners, through personal appeals. Prisoners' appeals are no longer submitted collectively, except for rare and insignificant cases. Most of the problems presented and the solutions reached pertain to individual prisoners. As a result, differences in living conditions and treatment by the authorities developed. However, collective punishments are given in cases of individual violations. This "collectivization" is aimed at directing prisoners' pressure against one another; prisoners thus become agents of the jailing authority, rather than comrades.

All these measures were taken in order to transform the Palestinian prisoner from an active subject, with his own personality and convictions, into a passive, receptive object, immersed in his basic material needs which are met according to his jailers' wish. These needs gradually turn into his main concern. The IPS enables the Palestinian prisoners to purchase food and even makes it necessary.[10] It is as if they tell the Palestinian prisoner: eat, drink, stay busy with such needs, as long as you don't become a subject, who understands and interprets his reality and thinks of his own destiny as well as that of his comrades.

The relatively reasonable material life turned into a trap for us, the Palestinian prisoners. This trap must be analyzed and its mechanism exposed: how material abundance turned into torture, while Israel presents it as an example of enlightened occupation responding to human rights discourse. Palestinian prisoners are probably the only prisoners in the history of the liberation movements, receiving monthly pensions to cover their expenses in prison, as if they were employees of the Palestinian Authority.[11] What makes the money transferred to the prisoners doubly suspicious is that Israel always takes great caution to track finances under the pretext of persecuting "terrorism-supporting finances"; yet it does not object to the transfer of these huge sums delivered to the prisoners. This calls into question the role of the money transfer and its consequences upon the prisoners and their role in the struggle.

The sums spent on the prisoners currently in custody[12]—for canteen expenses and monthly pensions—reach millions of dollars per month. To this we should add the financial fines imposed upon prisoners, which are also covered by the Palestinian Authority.[13] These are large sums in Palestinian terms. The problem is not that money is spent on prisoners and their families, so that their dignified living is secured. There is also nothing wrong with the prisoners having some material means. But when half of this sum is spent on the prisoners inside prison, this actually means that we are financing our own detention—we even make it profitable for Israel. The companies that provide the prisoners with food and cleaning supplies, according to the agreement signed with the Palestinian Ministry for Detainees Affairs, are Israeli. There are items consumed by the prisoner that they do not buy themselves, at their own expense; the IPS only supplies token quantities of those goods. The Palestinian Authority subsidizes the detention of Palestinian prisoners in Israeli prisons and is subsidized for this purpose by special grants coming from the European Union and the Donor Countries.[14] Not only is Israel thus relieved from the financial burden of the detention of the Palestinians, its detention policy is actually acknowledged. Moreover, the Palestinian Authority also covers the special needs of prisoners who are inhabitants of the Gaza Strip, because their families are prohibited from visiting them. It does this, instead of making Israel bear the responsibility of its detention policy, instead of prosecuting it in international courts and blaming it for violations of international accords.

The Palestinian prisoner, whose sole interest was the struggle for liberation, becomes a member of a sector, like the sector of government employees, with its own financial interests and demands. His struggle, thus, is no longer directed against the occupation government and its Prison Service, but against the Palestinian Authority, as his "employer"! In other words, we finance willingly an Israeli plan to transform the prisoners—the

Palestinian struggle's hard core—from a unified force with national concerns and shared values into individuals immersed in their private demands and concerns.

In addition, the material reality in which the prisoners live produces in them a state of social and mental disorder, for several prisoners live in much better material conditions than their families in the OPT, and certainly than that of the inhabitants of the Gaza Strip under the siege. The ordinary person becomes confused, because it is no longer clear where prison ends and freedom begins: outside, where the cantons and the enclaves are—or here, in the Israeli detention centers. When this reality is part of an intentional policy to empty the prisoners of vital content and to individualize them, shattering anything that might make them a collective, the chances to exploit the material abundance in order to raise the level of national consciousness are low. Still, this is not to be taken as an excuse.

The target is no longer the body of the prisoner, the torture is no longer material; it is the spirit, the mind, which is disfigured. In the postmodern era, material abundance is another tool, among others, in terms of torture. It is therefore necessary to re-identify torture and oppression and to expose their new complex components. The changes which occurred during a year in prison—in places, culture and people—are infinitely less than the changes occurring during a year *outside* of prison, in the present period. The loss of contact with reality outside prison, even after several months of imprisonment, becomes catastrophic. Nowadays, prisoners quickly lose contact with civilization, with values and social relations. After a few years in prison, they become relatively primitive in terms of outside reality. This loss of contact with reality is exploited by the Occupation and its mechanisms, including the IPS, in order to even deepen the disengagement, to sever the prisoners from any national project or collective thinking and push them into a state of exile, to a rejection of the struggle, or, at best, a situation of being a burden upon their national cause.

MODERN CONTROL: DANGEROUS ASPECTS OF THE NEW VALUES IN THE LIVES OF PALESTINIAN PRISONERS

The essence of modernity is the ability of the person to separate time from place. In the past, in order to have power over people, one had to control their locations; in modern times, this is no longer necessary: it is enough to control their time.[15] Prisoners no longer can organize their schedule according to their own plans. They cannot pass the time inside their cells, without interruption. Their days are broken up into units: apart from the slot for a courtyard walk, the prisoner in the Israeli prison is required to come out of his cell three times a day for security checks. Seven times a day, for an hour each, he must not use the bathroom: during the three security searches and four other role calls for counting prisoners.

This form of control bears many consequences over prisoners' lives, their self-esteem and their self-perception. It also reshapes the wardens' conduct and their understanding of their role within a bureaucratic mechanism such as the IPS. Control in the prisons of the Israeli Occupation is no longer direct, through wardens who are physically present, in the prison's courtyard, opening and closing doors. There are no more daily intensive encounters between prisoners and wardens. Such encounters became the exception, while the rule is that the warden is absent, and it is only his shadow that is present, by means of modern appliances and new technologies. There are cameras everywhere; doors and locks are controlled electronically. Thus one warden is enough for controlling a ward with 120 prisoners. Now this makes it appear as if prisoners control their own lives without interruption—they even close their cell doors themselves; yet in fact, the contrary is the case. Visible control was clear; it was possible to "cheat" it, "negotiate" with it and humanize it. Now even the wardens are under total surveillance and thus devoid of influence; there's no use in reasoning with them and all spontaneity is lost. Prisoners' individual skills and their social agility are useless and devoid of practical value. Dehumanization of the prisoner is easier, because the distance created by the technology of surveillance turns prisoners from subjects to objects on the screens.

The contradiction between the physical absence of wardens and the total control of any aspect in the prisoners' lives yields a cognitive dissonance between their wish to maintain their feeling of "control" and the fact that this control is nothing but an illusion. But dissonances, tensions and contradictions do not end here. The way prison's reality is depicted in literature, poetry and in the media, especially the Arab media, is taken from a different period altogether and is far from the present experience of the Palestinian prisoners. Although I believe reality now is harsher, there is no resemblance between the typical barbaric warden in the earlier literature and the 20-year-old girl who now sits in the surveillance center, controlling the lives of 120 prisoners. The language of literature and poetry cannot describe the present suffering and torture. There is a need for new tools for interpreting modern and complex torture, tools which might be taken from the science of sociology and philosophy. The resulting analysis should bestow on the Palestinian prisoners some certainty regarding the real source of their suffering. Given the political contradictions in which we live since the signing of the Oslo Accords, and especially after the second Intifada was crushed, this task is even harder. In the absence of such a scientific explanation, committed to the Palestinian cause, we are subject to Israeli interpretations, seeking to shatter our collective values and make consciousness molding easier.

It is crucial to understand the IPS strategy which centers on the enhancement of pre-national frameworks, that is, on primary affiliations like towns and cities, blood relations and geography. Until the mid 1990s, thinking and acting along the lines of local interests was considered shameful, something to be fought against, having no place among nationalists. Today, on the other hand, anyone who tries to think and act outside this pre-nationalistic framework is ostracized as a rebel against the authority of the faction, understood geographically. The power of this local authority is drawn from the IPS on one hand, through transfers of prisoners according to its interests, but on the other hand, it is also drawn from the Palestinian Authority, which gives power to the representatives of this local thinking, by turning them into the channel through which financial and social support flows. In this way, the Palestinian Authority strengthens, knowingly or unknowingly, the plan to break up the collective values of the prisoners.

As a result of this substantial change, some important behavioral patterns have emerged. Violence as a tool for resolving disputes is widespread, after having been taboo for many years. Some prisoners avoid politics altogether and concentrate on relaxing pastimes: there is a significant increase in the number of prisoners who are busy with physical fitness, while many watch television programs, as long as these have nothing to do with political affairs. In general, Palestinian prisoners read less and are now much less productive intellectually, compared to the past. Meetings, study circles, ideological discussions about national problems are much less frequent. Indeed, there is an increasing number of prisoners who take up academic studies (through the Israeli Open University), but their motivation is self-development and preparation for their own future after their release, rather than collective values and national concerns. It is simply one form of escape from reality.

As part of its control of the prisoners' consciousness, the IPS has limited the amount of books, with restrictions of contents, that prisoners are allowed to keep in their cells. Only religious books and some fictional works are allowed, but scientific, social and political studies are prohibited under the pretext of "agitation materials." Recently, among the popular books that one can find are astrology and trivia books. The IPS prohibits the consumption of Arab newspapers, especially political ones, such as *Fasl al-Maqal*, *Al-Ittihad* and *Sawt al-Haq*, the only exception being *Al-Quds* which only reaches the prisoners weeks after its publication. On the other hand, prisoners are allowed to read daily Hebrew newspapers. Only Israeli radio stations are allowed. Arab satellite channels are also limited: Al-Jazeera was banned, and only those channels which are considered as adhering to the "moderate Arab line" are now allowed.

The military takeover by Hamas in the Gaza strip complicated the situation further. Intelligence officers spread news and disinformation among the prisoners, in order to stir up conflicts and blast apart any national idea or collective value. As a result, there were several clashes between representatives of the two sides within prison. Although these were limited in scope, they were enough to inflate the security aspect, as a pretext to implementing the decision to separate the prisoners of the Islamic movements from those of the Fatah movement, especially in the southern prisons. One of the "fruits" of this Israeli policy was the silence with which the war against Gaza was received—a total silence throughout the prisons. Palestinian prisoners were sitting in front of television screens, watching the bloodbath on the Arab satellite channels (back then, Al-Jazeera was still allowed), but acting less than any Arab citizen, or any foreigner showing solidarity with the Palestinian people. No protest, nothing. The rudeness of the IPS reached a peak when it dared to order the prisoners to avoid mentioning the events in Gaza during the Friday sermons, because this might cause "agitation." This silence is salient, in particular, when considered against the historical background of the Palestinian National Prisoner Movement, which had always manifested its solidarity with every struggle for freedom around the world. In the past, prisoners protested in solidarity with Kurdish fighters on hunger strike in Turkish prison, or with Mandela and the ANC members in the prisons of racist South Africa. But now they sat there helpless, with neither a word nor deed, albeit symbolic, during the whole war against Gaza. Immediately after the war against Gaza, the IPS ordered the raising of the Israeli flag in every prison's courtyard. Such a step is closely connected with the prisoners' obvious helplessness during the war.

I point at this helplessness not in order to disgrace the fighters, or to castigate them. My purpose is to give objective proof to the extent of Israeli control over the prisoners through the whole system of policies, measures, arrangements and regulations, all constituting the process of consciousness molding. Though each of these actions is not critically significant, their totality is horrifying. The prison reality with all its complexities, the Israeli modern scientific effort to remold the consciousness of a whole generation, together with the political problems and crises in the Palestinian arena, made it impossible for the prisoners to emerge, on their own, from their state of helplessness and to act differently than they did during the war against Gaza. The responsibility to break out of this crisis is not that of the prisoners alone; it is primarily the responsibility of the political forces, the prisoners' committees and human rights committees.

At any rate, what happened during the war against Gaza is not the main issue; the principal problem is the contradiction and the inner conflict immanent to the prisoners' lives that were revealed then. The conflict is between the way the prisoner conceives of himself and his struggle and the inexplicability of the absence of that conception in his daily conduct. No one can assess the extent of moral and psychological damage resulting from this contradiction: the loss of self-esteem and its future repercussions on the national struggle. What we can feel today is the extent of the misery caused by this kind of mental torture.

In speaking about torture and the need for its re-identification, I refer among other things to the policies and non-sensual, indirect systems, which were mentioned above—the purpose of which is the gradual, creeping, coordinated brainwashing of the political collective, which is to be controlled. Yaakov Ganot, the former head of the IPS, expressed this desire to control in a speech he gave in 2006, in a courtyard of the Jalbu'a prison, after Minister of Internal Security Gideon Ezra took office. Addressing the minister—while he knew the prisoners could hear him—he said: "Don't worry, you can trust me that I'll make them raise the Israeli flag and sing Hatikva, Israel's national anthem."

NOTES

1. G. Levy, "Worse than Apartheid," *Ha'aretz*, July 10, 2008.
2. The declaration appeared in Israeli newspapers more than once; see, for example, an interview with Ari Shavit, *Ha'aretz*, 6 July, 2006.

3. B. Kimmerling, *Politicide: Ariel Sharon's War against the Palestinians*, London: Verso, 2003.
4. The following analysis draws on such seminal works as Jeremy Bentham's *Panopticon*, Michel Foucault's *Discipline and Punish*, Naomi Klein's *Shock Doctrine* and several writings by Zygmunt Bauman.
5. Strip searches and violating religious feelings were also used in Guantanamo and in Abu Ghraib, especially the use of dogs. See Naomi Klein, *The Shock Doctrine – The Rise of Disaster Capitalism*, Canada: Knopf, 2007, p. 140.
6. The story was reported widely in the Hebrew papers on August 15, 2004.
7. See Klein, *Shock Doctrine*.
8. The head of the IPS, Yaacov Ganot, said often that his goal was to make that strike the last one.
9. This term refers to the minority of Palestinians who remained in their homes during the 1947–49 war and eventually acquired Israeli citizenship in order to remain inside what then became Israel.
10. In addition to the prison's food, the prisoners are allowed to buy 2.5 kg per month of vegetables and fruit, and an identical quantity of chicken, meat and fish.
11. Each prisoner receives 500 NIS per month for his canteen expenses, on top of his monthly pension, which amounts to 1,500–6,000 Shekels (according to the numbers of years in prison, marital status, and so on).
12. There is a specific budget for released prisoners.
13. The fines imposed by Israeli courts upon the prisoners reached 2 million shekels in one of the payments transferred by the Palestinian Authority to Israel, according to the report of the Palestinian Ministry of Detainees Affairs, *Al-Quds*, no. 14378, p. 12.
14. Ibid.
15. See Z. Bauman, *Liquid Modernity*, Cambridge: Polity Press, 2000, p. 117f.

Index

Compiled by Sue Carlton